Houghton
Mifflin
Harcourt

Volume 1

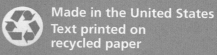

Made in the United States
Text printed on
recycled paper

Houghton Mifflin Harcourt

Printed in the U.S.A.

ISBN 978-0-544-43281-9

22 0928 23

4500864542   E F G

Dear Students and Families,

Welcome to **Go Math!**, Grade 6! In this exciting mathematics program, there are hands-on activities to do and real-world problems to solve. Best of all, you will write your ideas and answers right in your book. In **Go Math!**, writing and drawing on the pages helps you think deeply about what you are learning, and you will really understand math!

By the way, all of the pages in your **Go Math!** book are made using recycled paper. We wanted you to know that you can Go Green with **Go Math!**

Sincerely,

The Authors

Made in the United States
Text printed on recycled paper

GO MATH!

Authors

Juli K. Dixon, Ph.D.
Professor, Mathematics Education
University of Central Florida
Orlando, Florida

Edward B. Burger, Ph.D.
President, Southwestern University
Georgetown, Texas

Steven J. Leinwand
Principal Research Analyst
American Institutes for
    Research (AIR)
Washington, D.C.

Contributor

Rena Petrello
Professor, Mathematics
Moorpark College
Moorpark, CA

Matthew R. Larson, Ph.D.
K-12 Curriculum Specialist for
    Mathematics
Lincoln Public Schools
Lincoln, Nebraska

Martha E. Sandoval-Martinez
Math Instructor
El Camino College
Torrance, California

English Language Learners Consultant

Elizabeth Jiménez
CEO, GEMAS Consulting
Professional Expert on English
    Learner Education
Bilingual Education and
    Dual Language
Pomona, California

VOLUME 1
The Number System

 Critical Area Completing understanding of division of fractions and extending the notion of number to the system of rational numbers, which includes negative numbers

1 Whole Numbers and Decimals   3

Domain The Number System
COMMON CORE STATE STANDARDS 6.NS.B.2, 6.NS.B.3, 6.NS.B.4

2 Fractions   67

Domain The Number System
COMMON CORE STATE STANDARDS 6.NS.A.1, 6.NS.B.4, 6.NS.C.6c

GO DIGITAL

Go online! Your math lessons are interactive. Use *i*Tools, Animated Math Models, the Multimedia eGlossary, and more.

Chapter 1 Overview

In this chapter, you will explore and discover answers to the following **Essential Questions**:

- How do you solve real-world problems involving whole numbers and decimals?
- How does estimation help you solve problems involving decimals and whole numbers?
- How can you use the GCF and the LCM to solve problems?

Chapter 2 Overview

In this chapter, you will explore and discover answers to the following **Essential Questions**:

- How can you use the relationship between multiplication and division to divide fractions?
- What is a mixed number?
- How can you estimate products and quotients of fractions and mixed numbers?

In this chapter, you will explore and discover answers to the following **Essential Questions**:

- How do you write, interpret, and use rational numbers?
- How do you calculate the absolute value of a number?
- How do you graph an ordered pair?

Practice and Homework

Lesson Check and Spiral Review in every lesson

3 Rational Numbers 137

Domain The Number System

COMMON CORE STATE STANDARDS 6.NS.C.5, 6.NS.C.6a, 6.NS.C.6b, 6.NS.C.6c, 6.NS.C.7a, 6.NS.C.7b, 6.NS.C.7c, 6.NS.C.7d, 6.NS.C.8

© Houghton Mifflin Harcourt Publishing Company

Ratios and Rates

Critical Area Connecting ratio and rate to whole number multiplication and division and using concepts of ratio and rate to solve problems

Critical Area

GO DIGITAL

Go online! Your math lessons are interactive. Use *i*Tools, Animated Math Models, the Multimedia *e*Glossary, and more.

Chapter 4 Overview

In this chapter, you will explore and discover answers to the following **Essential Questions**:

• How can you use ratios to express relationships and solve problems?

• How can you write a ratio?

• What are equivalent ratios?

• How are rates related to ratios?

Chapter 5 Overview

In this chapter, you will explore and discover answers to the following **Essential Questions**:

• How can you use ratio reasoning to solve percent problems?

• How can you write a percent as a fraction?

• How can you use a ratio to find a percent of a number?

Personal Math Trainer
Online Assessment and Intervention

Chapter 6 Overview

In this chapter, you will explore and discover answers to the following **Essential Questions:**

- How can you use measurements to help you describe and compare objects?
- Why do you need to convert between units of measure?
- How can you use a ratio to convert units?
- How do you transform units to solve problems?

Practice and Homework

Lesson Check and Spiral Review in every lesson

6 Units of Measure

Domain Ratios and Proportional Relationships
COMMON CORE STATE STANDARDS 6.RP.A.3d

VOLUME 2
Expressions and Equations

 Critical Area Writing, interpreting, and using expressions and equations

Real World Project The Great Outdoors **354**

7 Algebra: Expressions   355

Domain Expressions and Equations
COMMON CORE STATE STANDARDS 6.EE.A.1, 6.EE.A.2a, 6.EE.A.2b, 6.EE.A.2c, 6.EE.A.3, 6.EE.A.4, 6.EE.B.6

GO DIGITAL

Go online! Your math lessons are interactive. Use *i*Tools, Animated Math Models, the Multimedia *e*Glossary, and more.

Chapter 7 Overview

In this chapter, you will explore and discover answers to the following **Essential Questions**:

- How do you write, interpret, and use algebraic expressions?

- How can you use expressions to represent real-world situations?

- How do you use the order of operations to evaluate expressions?

- How can you tell whether two expressions are equivalent?

Personal Math Trainer
Online Assessment and Intervention

Chapter 8 Overview

In this chapter, you will explore and discover answers to the following **Essential Questions**:

- How can you use equations and inequalities to represent situations and solve problems?
- How can you use Properties of Equality to solve equations?
- How do inequalities differ from equations?
- Why is it useful to describe situations by using algebra?

Practice and Homework

Lesson Check and Spiral Review in every lesson

Chapter 9 Overview

In this chapter, you will explore and discover answers to the following **Essential Questions**:

- How can you show relationships between variables?
- How can you determine the equation that gives the relationship between two variables?
- How can you use tables and graphs to visualize the relationship between two variables?

8 Algebra: Equations and Inequalities — 419

Domain Expressions and Equations
COMMON CORE STATE STANDARDS 6.EE.B.5, 6.EE.B.7, 6.EE.B.8

9 Algebra: Relationships Between Variables — 489

Domain Expressions and Equations
COMMON CORE STATE STANDARDS 6.EE.C.9

Geometry and Statistics

 Common Core **Critical Area** Solve real-world and mathematical problems involving area, surface area, and volume; and developing understanding of statistical thinking

Critical Area

GO DIGITAL

Go online! Your math lessons are interactive. Use *i*Tools, Animated Math Models, the Multimedia eGlossary, and more.

Chapter 10 Overview

In this chapter, you will explore and discover answers to the following **Essential Questions**:

- How can you use measurements to describe two-dimensional figures?
- What does area represent?
- How are the areas of rectangles and parallelograms related?
- How are the areas of triangles and trapezoids related?

Chapter 11 Overview

In this chapter, you will explore and discover answers to the following **Essential Questions**:

- How can you use measurements to describe three-dimensional figures?
- How can you use a net to find the surface area of a three-dimensional figure?
- How can you find the volume of a rectangular prism?

© Houghton Mifflin Harcourt Publishing Company

Critical Area

The Number System

CRITICAL AREA Completing understanding of division of fractions and extending the notion of number to the system of rational numbers, which includes negative numbers

Sweet Success

Businesses that sell food products need to combine ingredients in the correct amounts. They also need to determine what price to charge for the products they sell.

Get Started   WRITE ▸Math

A company sells Apple Cherry Mix. They make large batches of the mix that can be used to fill 250 bags each. Determine how many pounds of each ingredient should be used to make one batch of Apple Cherry Mix. Then decide how much the company should charge for each bag of Apple Cherry Mix, and explain how you made your decision.

Important Facts

Ingredients in Apple Cherry Mix (1 bag)
- $\frac{3}{4}$ pound of dried apples
- $\frac{1}{2}$ pound of dried cherries
- $\frac{1}{4}$ pound of walnuts

Cost of Ingredients
- dried apples: $2.80 per pound
- dried cherries: $4.48 per pound
- walnuts: $3.96 per pound

Completed by _____

Whole Numbers and Decimals

✓ Show What You Know

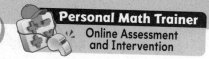

Personal Math Trainer
Online Assessment and Intervention

Check your understanding of important skills.

Name _____

▶ **Factors** Find all of the factors of the number. (4.OA.B.4)

1. 16 _____ 2. 27 _____

3. 30 _____ 4. 45 _____

▶ **Round Decimals** Round to the place of the underlined digit. (5.NBT.A.4)

5. 0.<u>3</u>23 6. 4.<u>0</u>96 7. 1<u>0</u>.67 8. 5.2<u>7</u>8

▶ **Multiply 3-Digit and 4-Digit Numbers** Multiply. (5.NBT.B.5)

9. 2,143
    ×   6

10. 375
     ×   8

11. 3,762
     ×   7

12. 603
     ×   9

Math in the Real World

Maxwell saved $18 to buy a fingerprinting kit that costs $99. He spent 0.25 of his savings to buy a magnifying glass. Help Maxwell find out how much more he needs to save to buy the fingerprinting kit.

Vocabulary Builder

▶ **Visualize It** •

Complete the Flow Map using the words with a ✓.

Estimation

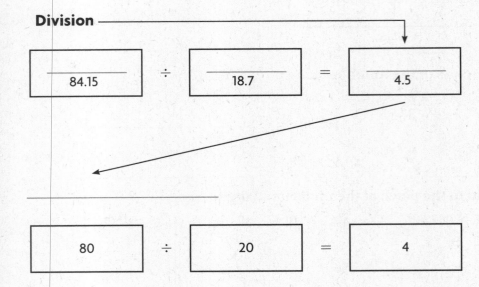

Division

| 84.15 | ÷ | 18.7 | = | 4.5 |

| 80 | ÷ | 20 | = | 4 |

▶ **Understand Vocabulary** • • • • • • • • • • • • • • • • • • •

Complete the sentences using the preview words.

1. The least number that is a common multiple of two or more

   numbers is the _____.

2. The greatest factor that two or more numbers have in common

   is the _____.

3. A number that is a factor of two or more numbers is a

   _____.

4. A number written as the product of its prime factors is the

   _____ of the number.

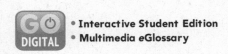

• Interactive Student Edition
• Multimedia eGlossary

Chapter 1 Vocabulary

common factor

factor común

12

dividend

dividendo

23

divisor

divisor

25

factor

factor

33

greatest common factor (*GCF*)

máximo común divisor (MCD)

38

least common multiple (*LCM*)

mínimo común múltiplo (m.c.m.)

48

prime factorization

descomposición en factores primos

77

prime number

número primo

78

The number that is to be divided in a division problem

$$18 \div 6 \qquad 6\overline{)18}$$

dividend · · · · · · · · · dividend

A number that is a factor of two or more numbers

Example:

Factors of 16: (1, (2, (4,   8,   16

Factors of 20: (1, (2, (4,   5,   10,   20

A number multiplied by another number to find a product

$$2 \times 3 \times 7 = 42$$

factors

The number that divides the dividend

$$18 \div 6 \qquad 6\overline{)18}$$

divisor · · · · · · · · · divisor

The least number that is a common multiple of two or more numbers

Example:

Multiples of 4: 4, 8, (12,)16, 20,(24,)28, 32,(36)

Multiples of 6: 6,(12,)18,(24,)30,(36,)42

The LCM of 4 and 6 is 12.

The greatest factor that two or more numbers have in common

Example:

Factors of 18:(1,)(2,)(3,)(6,)9, 18

Factors of 30:(1,)(2,)(3,)5,(6,)10, 15, 30

The GCF of 18 and 30 is 6.

A number that has exactly two factors: 1 and itself

Examples: 2, 3, 5, 7, 11, 13, 17, and 19 are prime numbers. 1 is not a prime number.

A number written as the product of all its prime factors

Example:

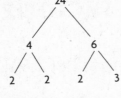

$$24 = 2 \times 2 \times 2 \times 3$$

Going to Washington, DC

For 2 to 4 players

Materials

- 3 of 1 color per player: red, blue, green, and yellow playing pieces
- 1 number cube

How to Play

1. Put your 3 playing pieces in the START circle of the same color.
2. To get a playing piece out of START, you must toss a 6.
   - If you toss a 6, move 1 of your playing pieces to the same-colored circle on the path. If you do not toss a 6, wait until your next turn.
3. Once you have a playing piece on the path, toss the number cube to take a turn. Move the playing piece that many tan spaces. You must get all three of your playing pieces on the path.
4. If you land on a space with a question, answer it. If you are correct, move ahead 1 space.
5. To reach FINISH move your playing pieces up the path that is the same color as your playing pieces. The first player to get all three playing pieces on FINISH wins.

Word Box

common factor

dividend

divisor

factor

greatest common
   factor (GCM)

least common
   multiple (LCM)

prime factorization

prime number

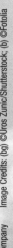

START

How can you use a list to find the least common multiple of two numbers?

Explain how to use prime factorization to find a least common multiple.

Name two common factors for 32 and 40.

How many factors does a prime number have?

FINISH

What is the greatest common factor of 28 and 49?

Explain two ways to find the prime factorization of 210.

True or false: The LCM of 7 and 14 is 42. Explain how you know.

How can you find the common factors of two numbers?

START

START

Explain why a prime factorization may be used as a secret code.

$2 \times 2 \times 3 \times 5$ is the prime factorization of what number?

FINISH

What is the least common multiple of 4 and 10?

What is the dividend in 48 ÷ 8?

What is a least common multiple?

What is a greatest common factor?

Why might you estimate when a dividend has a decimal?

How can you change a divisor such as 16.3 into a whole number?

START

The Write Way

Reflect

Choose one idea. Write about it.

- Explain how to find the prime factorization of 140.
- Two students found the least common multiple of 6 and 16. Tell how you know which student's answer is correct.

  Student A: The LCM of 6 and 16 is 96.

  Student B: The LCM of 6 and 16 is 48.
- Describe two ways to find the greatest common factor of 36 and 42.
- Write and solve a word problem that uses a whole number as a divisor and a decimal as a dividend.

_____

_____

_____

_____

_____

_____

_____

_____

_____

_____

_____

_____

_____

_____

_____

Divide Multi-Digit Numbers

Essential Question How do you divide multi-digit numbers?

Common Core **The Number System—**
6.NS.B.2

MATHEMATICAL PRACTICES
MP1, MP2, MP6

Unlock the Problem

When you watch a cartoon, the frames of film seem to blend together to form a moving image. A cartoon lasting just 92 seconds requires 2,208 frames. How many frames do you see each second when you watch a cartoon?

Divide 2,208 ÷ 92.

Estimate using compatible numbers. _____ ÷ _____ = _____

$$\begin{array}{r} 2 \\ 92\overline{)2{,}208} \\ -184\!\downarrow \\ \hline 368 \\ - \\ \hline \end{array}$$

Divide the tens.

Divide the ones.

Compare your estimate with the quotient. Since the estimate, _____,

is close to _____, the answer is reasonable.

So, you see _____ frames each second when you watch a cartoon.

Example 1 Divide 12,749 ÷ 18.

Estimate using compatible numbers. _____ ÷ _____ = _____

STEP 1 Divide.

$$\begin{array}{r} 70r5 \\ 18\overline{)12{,}749} \\ -126\!\downarrow \\ \hline 14 \\ -0\!\downarrow \\ \hline 149 \\ - \\ \hline \end{array}$$

STEP 2 Check your answer.

$$\begin{array}{r} \\ \times 18 \\ \hline \\ + \\ \hline \\ + \\ \hline 12{,}749 \end{array}$$

Multiply the whole number part of the quotient by the divisor.

Add the remainder.

Math Idea

You can write a remainder with an r, as a fractional part of the divisor, or as a decimal. For 131 ÷ 5, the quotient can be written as 26 r1, $26\frac{1}{5}$, or 26.2.

So, 12,749 ÷ 18 = _____.

🔓 Example 2

Divide 59,990 ÷ 280. Write the remainder as a fraction.

Estimate using compatible numbers. _____ ÷ _____ = _____

STEP 1 Divide.

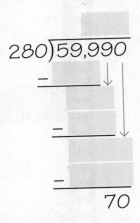

$$280\overline{)59{,}990}$$

70

STEP 2 Write the remainder as a fraction.

$$\frac{\text{remainder}}{\text{divisor}} = \frac{\boxed{}}{280}$$

Write the remainder over the divisor.

$$\frac{70 \div \boxed{}}{280 \div \boxed{}} = \frac{\boxed{}}{\boxed{}}$$

Simplify.

Compare your estimate with the quotient. Since the estimate, _____

is close to _____, the answer is reasonable.

So, 59,990 ÷ 280 = _____.

MATHEMATICAL PRACTICE ① **Describe** two ways to check your answer in Example 2.

_____

_____

_____

Share and Show

Estimate. Then find the quotient. Write the remainder, if any, with an r.

1. $29\overline{)986}$ Think: 30 × 3 = 90

2. $37\overline{)3{,}786}$

_____   _____

Name _____

Estimate. Then find the quotient. Write the remainder, if any, as a fraction.

☑ 3. 6,114 ÷ 63

☑ 4. 11,050 ÷ 26

_____

MATHEMATICAL PRACTICES ⑥

Explain why you can use multiplication to check a division problem.

On Your Own

Estimate. Then find the quotient. Write the remainder, if any, as a fraction.

5. 3,150 ÷ 9

6. 2,115 ÷ 72

7. 20,835 ÷ 180

_____

_____

_____

8. Find the least whole number that can replace ■ to make the statement true.

$110 < ■ ÷ 47$

_____

9. **MATHEMATICAL PRACTICE ②** **Use Reasoning** Name two whole numbers that can replace ■ to make both statements true.

$2 × ■ < 1,800 ÷ 12$ $■ > 3,744 ÷ 52$

_____

10. **GO DEEPER** The 128 employees of a company volunteer 12,480 hours in 26 weeks. On average, how many hours do they all volunteer per week? On average, how many hours does each employee volunteer per week?

_____

11. **GO DEEPER** A factory produces 30,480 bolts in 12 hours. If the same number of bolts are produced each hour, how many bolts does the factory produce in 5 hours?

_____

Problem Solving • Applications (Real World)

Use the table for 12–15.

12. A Smooth Flight jet carried 6,045 passengers last week, and all of its flights were full. How many flights did the jet make last week?

   _____

13. GO DEEPER Last month an airline made 6,322 reservations for flights from Newark, New Jersey, to Frankfurt, Germany. If there were 21 full flights and 64 reservations cancelled, which airplane made the flights?

   _____

Airplane Passenger Seats

Type of Plane	Seats
Jet Set	298
Smooth Flight	403
Blue Skies	160
Cloud Mover	70

14. THINK SMARTER An airline carries about 750 passengers from Houston to Chicago each day. How many Blue Sky jets would be needed to carry this many passengers, and how many empty seats would there be?

   _____

Math on the Spot

| WRITE ▸ Math • **Show Your Work**

15. THINK SMARTER **Pose a Problem** Refer back to Problem 12. Use the information in the table to write a similar problem involving airplane passenger seats.

   _____

   _____

16. THINK SMARTER For numbers 16a–16d, choose Yes or No to indicate whether the equation is correct.

   16a. $1,350 \div 5 = 270$ ○ Yes   ○ No

   16b. $3,732 \div 4 = 933$ ○ Yes   ○ No

   16c. $4,200 \div 35 = 12$ ○ Yes   ○ No

   16d. $1,586 \div 13 = 122$ ○ Yes   ○ No

Name _____

Divide Multi-Digit Numbers

COMMON CORE STANDARD—6.NS.B.2
Compute fluently with multi-digit numbers and find common factors and multiples.

Estimate. Then find the quotient. Write the remainder, if any, with an r.

1.
$$\begin{array}{r} 13 \\ 55\overline{)715} \\ \underline{55} \\ 165 \\ \underline{165} \\ 0 \end{array}$$

Estimate:
$700 \div 50 = 15$

2. $19\overline{)800}$

3. $68\overline{)1,025}$

Estimate. Then find the quotient. Write the remainder, if any, as a fraction.

4. $20\overline{)1,683}$

5. $14,124 \div 44$

6. $11,629 \div 29$

Find the least whole number that can replace ▪ to make the statement true.

7. ▪ $\div 7 > 800$

8. ▪ $\div 21 > 13$

9. $15 <$ ▪ $\div 400$

Problem Solving Real World

10. A plane flew a total of 2,220 miles. Its average speed was 555 miles per hour. How many hours did the plane fly?

11. A van is carrying 486 pounds. There are 27 boxes in the van. What is the average weight of each box in the van?

12. **WRITE** ▸*Math* Find $56,794 \div 338$. Write the quotient twice, once with the remainder as a fraction and once with an r.

Lesson Check (6.NS.B.2)

1. A caterer's fee is based on the number of meals she provides. How much is the price per meal if the total fee is $1,088 for 64 meals?

2. Amelia needs 24 grams of beads to make a bracelet. She has 320 grams of beads. How many bracelets can she make?

_____

_____

Spiral Review (5.NBT.A.2, 5.NBT.A.3b, 5.NBT.B.7)

3. Hank bought 2.4 pounds of apples. Each pound cost $1.95. How much did Hank spend on the apples?

4. Gavin bought 4 packages of cheese. Each package weighed 1.08 kilograms. How many kilograms of cheese did Gavin buy?

_____

_____

5. Mr. Thompson received a water bill for $85.98. The bill covered three months of service. He used the same amount of water each month. How much does Mr. Thompson pay for water each month?

6. Layla used 0.482 gram of salt in her experiment. Maurice use 0.51 gram of salt. Who used the greater amount of salt?

_____

_____

FOR MORE PRACTICE
GO TO THE
Personal Math Trainer

Prime Factorization

Essential Question How do you write the prime factorization of a number?

Common Core The Number System—
6.NS.B.4

MATHEMATICAL PRACTICES
MP1, MP3, MP6, MP7

❗Unlock the Problem Real World

Secret codes are often used to send information over the Internet. Many of these codes are based on very large numbers. For some codes, a computer must determine the prime factorization of these numbers to decode the information.

The **prime factorization** of a number is the number written as a product of all of its prime factors.

🔢 One Way Use a factor tree.

The key for a code is based on the prime factorization of 180. Find the prime factorization of 180.

Choose any two factors whose product is 180. Continue finding factors until only prime factors are left.

Remember

A prime number is a whole number greater than 1 that has exactly two factors: itself and 1.

A Use a basic fact.

Think: 10 times what number is equal to 180?

$10 \times$ _____ $= 180$

```
        180
       /    \
      10     [ ]
     /  \   /  \
    2   [ ] 6   [ ]
   /   / \ / \   \
  2  [ ][ ] 3  [ ]
```

B Use a divisibility rule.

Think: 180 is even, so it is divisible by 2.

$2 \times$ _____ $= 180$

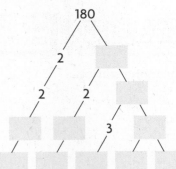

List the prime factors from least to greatest.

$180 =$ _____ $\times$ _____ $\times$ _____ $\times$ _____ $\times$ _____

So, the prime factorization of 180 is _____ $\times$ _____ $\times$ _____ $\times$ _____ $\times$ _____ .

Math Talk

MATHEMATICAL PRACTICES ❸

Apply How can you apply divisibility rules to make the factor tree on the left?

🔒 Another Way Use a ladder diagram.

The key for a code is based on the prime factorization of 140. Find the prime factorization of 140.

Choose a prime factor of 140. Continue dividing by prime factors until the quotient is 1.

Ⓐ Use the divisibility rule for 2.

Think: 140 is even, so 140 is divisible by 2.

```
2 │ 140  ←─── 140 ÷ 2 = 70
  ─┼───
7 │ 70
  ─┼───
  │ 10
  ─┼───
  │ 2
  ─┴───
    1
```

prime factors

140 = _____ × _____ × _____ × _____

So, the prime factorization of 140 is _____ × _____ × _____ × _____ .

Ⓑ Use the divisibility rule for 5.

Think: The last digit is 0, so 140 is divisible by 5.

```
5 │ 140
  ─┼───
2 │
  ─┼───
  │ 14
  ─┼───
  │ 2
  ─┴───
```

List the prime factors from least to greatest.

Share and Show MATH BOARD

Math Talk MATHEMATICAL PRACTICES ①

Describe a different strategy you could use to find the prime factorization of 140.

Find the prime factorization.

1. 18

18 = _____ × _____ × _____

2. 42

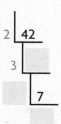

```
2 │ 42
  ─┼───
3 │
  ─┼───
  │ 7
  ─┴───
```

42 = _____ × _____ × _____

Name _____

Find the prime factorization.

3. 75

 4. 12

 5. 65

Math Talk

MATHEMATICAL PRACTICES 6

Explain why a prime number cannot be written as a product of prime factors.

On Your Own

Write the number whose prime factorization is given.

6. $2 \times 2 \times 2 \times 7$

7. $2 \times 2 \times 5 \times 5$

8. $2 \times 2 \times 2 \times 2 \times 3 \times 3$

Practice: Copy and Solve **Find the prime factorization.**

9. 45

10. 50

11. 32

12. 76

13. 108

14. 126

15. The area of a rectangle is the product of its length and width. A rectangular poster has an area of 260 square inches. The width of the poster is greater than 10 inches and is a prime number. What is the width of the poster?

16. MATHEMATICAL PRACTICE 7 **Look for Structure** Dani says she is thinking of a secret number. As a clue, she says the number is the least whole number that has three different prime factors. What is Dani's secret number? What is its prime factorization?

© Houghton Mifflin Harcourt Publishing Company

Problem Solving • Applications

Use the table for 17–19. Agent Sanchez must enter a code on a keypad to unlock the door to her office.

17. In August, the digits of the code number are the prime factors of 150. What is the code number for the office door in August?

_____

18. **GO DEEPER** In September, the fourth digit of the code number is 2 more than the fourth digit of the code number based on the prime factors of 225. The prime factors of what number were used for the code in September?

_____

19. **THINK SMARTER** One day in October, Agent Sanchez enters the code 3477. How do you know that this code is incorrect and will not open the door?

_____

_____

Code Number Rules

1. The code is a 4-digit number.

2. Each digit is a prime number.

3. The prime numbers are entered from least to greatest.

4. The code number is changed at the beginning of each month.

WRITE *Math* • **Show Your Work**

20. **THINK SMARTER** Use the numbers to complete the factor tree. You may use a number more than once.

| 2 | 3 | 6 | 9 | 18 |

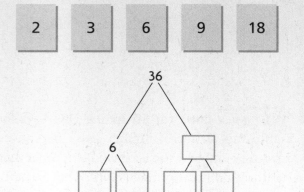

Write the prime factorization of 36.

_____

Prime Factorization

Common Core

COMMON CORE STANDARD—6.NS.B.4
Compute fluently with multi-digit numbers and find common factors and multiples.

Find the prime factorization.

1. 44

$$2 \times 2 \times 11$$

2. 90

_____

3. 48

_____

4. 204

_____

5. 400

_____

6. 112

_____

Problem Solving Real World

7. A computer code is based on the prime factorization of 160. Find the prime factorization of 160.

_____

8. The combination for a lock is a 3-digit number. The digits are the prime factors of 42 listed from least to greatest. What is the combination for the lock?

_____

9. **WRITE** ▸ *Math* Describe two methods for finding the prime factorization of a number.

_____

_____

_____

Lesson Check (6.NS.B.4)

1. Maritza remembers her PIN because it is between 1,000 and 1,500 and it is the product of two consecutive prime numbers. What is her PIN?

_____

_____

2. Brent knows that the 6-digit number he uses to open his computer is the prime factorization of 5005. If each digit of the code increases from left to right, what is his code?

_____

_____

Spiral Review (5.OA.A.2, 5.NBT.A.1, 5.NBT.B.6)

3. Piano lessons cost $15. What expressions could be used to find the cost in dollars of 5 lessons?

_____

4. A jet plane costs an airline $69,500,000. What is the place value of the digit 5 in this number?

_____

5. A museum has 13,486 butterflies, 1,856 ants, and 13,859 beetles. What is the order of the insects from least number to greatest number?

_____

6. Juan is reading a 312-page book for school. He reads 12 pages each day. How long will it take him to finish the book?

_____

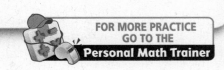

FOR MORE PRACTICE
GO TO THE
Personal Math Trainer

Name _____

Least Common Multiple

Essential Question How can you find the least common multiple of two whole numbers?

 Common Core The Number System— 6.NS.B.4
MATHEMATICAL PRACTICES
MP2, MP3, MP4, MP6

 Unlock the Problem Real World

In an experiment, each flowerpot will get one seed. If the flowerpots are in packages of 6 and the seeds are in packets of 8, what is the least number of plants that can be grown without any seeds or pots left over?

The **least common multiple**, or **LCM**, is the least number that is a common multiple of two or more numbers.

- Explain why you cannot buy the same number of packages of each item.

_____

_____

_____

🔒 One Way Use a list.

Make a list of the first eight nonzero multiples of 6 and 8. Circle the common multiples. Then find the least common multiple.

Multiples of 6: 6, 12, 18, _____,_____,_____,_____,_____

Multiples of 8: 8, 16, 24, _____,_____,_____,_____,_____

The least common multiple, or LCM, is _____.

🔒 Another Way Use prime factorization and a Venn diagram.

Write the prime factorization of each number.

$6 = 2 \times$ _____

$8 = 2 \times$ _____ $\times$ _____

List the common prime factors of the numbers, if any.

6 and 8 have one prime factor of _____ in common.

Place the prime factors of the numbers in the appropriate parts of the Venn diagram.

To find the LCM, find the product of all of the prime factors in the Venn diagram.

$3 \times 2 \times 2 \times 2 =$ _____

The LCM is _____.

So, the least number of plants is _____.

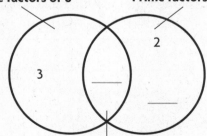

Prime factors of 6   **Prime factors of 8**

3   _____   2

_____

Common prime factors

 Math Talk   MATHEMATICAL PRACTICES ④

Model How does the diagram help you find the LCM of 6 and 8?

🔓 Example Use prime factorization to find the LCM of 12 and 18.

Write the prime factorization of each number.

Line up the common factors.

Multiply one number from each column.

$12 = 2 \times 2 \times$ _____

$18 = 2$ | $\times$ 3 $\times$ _____

$2 \times 2 \times$ 3 $\times$ $3 = 36$

Math Idea

The factors in the prime factorization of a number are usually listed in order from least to greatest.

So, the LCM of 12 and 18 is _____.

Try This! Find the LCM.

Ⓐ 10, 15, and 25

Use prime factorization.

10 = _____

15 = _____

25 = _____

_____

The LCM is _____.

Ⓑ 3 and 12

Use a list.

Multiples of 3: _____

Multiples of 12: _____

The LCM is _____.

1. How can you tell whether the LCM of a pair of numbers is one of the numbers? Give an example.

_____

_____

2. **MATHEMATICAL PRACTICE ⑥** **Explain** one reason why you might use prime factorization instead of making a list of multiples to find the LCM of 10, 15, and 25.

_____

_____

Share and Show MATH BOARD

✓ 1. List the first six nonzero multiples of 6 and 9. Circle the common multiples. Then find the LCM.

Multiples of 6: _____

Multiples of 9: _____

The LCM of 6 and 9 is _____.

Name _____

Find the LCM.

2. 3, 5

_____

3. 3, 9

_____

☑ **4.** 9, 15

_____

On Your Own

Find the LCM.

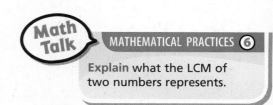

Math Talk — MATHEMATICAL PRACTICES ⑥

Explain what the LCM of two numbers represents.

5. 5, 10

_____

6. 3, 8

_____

7. 9, 12

_____

MATHEMATICAL PRACTICE ② **Use Reasoning** **Algebra** **Write the unknown number for the** ■.

8. 5, 8   LCM: ■

■ = _____

9. ■, 6   LCM: 42

■ = _____

10. THINK SMARTER How can you tell when the LCM of two numbers will equal one of the numbers or equal the product of the numbers?

_____

_____

11. MATHEMATICAL PRACTICE ③ **Verify the Reasoning of Others** Mr. Haigwood is shopping for a school picnic. Veggie burgers come in packages of 15, and buns come in packages of 6. He wants to serve veggie burgers on buns and wants to have no items left over. Mr. Haigwood says that he will have to buy at least 90 of each item, since 6 × 15 = 90. Do you agree with his reasoning? Explain.

_____

_____

12. GO DEEPER A deli has a special one-day event to celebrate its anniversary. On the day of the event, every eighth customer receives a free drink. Every twelfth customer receives a free sandwich. If 200 customers show up for the event, how many of the customers will receive both a free drink and a free sandwich?

© Houghton Mifflin Harcourt Publishing Company

⚷ Unlock the Problem (Real World)

13. Katie is making hair clips to sell at the craft fair. To make each hair clip, she uses 1 barrette and 1 precut ribbon. The barrettes are sold in packs of 12, and the precut ribbons are sold in packs of 9. How many packs of each item does she need to buy to make the least number of hair clips with no supplies left over?

a. What information are you given? _____

_____

b. What problem are you being asked to solve? _____

_____

c. Show the steps you use to solve the problem.

d. Complete the sentences.

The least common multiple of

12 and 9 is _____ .

Katie can make _____ hair clips with no supplies left over.

To get 36 barrettes and 36 ribbons, she

needs to buy _____ packs of barrettes

and _____ packs of precut ribbons.

14. THINK SMARTER Reptile stickers come in sheets of 6 and fish stickers come in sheets of 9. Antonio buys the same number of both types of stickers and he buys at least 100 of each type. What is the least number of sheets of each type he might buy?

_____

_____

15. THINK SMARTER For numbers 15a–15d, choose Yes or No to indicate whether the LCM of the two numbers is 16.

15a. 2, 8   ○ Yes   ○ No

15b. 2, 16   ○ Yes   ○ No

15c. 4, 8   ○ Yes   ○ No

15d. 8, 16   ○ Yes   ○ No

Name _____

Least Common Multiple

Common Core

COMMON CORE STANDARD—6.NS.B.4
Compute fluently with multi-digit numbers and find common factors and multiples.

Find the LCM.

1. 2, 7

Multiples of 2: 2, 4, 6, 8, 10, 12, 14
Multiples of 7: 7, 14

    LCM: ____14____

2. 4, 12

    LCM: _____

3. 6, 9

    LCM: _____

4. 5, 4

    LCM: _____

5. 5, 8, 4

    LCM: _____

6. 12, 8, 24

    LCM: _____

Write the unknown number for the .

7. 3, ■   LCM: 21

8. ■, 7   LCM: 63

9. 10, 5   LCM: ■

    ■ = _____

    ■ = _____

    ■ = _____

Problem Solving · Real World

10. Juanita is making necklaces to give as presents. She plans to put 15 beads on each necklace. Beads are sold in packages of 20. What is the least number of packages she can buy to make necklaces and have no beads left over?

_____

11. Pencils are sold in packages of 10, and erasers are sold in packages of 6. What is the least number of pencils and erasers you can buy so that there is one pencil for each eraser with none left over?

_____

12. **WRITE** ▸*Math* Explain when you would use each method (finding multiples or prime factorization) for finding the LCM and why.

_____

_____

_____

Lesson Check (6.NS.B.4)

1. Martha is buying hot dogs and buns for the class barbecue. The hot dogs come in packages of 10. The buns come in packages of 12. What is the least number she can buy of each so that she has exactly the same number of hot dogs and buns? How many packages of each should she buy?

_____

_____

_____

_____

2. Kevin makes snack bags that each contain a box of raisins and a granola bar. Each package of raisins contains 9 boxes. The granola bars come 12 to a package. What is the least number he can buy of each so that he has exactly the same number of granola bars and boxes of raisins? How many packages of each should he buy?

_____

_____

_____

_____

Spiral Review (5.NBT.B.6, 5.NF.A.1, 5.NF.B.7c)

3. John has 2,456 pennies in his coin collection. He has the same number of pennies in each of 3 boxes. Estimate to the nearest hundred the number of pennies in each box.

_____

4. What is the distance around a triangle that has sides measuring $2\frac{1}{8}$ feet, $3\frac{1}{2}$ feet, and $2\frac{1}{2}$ feet?

_____

5. The 6th grade class collects $1,575. The class wants to give the same amount of money to each of 35 charities. How much will each charity receive?

_____

6. Jean needs $\frac{1}{3}$ cup of walnuts for each serving of salad she makes. She has 2 cups of walnuts. How many servings can she make?

_____

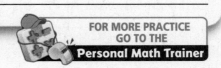

FOR MORE PRACTICE GO TO THE Personal Math Trainer

Name _____

Greatest Common Factor

Essential Question How can you find the greatest common factor of two whole numbers?

 Common Core **The Number System—**
6.NS.B.4
MATHEMATICAL PRACTICES
MP1, MP4, MP7

A **common factor** is a number that is a factor of two or more numbers. The numbers 16 and 20 have 1, 2, and 4 as common factors.

Factors of 16: 1, 2, 4, 8, 16

Factors of 20: 1, 2, 4, 5, 10, 20

The **greatest common factor**, or **GCF**, is the greatest factor that two or more numbers have in common. The greatest common factor of 16 and 20 is 4.

> **Remember**
> A number that is multiplied by another number to find a product is a factor.
> Factors of 6: 1, 2, 3, 6
> Factors of 9: 1, 3, 9
> Every number has 1 as a factor.

Unlock the Problem (Real World)

Jim is cutting two strips of wood to make picture frames. The wood strips measure 12 inches and 18 inches. He wants to cut the strips into equal lengths that are as long as possible. Into what lengths should he cut the wood?

12 inches

18 inches

Find the greatest common factor, or GCF, of 12 and 18.

One Way Use a list.

Factors of 12: 1, 2, _____, _____, _____, 12

Factors of 18: 1, _____, _____, _____, _____, _____

The greatest common factor, or GCF, is _____.

> **Math Talk**   MATHEMATICAL PRACTICES ①
> **Analyze** Into what other lengths could Jim cut the wood to obtain equal lengths?

Another Way Use prime factorization.

Write the prime factorization of each number.

12 = 2 × _____ × 3

18 = _____ × 3 × _____

Place the prime factors of the numbers in the appropriate parts of the Venn diagram.

To find the GCF, find the product of the common prime factors.

2 × 3 = _____   The GCF is _____.

So, Jim should cut the wood into _____-inch lengths.

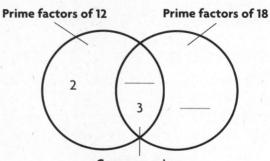

Prime factors of 12   Prime factors of 18

2   _____

3   _____

Common prime factors

Distributive Property

Multiplying a sum by a number is the same as multiplying each addend by the number and then adding the products.	$5 \times (8 + 6) = (5 \times 8) + (5 \times 6)$

You can use the Distributive Property to express the sum of two whole numbers as a product if the numbers have a common factor.

Example Use the GCF and the Distributive Property to express 36 + 27 as a product.

Find the GCF of 36 and 27. GCF: _____

Write each number as the product of the GCF and another factor.

$$36 + 27$$

$$(9 \times \rule{1cm}{0.4pt}) + (9 \times \rule{1cm}{0.4pt})$$

Use the Distributive Property to write 36 + 27 as a product.

$$9 \times (4 + \rule{1cm}{0.4pt})$$

Check your answer.

$$36 + 27 = \rule{1.5cm}{0.4pt}$$

$$9 \times (4 + \rule{1cm}{0.4pt}) = 9 \times \rule{1cm}{0.4pt} = \rule{1.5cm}{0.4pt}$$

So, $36 + 27 = \rule{1.5cm}{0.4pt} \times (\rule{1.5cm}{0.4pt} + \rule{1.5cm}{0.4pt})$.

---

1. Explain two ways to find the GCF of 36 and 27.

_____

_____

2. **MATHEMATICAL PRACTICE ④** **Use Diagrams** Describe how the figure at the right shows that $36 + 27 = 9 \times (4 + 3)$.

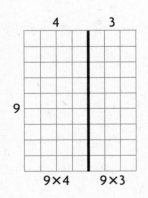

_____

_____

_____

_____

_____

Name _____

1. List the factors of 12 and 20. Circle the GCF.

Factors of 12: _____

Factors of 20: _____

Find the GCF.

2. 16, 18

3. 25, 40

 4. 24, 40

5. 14, 35

Use the GCF and the Distributive Property to express the sum as a product.

6. 21 + 28

7. 15 + 27

8. 40 + 15

9. 32 + 20

Math Talk MATHEMATICAL PRACTICES ①

Analyze Describe how to use the prime factorization of two numbers to find their GCF.

On Your Own

Find the GCF.

10. 8, 25

11. 31, 32

12. 56, 64

13. 150, 275

Use the GCF and the Distributive Property to express the sum as a product.

14. 24 + 30

15. 49 + 14

16. 63 + 81

17. 60 + 12

18. MATHEMATICAL PRACTICE ① Describe the difference between the LCM and the GCF of two numbers.

Problem Solving • Applications (Real World)

Use the table for 19–22. Teachers at the Scott School of Music teach only one instrument in each class. No students take classes for more than one instrument.

19. Francisco teaches group lessons to all of the violin and viola students at the Scott School of Music. All of his classes have the same number of students. What is the greatest number of students he can have in each class?

_____

Scott School of Music	
Instrument	**Number of Students**
Bass	20
Cello	27
Viola	30
Violin	36

20. **GO DEEPER** Amanda teaches all of the bass and viola students. All her classes have the same number of students. Each class has the greatest possible number of students. How many of these classes does she teach?

_____

21. **THINK SMARTER** Mia teaches jazz classes. She has 9 students in each class, and she teaches all the classes for two of the instruments. Which two instruments does she teach, and how many students are in her classes?

_____

22. **WRITE ▸ Math** Explain how you could use the GCF and the Distributive Property to express the sum of the number of bass students and the number of violin students as a product.

_____

_____

_____

23. **THINK SMARTER** The prime factorization of each number is shown.

$6 = 2 \times 3$
$12 = 2 \times 2 \times 3$

Using the prime factorization, complete the Venn diagram and write the GCF of 6 and 12.

GCF = _____

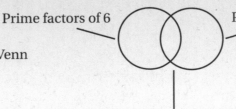

Prime factors of 6   Prime factors of 12

Common prime factors

Name _____

Greatest Common Factor

COMMON CORE STANDARD—6.NS.B.4
Compute fluently with multi-digit numbers and find common factors and multiples.

List the common factors. Circle the greatest common factor.

1. 25 and 10

2. 36 and 90

3. 45 and 60

_____ 1,⑤ _____

_____

_____

Find the GCF.

4. 14, 18

5. 6, 48

6. 16, 100

_____

_____

_____

Use the GCF and the Distributive Property to express the sum as a product.

7. 20 + 35

8. 18 + 27

9. 64 + 40

_____

_____

_____

10. Jerome is making prizes for a game at the school fair. He has two bags of different pins, one with 15 square pins and one with 20 round pins. Every prize will have one kind of pin. Each prize will have the same number of pins. What is the greatest number of pins Jerome can put in each prize?

11. There are 24 sixth graders and 40 seventh graders. Mr. Chan wants to divide both grades into groups of equal size, with the greatest possible number of students in each group. How many students should be in each group?

_____

_____

12. **WRITE** ▸*Math* Write a short paragraph to explain how to use prime factorization and the Distributive Property to express the sum of two whole numbers as a product.

_____

_____

Lesson Check (6.NS.B.4)

1. There are 15 boys and 10 girls in Miss Li's class. She wants to group all the students so that each group has the same number of boys and the same number of girls. What is the greatest number of groups she can have?

2. A pet shop manager wants the same number of birds in each cage. He wants to use as few cages as possible, but can only have one type of bird in each cage. If he has 42 parakeets and 18 canaries, how many birds will he put in each cage?

Spiral Review (5.NBT.A.1, 5.NBT.B.6, 5.NF.B.7c, 6.NS.B.2)

3. There are 147 people attending a dinner party. If each table can seat 7 people, how many tables are needed for the dinner party?

4. Sammy has 3 pancakes. He cuts each one in half. How many pancake halves are there?

5. The Cramer Company had a profit of $8,046,890 and the Coyle Company had a profit of $8,700,340 last year. Which company had the greater profit?

6. There are 111 guests attending a party. There are 15 servers. Each server has the same number of guests to serve. Jess will serve any extra guests. How many guests will Jess be serving?

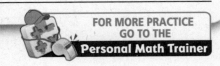

FOR MORE PRACTICE
GO TO THE
Personal Math Trainer

Name _____

Problem Solving • Apply the Greatest Common Factor

Essential Question How can you use the strategy *draw a diagram* to help you solve problems involving the GCF and the Distributive Property?

 The Number System—6.NS.B.4

MATHEMATICAL PRACTICES
MP1, MP5, MP6

Unlock the Problem

A trophy case at Riverside Middle School holds 18 baseball trophies and 24 soccer trophies. All shelves hold the same number of trophies. Only one sport is represented on each shelf. What is the greatest number of trophies that can be on each shelf? How many shelves are there for each sport?

Use the graphic organizer to help you solve the problem.

Read the Problem

What do I need to find?

I need to find _____

_____

_____

What information do I need to use?

I need to use _____

_____

How will I use the information?

I can find the GCF of _____ and use it to draw a diagram representing

the _____ of the trophy case.

Solve the Problem

Total trophies = baseball + soccer

$$18 + 24$$

Find the GCF of 18 and 24.   GCF: _____

Write each number as the product of the GCF and another factor.

$$18 + 24$$
$$(6 \times \text{\_\_\_\_\_}) + (6 \times \text{\_\_\_\_\_})$$

Use the Distributive Property to write 18 + 24 as a product.

$$6 \times (\text{\_\_\_\_\_} + \text{\_\_\_\_\_})$$

Use the product to draw a diagram of the trophy case. Use B's to represent baseball trophies. Use S's to represent soccer trophies.

```
B B B B B B




S S S S S S

```

 Math Talk

MATHEMATICAL PRACTICES ⑤

Use Tools Explain how the Distributive Property helped you solve the problem.

So, there are _____ trophies on each shelf. There are _____ shelves of

baseball trophies and _____ shelves of soccer trophies.

🔑 Try Another Problem

Delia is bagging 24 onion bagels and 16 plain bagels for her bakery customers. Each bag will hold only one type of bagel. Each bag will hold the same number of bagels. What is the greatest number of bagels she can put in each bag? How many bags of each type of bagel will there be?

Use the graphic organizer to help you solve the problem.

Read the Problem	Solve the Problem
What do I need to find?	
What information do I need to use?	
How will I use the information?	

So, there will be _____ bagels in each bag. There will be

_____ bags of onion bagels and _____ bags of plain bagels.

- **MATHEMATICAL PRACTICE 6** **Explain** how knowing that the GCF of 24 and 16 is 8 helped you solve the bagel problem.

_____

_____

Name _____

Share and Show

Unlock the Problem

√ Circle important facts.
√ Check to make sure you answered the question.
√ Check your answer.

1. Toby is packaging 21 baseball cards and 12 football cards to sell at a swap meet. Each packet will have the same number of cards. Each packet will have cards for only one sport. What is the greatest number of cards he can place in each packet? How many packets will there be for each sport?

   First, find the GCF of 21 and 12.

   _____

   Next, use the Distributive Property to write $21 + 12$ as a product, with the GCF as one of the factors.

   _____

   So, there will be _____ packets of baseball cards and

   _____ packets of football cards. Each packet will

   contain _____ cards.

2. **THINK SMARTER** **What if** Toby had decided to keep one baseball card for himself and sell the rest? How would your answers to the previous problem have changed?

   _____
   _____
   _____
   _____

3. Melissa bought 42 pine seedlings and 30 juniper seedlings to plant in rows on her tree farm. She wants each row to have the same number of seedlings. She wants only one type of seedling in each row. What is the greatest number of seedlings she can plant in each row? How many rows of each type of tree will there be?

   _____
   _____
   _____

WRITE Math
Show Your Work

On Your Own

4. **MATHEMATICAL PRACTICE ❶ Make Sense of Problems** A drum and bugle marching band has 45 members who play bugles and 27 members who play drums. When they march, each row has the same number of players. Each row has only bugle players or only drummers. What is the greatest number of players there can be in each row? How many rows of each type of player can there be?

_____

_____

WRITE ✏ *Math* · **Show Your Work**

5. **THINK SMARTER** The "color guard" of a drum and bugle band consists of members who march with flags, hoops, and other props. How would your answers to Exercise 4 change if there were 21 color guard members marching along with the bugle players and drummers?

_____

_____

_____

_____

6. **GO DEEPER** If you continue the pattern below so that you write all of the numbers in the pattern less than 500, how many even numbers will you write?

$$4, 9, 14, 19, 24, 29…$$

_____

Personal Math Trainer

7. **THINK SMARTER +** Mr. Yaw's bookcase holds 20 nonfiction books and 15 fiction books. Each shelf holds the same number of books and contains only one type of book. How many books will be on each shelf if each shelf has the **greatest** possible number of books? Show your work.

_____

_____

_____

_____

Problem Solving • Apply the Greatest Common Factor

COMMON CORE STANDARD—6.NS.B.4
Compute fluently with multi-digit numbers
and find common factors and multiples.

Read the problem and solve.

1. Ashley is bagging 32 pumpkin muffins and 28 banana muffins for some friends. Each bag will hold only one type of muffin. Each bag will hold the same number of muffins. What is the greatest number of muffins she can put in each bag? How many bags of each type of muffin will there be?

GCF: 4

$32 = 4 \times 8$

$28 = 4 \times 7$

$32 + 28 = 4 \times (8 + 7)$

So, there will be __8__ bags of pumpkin muffins and __7__ bags of banana muffins, with __4__ muffins in each bag.

2. Patricia is separating 16 soccer cards and 22 baseball cards into groups. Each group will have the same number of cards, and each group will have only one kind of sports card. What is the greatest number of cards she can put in each group? How many groups of each type will there be?

_____

3. Bryan is setting chairs in rows for a graduation ceremony. He has 50 black chairs and 60 white chairs. Each row will have the same number of chairs, and each row will have the same color chair. What is the greatest number of chairs that he can fit in each row? How many rows of each color chair will there be?

_____

4. A store clerk is bagging spices. He has 18 teaspoons of cinnamon and 30 teaspoons of nutmeg. Each bag needs to contain the same number of teaspoons, and each bag can contain only one spice. What is the maximum number of teaspoons of spice the clerk can put in each bag? How many bags of each spice will there be?

_____

5. **WRITE** ▸*Math* Write a problem in which you need to put as many of two different types of objects as possible into equal groups. Then use the GCF, Distributive Property, and a diagram to solve your problem.

_____

Lesson Check (6.NS.B.4)

1. Fred has 36 strawberries and 42 blueberries. He wants to use them to garnish desserts so that each dessert has the same number of berries, but only one type of berry. He wants as much fruit as possible on each dessert. How many berries will he put on each dessert? How many desserts with each type of fruit will he have?

_____

_____

_____

2. Dolores is arranging coffee mugs on shelves in her shop. She wants each shelf to have the same number of mugs. She only wants one color of mug on each shelf. If she has 49 blue mugs and 56 red mugs, what is the greatest number she can put on each shelf? How many shelves does she need for each color?

_____

_____

_____

Spiral Review (5.NF.A.1, 5.NF.A.2, 6.NS.B.4)

3. A rectangle is $3\frac{1}{3}$ feet long and $2\frac{1}{3}$ feet wide. What is the distance around the rectangle?

_____

4. Lowell bought $4\frac{1}{4}$ pounds of apples and $3\frac{3}{5}$ pounds of oranges. How many pounds of fruit did Lowell buy?

_____

5. How much heavier is a $9\frac{1}{8}$ pound box than a $2\frac{5}{6}$ pound box?

6. The combination of Clay's locker is the prime factors of 102 in order from least to greatest. What is the combination of Clay's locker?

_____

_____

FOR MORE PRACTICE
GO TO THE
Personal Math Trainer

Name _____

Vocabulary

Choose the best term from the box to complete the sentence.

Vocabulary
greatest common factor
least common multiple
prime number

1. The _____ of two numbers is greater than or equal to the numbers. (p. 17)

2. The _____ of two numbers is less than or equal to the numbers. (p. 23)

Concepts and Skills

Estimate. Then find the quotient. Write the remainder, if any, with an r. (6.NS.B.2)

3. 2,800 ÷ 25

4. 19,129 ÷ 37

5. 32,111 ÷ 181

_____ _____ _____

Find the prime factorization. (6.NS.B.4)

6. 44

7. 36

8. 90

_____ _____ _____

Find the LCM. (6.NS.B.4)

9. 8, 10

10. 4, 14

11. 6, 9

_____ _____ _____

Find the GCF. (6.NS.B.4)

12. 16, 20

13. 8, 52

14. 36, 54

_____ _____ _____

15. A zookeeper divided 2,440 pounds of food equally among 8 elephants. How many pounds of food did each elephant receive? (6.NS.B.2)

_____

16. DVD cases are sold in packages of 20. Padded mailing envelopes are sold in packets of 12. What is the least number of cases and envelopes you could buy so that there is one case for each envelope with none left over? (6.NS.B.4)

_____

17. `GO DEEPER` Max bought two deli sandwich rolls measuring 18 inches and 30 inches. He wants them to be cut into equal sections that are as long as possible. Into what lengths should the rolls be cut? How many sections will there be in all? (6.NS.B.4)

_____

18. Susan is buying supplies for a party. If spoons only come in bags of 8 and forks only come in bags of 6, what is the least number of spoons and the least number of forks she can buy so that she has the same number of each? (6.NS.B.4)

_____

19. `GO DEEPER` Tina is placing 30 roses and 42 tulips in vases for table decorations in her restaurant. Each vase will hold the same number of flowers. Each vase will have only one type of flower. What is the greatest number of flowers she can place in each vase? If Tina has 24 tables in her restaurant, how many flowers can she place in each vase? (6.NS.B.4)

_____

Add and Subtract Decimals

Essential Question How do you add and subtract multi-digit decimals?

Common Core **The Number System—
6.NS.B.3**
MATHEMATICAL PRACTICES
MP3, MP6, MP7

CONNECT The place value of a digit in a number shows the value of the digit. The number 2.358 shows 2 ones, 3 tenths, 5 hundredths, and 8 thousandths.

Place Value						
Thousands	Hundreds	Tens	Ones	Tenths	Hundredths	Thousandths
			2 .	3	5	8

Unlock the Problem Real World

Amanda and three of her friends volunteer at the local animal shelter. One of their jobs is to weigh the puppies and kittens and chart their growth. Amanda's favorite puppy weighed 2.358 lb last month. If it gained 1.08 lb, how much does it weigh this month?

- How do you know whether to add or subtract the weights given in the problem?

_____

_____

 Add 2.358 + 1.08.

Estimate the sum. _____ + _____ = _____

$$2.358$$
$$+ 1.08$$
_____

Compare your estimate with the sum. Since the estimate,

_____, is close to _____, the answer is reasonable.

So, the puppy weighs _____ lb this month.

---

1. **MATHEMATICAL PRACTICE 7** **Look for Structure** Is it necessary to write a zero after 1.08 to find the sum? Explain.

_____

_____

2. Explain how place value can help you add decimals.

_____

🔒 Example 1

A bee hummingbird, the world's smallest bird, has a mass of 1.836 grams. A new United States nickel has a mass of 5 grams. What is the difference in grams between the mass of a nickel and the mass of a bee hummingbird?

Subtract 5 − 1.836.

Estimate the difference. _____ − _____ = _____

Think: 5 = 5._____

Subtract the thousandths first.

Then subtract the hundredths, tenths, and ones.

Regroup as needed.

$$5.\ \rule{1cm}{0.4pt}$$
$$-1.836$$

Bee hummingbird

Compare your estimate with the difference. Since the estimate,

_____, is close to _____, the answer is reasonable.

So, the mass of a new nickel is _____ grams more than the mass of a bee hummingbird.

U.S. Nickel

Math Talk

MATHEMATICAL PRACTICES ⑥

Explain how to use inverse operations to check your answer to 5 − 1.836.

🔒 Example 2 Evaluate (6.5 − 1.97) + 3.461 using the order of operations.

Write the expression.

$$(6.5 - 1.97) + 3.461$$

Perform operations in parentheses.

$$6.50$$
$$-1.97$$

Add.

$$+\ 3.461$$

So, the value of the expression is _____.

Math Talk

MATHEMATICAL PRACTICES ⑦

Look for Structure Describe how adding and subtracting decimals is like adding and subtracting whole numbers.

Name _____

Share and Show MATH BOARD

1. Find $3.42 - 1.9$.

Estimate.

_____ − _____ = _____

Subtract the _____ first.

$$\begin{array}{r} 3.42 \\ -1.90 \\ \hline \end{array}$$

Estimate. Then find the sum or difference.

2. $2.3 + 5.68 + 21.047$

3. $33.25 - 21.463$

4. Evaluate
$(8.54 + 3.46) - 6.749$.

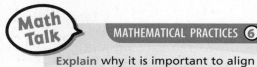

Math Talk MATHEMATICAL PRACTICES ⑥

Explain why it is important to align the decimal points when you add or subtract decimals.

On Your Own

Estimate. Then find the sum or difference.

5. $57.08 + 34.71$

6. $20.11 - 13.27$

7. $62 - 9.817$

8. $35.1 + 4.89$

Practice: Copy and Solve Evaluate using the order of operations.

9. $8.01 - (2.2 + 4.67)$

10. $54 + (9.2 - 1.413)$

11. $21.3 - (19.1 - 3.22)$

12. MATHEMATICAL PRACTICE ③ **Make Arguments** A student evaluated $19.1 + (4.32 + 6.9)$ and got 69.2. How can you use estimation to convince the student that this answer is not reasonable?

_____

13. THINK SMARTER Lynn paid $4.75 for cereal, $8.96 for chicken, and $3.25 for soup. Show how she can use properties and compatible numbers to evaluate $(4.75 + 8.96) + 3.25$ to find the total cost.

_____

14. **THINK SMARTER** For numbers 14a–14d, select True or
False for each equation.

14a. $3.76 + 2.7 = 6.46$ ○ True ○ False

14b. $4.14 + 1.8 = 4.32$ ○ True ○ False

14c. $2.01 - 1.33 = 0.68$ ○ True ○ False

14d. $51 - 49.2 = 1.8$ ○ True ○ False

Connect [to] Science

Comparing Eggs

Different types of birds lay eggs of different sizes. Small
birds lay eggs that are smaller than those that are laid
by larger birds. The table shows the average lengths and
widths of five different birds' eggs.

Average Dimensions of Bird Eggs		
Bird	**Length (m)**	**Width (m)**
Canada Goose	0.086	0.058
Hummingbird	0.013	0.013
Raven	0.049	0.033
Robin	0.019	0.015
Turtledove	0.031	0.023

Canada Goose

Use the table for 15–17.

15. What is the difference in average length between the longest egg
and the shortest egg?

_____

16. **GO DEEPER** Which egg has a width that is eight thousandths of a meter shorter
than its length?

_____

17. **THINK SMARTER** How many robin eggs, laid end to end, would be
about equal in length to two raven eggs? Justify your answer.

_____

_____

_____

Name _____

Add and Subtract Decimals

COMMON CORE STANDARD—6.NS.B.3
*Compute fluently with multi-digit numbers and
find common factors and multiples.*

Estimate. Then find the sum or difference.

1. 43.53 + 27.67

    40 + 30 = 70

         43.53
       + 27.67
       ――――――
         71.20

2. 17 + 3.6 + 4.049

_____

3. 3.49 − 2.75

_____

4. 5.07 − 2.148

_____

5. 3.92 + 16 + 0.085

_____

6. 41.98 + 13.5 + 27.338

_____

Evaluate using the order of operations.

7. 8.4 + (13.1 − 0.6)

_____

8. 34.7 − (12.07 + 4.9)

_____

9. (32.45 − 4.8) − 2.06

_____

Problem Solving · Real World

10. The average annual rainfall in Clearview is 38 inches. This year, 29.777 inches fell. How much less rain fell this year than falls in an average year?

_____

11. At the theater, the Worth family spent $18.00 on adult tickets, $16.50 on children's tickets, and $11.75 on refreshments. How much did they spend in all?

_____

12. **WRITE** ▸*Math* Write a word problem that involves adding or subtracting decimals. Include the solution.

_____

_____

_____

Lesson Check (6.NS.B.3)

1. Alden fills his backpack with 0.45 kg of apples, 0.18 kg of cheese, and a water bottle that weighs 1.4 kg. How heavy are the contents of his backpack?

_____

_____

2. Gabby plans to hike 6.3 kilometers to see a waterfall. She stops to rest after hiking 4.75 kilometers. How far does she have left to hike?

_____

_____

Spiral Review (5.NBT.B.5, 5.NBT.B.6, 6.NS.B.4)

3. A 6-car monorail train can carry 78 people. If one train makes 99 trips during the day, what is the greatest number of people the train can carry in one day?

_____

4. An airport parking lot has 2,800 spaces. If each row has 25 spaces, how many rows are there?

_____

5. Evan brought 6 batteries that cost $10 each and 6 batteries that cost $4 each. The total cost was the same as he would have spent buying 6 batteries that cost $14 each. So, $6 \times \$14 = (6 \times 10) + (6 \times 4)$. What property does the equation illustrate?

_____

6. Cups come in packages of 12 and lids come in packages of 15. What is the least number of cups and lids that Corrine can buy if she wants to have the same number of cups and lids?

_____

FOR MORE PRACTICE
GO TO THE
Personal Math Trainer

Multiply Decimals

Essential Question How do you multiply multi-digit decimals?

 Common Core The Number System—
6.NS.B.3

MATHEMATICAL PRACTICES
MP2, MP6, MP8

 Unlock the Problem Real World

Last summer Rachel worked 38.5 hours per week at a grocery store. She earned $9.70 per hour. How much did she earn in a week?

🔑 **Multiply** $9.70 × 38.5.

First estimate the product. $10 × 40 = _____

- How can you estimate the product?

_____

_____

You can use the estimate to place the decimal in a product.

$9.70
× 38.5

Multiply as you would with whole numbers.

+ _____
$ _____

The estimate is about $ _____,

so the decimal point should be

placed after $ _____.

Since the estimate, _____, is close to _____, the answer is reasonable.

So, Rachel earned _____ per week.

1. Explain how your estimate helped you know where to place the decimal in the product.

_____

_____

Try This! **What if** Rachel gets a raise of $1.50 per hour? How much will she earn when she works 38.5 hours?

Counting Decimal Places Another way to place the decimal in a product is to add the numbers of decimal places in the factors.

Example 1 Multiply 0.084 × 0.096.

$$
\begin{array}{r}
0.084 \\
\times\,0.096 \\
\hline
\end{array}
$$

_____ decimal places

_____ decimal places

Multiply as you would with whole numbers.

_____ + _____, or _____ decimal places

Example 2 Evaluate 0.35 × (0.48 + 1.24) using the order of operations.

Write the expression.

$$0.35 \times (0.48 + 1.24)$$

Perform operations in parentheses.

$$0.35 \times \text{_____}$$

Multiply.

0.35   _____ decimal places

×   _____ decimal places

_____ + _____, or _____ decimal places

So, the value of the expression is _____.

Math Talk

MATHEMATICAL PRACTICES ②

Reasoning Is the product of 0.5 and 3.052 greater than or less than 3.052?

2. **MATHEMATICAL PRACTICE ⑧** **Use Repeated Reasoning** Look for a pattern. Explain.

0.645 × 1 = 0.645

0.645 × 10 = 6.45   The decimal point moves _____ place to the right.

0.645 × 100 = _____   The decimal point moves _____ places to the right.

0.645 × 1,000 = _____ The decimal point moves _____ places to the right.

_____

_____

Name _____

Estimate. Then find the product.

1. 12.42×28.6

_____ × _____ = _____

$$\begin{array}{r} 12.42 \\ \times\ 28.6 \\ \hline \end{array}$$

Estimate.

Think: The estimate is about _____, so the decimal point should be placed after _____.

2. 32.5×7.4

_____

MATHEMATICAL PRACTICE 6 **Attend to Precision** **Algebra** **Evaluate using the order of operations.**

3. $0.24 \times (7.3 + 2.1)$

_____

4. $0.075 \times (9.2 - 0.8)$

_____

5. $2.83 + (0.3 \times 2.16)$

_____

On Your Own

Estimate. Then find the product.

6. 29.14×5.2

_____

7. 6.95×12

_____

8. 0.055×1.82

_____

MATHEMATICAL PRACTICE 6 **Attend to Precision** **Algebra** **Evaluate using the order of operations.**

9. $(3.62 \times 2.1) - 0.749$

_____

10. $5.8 - (0.25 \times 1.5)$

_____

11. $(0.83 + 1.27) \times 6.4$

_____

12. GO DEEPER Jamal is buying ingredients to make a large batch of granola to sell at a school fair. He buys 3.2 pounds of walnuts for $4.40 per pound and 2.4 pounds of cashews for $6.25 per pound. How much change will he receive if he pays with two $20 bills?

_____

Unlock the Problem

The table shows some currency exchange rates for 2009.

Major Currency Exchange Rates in 2009				
Currency	U.S. Dollar	Japanese Yen	European Euro	Canadian Dollar
U.S. Dollar	1	88.353	0.676	1.052
Japanese Yen	0.011	1	0.008	0.012
European Euro	1.479	130.692	1	1.556
Canadian Dollar	0.951	83.995	0.643	1

Denominations of Euro

13. **THINK SMARTER** When Cameron went to Canada in 2007, he exchanged 40 U.S. dollars for 46.52 Canadian dollars. If Cameron exchanged 40 U.S. dollars in 2009, did he receive more or less than he received in 2007? How much more or less?

a. What do you need to find?

_____

_____

b. How will you use the table to solve the problem?

_____

_____

_____

_____

c. Complete the sentences.

40 U.S. dollars were worth _____ Canadian dollars in 2009.

So, Cameron would receive _____

_____ Canadian dollars in 2009.

14. **THINK SMARTER +** At a convenience store, the Jensen family puts 12.4 gallons of gasoline in their van at a cost of $3.80 per gallon. They also buy 4 water bottles for $1.99 each, and 2 snacks for $1.55 each. Complete the table to find the cost for each item.

Personal Math Trainer

Item	Calculation	Cost
Gasoline	12.4 × $3.80	
Water bottles	4 × $1.99	
Snacks	2 × $1.55	

Mrs. Jensen says the total cost for everything before tax is $56.66. Do you agree with her? Explain why or why not.

_____

Name _____

Multiply Decimals

COMMON CORE STANDARD—6.NS.B.3
Compute fluently with multi-digit numbers and find common factors and multiples.

Estimate. Then find the product.

1. 5.69×7.8

$6 \times 8 = 48$

$$
\begin{array}{r}
5.69 \\
\times\ 7.8 \\
\hline
4552 \\
39830 \\
\hline
44.382
\end{array}
$$

2. 3.92×0.051

3. 2.365×12.4

4. 305.08×1.5

Evaluate the expression using the order of operations.

5. $(61.8 \times 1.7) + 9.5$

6. $205 - (35.80 \times 5.6)$

7. $1.9 \times (10.6 - 2.17)$

Problem Solving Real World

8. Blaine exchanges $100 for yen before going to Japan. If each U.S. dollar is worth 88.353 yen, how many yen should Blaine receive?

9. A camera costs 115 Canadian dollars. If each Canadian dollar is worth 0.952 U.S. dollars, how much will the camera cost in U.S. dollars?

10. **WRITE** ▸*Math* Explain how to mentally multiply a decimal number by 100.

_____

_____

Lesson Check (6.NS.B.3)

Estimate each product. Then find the exact product for each question.

1. A gallon of water at room temperature weighs about 8.35 pounds. Lena puts 4.5 gallons in a bucket. How much does the water weigh?

   _____

   _____

   _____

2. Shawn's rectangular mobile home is 7.2 meters wide and 19.5 meters long. What is its area?

   _____

   _____

   _____

   _____

Spiral Review (5.OA.A.1, 6.NS.B.2, 6.NS.B.4)

3. Last week, a store sold laptops worth a total of $3,885. Each laptop cost $555. How many laptops did the store sell last week?

   _____

4. Kyle drives his truck 429 miles on 33 gallons of gas. How many miles can Kyle drive on 1 gallon of gas?

   _____

5. Seven busloads each carrying 35 students arrived at the game, joining 23 students who were already there. Evaluate the expression $23 + (7 \times 35)$ to find the total number of students at the game.

   _____

6. A store is giving away a $10 coupon to every 7th person to enter the store and a $25 coupon to every 18th person to enter the store. Which person will be the first to get both coupons?

   _____

FOR MORE PRACTICE
GO TO THE
Personal Math Trainer

Divide Decimals by Whole Numbers

Essential Question How do you divide decimals by whole numbers?

Common Core The Number System—
6.NS.B.3

MATHEMATICAL PRACTICES
MP1, MP5, MP6, MP8

Unlock the Problem Real World

Dan opened a savings account at a bank to save for a new snowboard. He earned $3.48 interest on his savings account over a 3-month period. What was the average amount of interest Dan earned per month on his savings account?

 Divide $3.48 ÷ 3.

First estimate. 3 ÷ 3 = _____

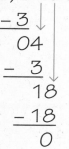

Think: 3.48 is shared among 3 groups.

Divide the ones. Place a decimal point after the ones place in the quotient.

Divide the tenths and then the hundredths. When the remainder is zero and there are no more digits in the dividend, the division is complete.

> **Remember**
> Quotient
> ↓
> 1.23
> Divisor → 2)2.46 ← Dividend

Check your answer.

$
×   3
——————
$3.48

Multiply the quotient by the divisor to check your answer.

So, Dan earned an average of _____ in interest per month.

Math Talk

MATHEMATICAL PRACTICES ⑥
Explain how you know your answer is reasonable.

1. **MATHEMATICAL PRACTICE ①** **Analyze Relationships** What if the same amount of interest was gained over 4 months? Explain how you would solve the problem.

_____

🔑 Example **Divide 42.133 ÷ 7.**

First estimate. 42 ÷ 7 = _____

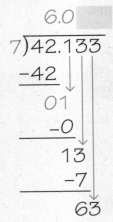

```
        6.0
      _____
   7 ) 42.133
      -42
      _____
        01
        -0
      _____
        13
        -7
      _____
        63
        -
      _____
```

Think: 42.133 is shared among 7 groups.

Divide the ones. Place a decimal point after the ones place in the quotient.

Divide the tenths. Since 1 tenth cannot be shared among 7 groups, write a zero in the quotient. Regroup the 1 tenth as 10 hundredths. Now you have 13 hundredths.

Continue to divide until the remainder is zero and there are no more digits in the dividend.

Check your answer.

```
     6.019
   ×     7
   _____
```

Multiply the quotient by the divisor to check your answer.

So, 42.133 ÷ 7 = _____.

---

2. Explain how you know which numbers to multiply when checking your answer.

_____

_____

Share and Show MATH BOARD

1. Estimate 24.186 ÷ 6. Then find the quotient. Check your answer.

Estimate. _____ ÷ _____ = _____

Think: Place a decimal point after the ones place in the quotient.

```
   6 ) 24.186
```

```
   ×        6
```

Name _____

Estimate. Then find the quotient.

2. $7\overline{)\$17.15}$

✓ 3. $4\overline{)1.068}$

4. $12\overline{)60.84}$

✓ 5. $18.042 \div 6$

_____ _____ _____ _____

Math Talk

MATHEMATICAL PRACTICES ⑧

Generalize Explain how you know where to place the decimal point in the quotient when dividing a decimal by a whole number.

On Your Own

Estimate. Then find the quotient.

6. $\$21.24 \div 6$

7. $28.63 \div 7$

8. $1.505 \div 35$

9. $0.108 \div 18$

_____ _____ _____ _____

MATHEMATICAL PRACTICE ⑥ **Attend to Precision** **Algebra** Evaluate using the order of operations.

10. $(3.11 + 4.0) \div 9$

11. $(6.18 - 1.32) \div 3$

12. $(18 - 5.76) \div 6$

_____ _____ _____

13. **MATHEMATICAL PRACTICE ⑤** **Use Appropriate Tools** Find the length of a dollar bill to the nearest tenth of a centimeter. Then show how to use division to find the length of the bill when it is folded in half along the portrait of George Washington.

_____

_____

14. **GO DEEPER** Emilio bought 5.65 pounds of green grapes and 3.07 pounds of red grapes. He divided the grapes equally into 16 bags. If each bag of grapes has the same weight, how much does each bag weigh?

_____

Problem Solving • Applications Real World

Pose a Problem

15. **THINK SMARTER** This table shows the average height in inches for girls and boys at ages 8, 10, 12, and 14 years.

Average Height (in.)				
	Age 8	Age 10	Age 12	Age 14
Girls	50.75	55.50	60.50	62.50
Boys	51.00	55.25	59.00	65.20

To find the average growth per year for girls from age 8 to age 12, Emma knew she had to find the amount of growth between age 8 and age 12, then divide that number by the number of years between age 8 and age 12.

Emma used this expression: $(60.50 - 50.75) \div 4$

She evaluated the expression using the order of operations.

Write the expression.	$(60.50 - 50.75) \div 4$
Perform operations in parentheses.	$9.75 \div 4$
Divide.	2.4375

So, the average annual growth for girls ages 8 to 12 is 2.4375 inches.

Write a new problem using the information in the table for the average height for boys. Use division in your problem.

Pose a Problem

_____

_____

_____

Solve Your Problem

16. **THINK SMARTER** The table shows the number of books each of three friends bought and the cost. On average, which friend spent the most per book? Use numbers and words to explain your answer.

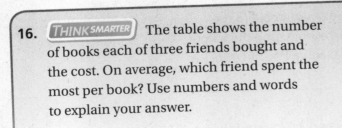

Friend	Number of books Purchased	Total Cost (in dollars)	Average Cost (in dollars)
Joyce	1	$10.95	
Nabil	2	$40.50	
Kenneth	3	$51.15	

_____

_____

_____

Divide Decimals by Whole Numbers

COMMON CORE STANDARD—6.NS.B.3
Compute fluently with multi-digit numbers
and find common factors and multiples.

Estimate. Then find the quotient.

1. $1.284 \div 12$

$1.2 \div 12 = 0.1$

$$\begin{array}{r} 0.107 \\ 12\overline{)1.284} \\ -12 \\ \hline -8 \\ \hline 0 \\ \hline 84 \\ -84 \\ \hline 0 \end{array}$$

2. $9\overline{)2.43}$

3. $25.65 \div 15$

4. $12\overline{)2.436}$

Evaluate using the order of operations.

5. $(8 - 2.96) \div 3$

6. $(7.772 - 2.38) \div 8$

7. $(53.2 + 35.7) \div 7$

Problem Solving · Real World

8. Jake earned $10.44 interest on his savings account for an 18-month period. What was the average amount of interest Jake earned on his savings account per month?

9. Gloria worked for 6 hours a day for 2 days at the bank and earned $114.24. How much did she earn per hour?

10. **WRITE** ▸ *Math* Explain the importance of correctly placing the decimal point in the quotient of a division problem.

Lesson Check (6.NS.B.3)

Estimate each quotient. Then find the exact quotient for each question.

1. Ron divided 67.6 fluid ounces of orange juice evenly among 16 glasses. How much did he pour into each glass?

2. The cost of a $12.95 pizza was shared evenly by 5 friends. How much did each person pay?

_____

_____

_____

_____

_____

_____

Spiral Review (5.NBT.A.1, 5.NBT.B.6, 6.NS.B.2, 6.NS.B.4)

3. What is the value of the digit 6 in 968,743,220?

4. The Tama, Japan, monorail carries 92,700 riders each day. If the monorail runs 18 hours each day, what is the average number of passengers riding each hour?

_____

_____

5. Ray paid $812 to rent music equipment that costs $28 per hour. How many hours did he have the equipment?

6. Jan has 35 teaspoons of chocolate cocoa mix and 45 teaspoons of french vanilla cocoa mix. She wants to put the same amount of mix into each jar, and she only wants one flavor of mix in each jar. She wants to fill as many jars as possible. How many jars of french vanilla cocoa mix will Jan fill?

_____

_____

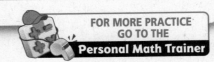

FOR MORE PRACTICE
GO TO THE
Personal Math Trainer

Divide with Decimals

Essential Question How do you divide whole numbers and decimals by decimals?

Common Core — The Number System—
6.NS.B.3
MATHEMATICAL PRACTICES
MP1, MP6, MP8

CONNECT Find each quotient to discover a pattern.

$4 \div 2 =$ _____

$40 \div 20 =$ _____

$400 \div 200 =$ _____

When you multiply both the dividend and the divisor by the same

power of _____, the quotient is the _____. You can use this
fact to help you divide decimals.

Unlock the Problem Real World

Tami is training for a triathlon. In a triathlon, athletes compete in three events: swimming, cycling, and running. She cycled 66.5 miles in 3.5 hours. If she cycled at a constant speed, how far did she cycle in 1 hour?

Remember
Compatible numbers are pairs of numbers that are easy to compute mentally.

🔑 **Divide 66.5 ÷ 3.5.**

Estimate using compatible numbers.

$60 \div 3 =$ _____

STEP 1

Make the divisor a whole number by multiplying the divisor and dividend by 10.

$3.5 \overline{)66.5}$

Think: $3.5 \times 10 = 35$ $66.5 \times 10 = 665$

STEP 2

Divide.

$35 \overline{)665}$

So, Tami cycled _____ in 1 hour.

• **MATHEMATICAL PRACTICE ①** **Evaluate Reasonableness** Explain whether your answer is reasonable.

🔑 Example 1 Divide 17.25 ÷ 5.75. Check.

STEP 1

Make the divisor a whole number by multiplying the divisor and dividend by _____.

5.75 × _____ = _____

17.25 × _____ = _____

$$5.75\overset{\frown}{)}17.25\,\,$$

STEP 2

Divide.

$$575\overline{)1{,}725}$$

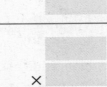

STEP 3

Check.

So, 17.25 ÷ 5.75 = _____.

🔑 Example 2 Divide 37.8 ÷ 0.14.

STEP 1

Make the divisor a whole number by multiplying the divisor and dividend by _____.

_____ × _____ = _____

_____ × _____ = _____

$$0.14\overset{\frown}{)}37.80\,\,$$

Think: Write a zero to the right of the dividend so that you can move the decimal point.

STEP 2

Divide.

$$14\overline{)3{,}780}$$

So, 37.8 ÷ 0.14 = _____.

> **! ERROR Alert**
>
> Be careful to move the decimal point in the dividend the same number of places that you moved the decimal point in the divisor.

Math Talk

 MATHEMATICAL PRACTICES ⑥

Explain How can you check that the quotient is reasonable? How can you check that it is accurate?

Name _____

1. Find the quotient.

Think: Make the divisor a whole number by

multiplying the divisor and dividend by _____.

$$14.8\overline{)99.456}$$

Estimate. Then find the quotient.

2. $10.80 ÷ $1.35

3. 26.4 ÷ 1.76

4. $8.7\overline{)53.07}$

MATHEMATICAL PRACTICES ⑧

Generalize Explain how you know how many places to move the decimal point in the divisor and the dividend.

On Your Own

Estimate. Then find the quotient.

5. 75 ÷ 12.5

6. 544.6 ÷ 1.75

7. $0.78\overline{)0.234}$

MATHEMATICAL PRACTICE ⑥ Attend to Precision Algebra Evaluate using the order of operations.

8. 36.4 + (9.2 − 4.9 ÷ 7)

9. 16 ÷ 2.5 − 3.2 × 0.043

10. 142 ÷ (42 − 6.5) × 3.9

11. **GO DEEPER** Marcus can buy 0.3 pound of sliced meat from a deli for $3.15. How much will 0.7 pound of sliced meat cost?

_____

12. The table shows the earnings and the number of hours worked for three employees. Complete the table by finding the missing values. Which employee earned the least per hour? Explain.

_____

_____

Employee	Total Earned (in dollars)	Number of Hours Worked	Earnings per Hour (in dollars)
1	$34.02		$9.72
2	$42.75	4.5	
3	$52.65		$9.75

Connect to Science

Amoebas

Amoebas are tiny one-celled organisms. Amoebas can range in size from 0.01 mm to 5 mm in length. You can study amoebas by using a microscope or by studying photographic enlargements of them.

Jacob has a photograph of an amoeba that has been enlarged 1,000 times. The length of the amoeba in the photo is 60 mm. What is the actual length of the amoeba?

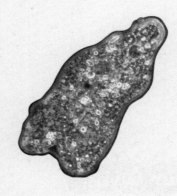

Divide 60 ÷ 1,000 by looking for a pattern.

$60 \div 1 = 60$

$60 \div 10 = 6.0$ The decimal point moves _____ place to the left.

$60 \div 100 =$ _____   The decimal point moves _____ places to the left.

$60 \div 1,000 =$ _____   The decimal point moves _____ places to the left.

So, the actual length of the amoeba is _____ mm.

13.  Explain the pattern.

_____

_____

14. GO DEEPER _Pelomyxa palustris_ is an amoeba with a length of 4.9 mm. _Amoeba proteus_ has a length of 0.7 mm. How many _Amoeba proteus_ would you have to line up to equal the length of three _Pelomyxa palustris_? Explain.

_____

_____

Common Core

COMMON CORE STANDARD—6.NS.B.3
Compute fluently with multi-digit numbers and find common factors and multiples.

Estimate. Then find the quotient.

1. $43.18 \div 3.4$

   $\underline{44 \div 4 = 11}$

   $$
   \begin{array}{r}
   12.7 \\
   34 \overline{)431.8} \\
   -34 \\
   \hline
   91 \\
   -68 \\
   \hline
   238 \\
   -238 \\
   \hline
   0
   \end{array}
   $$

2. $4.185 \div 0.93$

3. $6.3\overline{)25.83}$

4. $0.143 \div 0.55$

Evaluate using the order of operations.

5. $4.92 \div (0.8 - 0.12 \div 0.3)$

6. $0.86 \div 5 - 0.3 \times 0.5$

7. $17.28 \div (1.32 - 0.24) \times 0.6$

Problem Solving ·Real· ·World·

8. If Amanda walks at an average speed of 2.72 miles per hour, how long will it take her to walk 6.8 miles?

9. Chad cycled 62.3 miles in 3.5 hours. If he cycled at a constant speed, how far did he cycle in 1 hour?

10. **WRITE** ▸*Math* Explain how dividing by a decimal is different from dividing by a whole number and how it is similar.

Lesson Check (6.NS.B.3)

1. Elliot drove 202.8 miles and used 6.5 gallons of gasoline. How many miles did he travel per gallon of gasoline?

2. A package of crackers weighing 8.2 ounces costs $2.87. What is the cost per ounce of crackers?

Spiral Review (5.NBT.B.5, 5.NBT.B.7, 5.NF.B.3)

3. Four bags of pretzels were divided equally among 5 people. How much of a bag did each person get?

4. A zebra ran at a speed of 20 feet per second. What operation should you use to find the distance the zebra ran in 10 seconds?

5. Nira has $13.50. She receives a paycheck for $55. She spends $29.40. How much money does she have now?

6. A piece of cardboard is 24 centimeters long and 15 centimeters wide. What is its area?

© Houghton Mifflin Harcourt Publishing Company

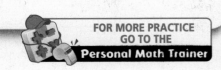

FOR MORE PRACTICE
GO TO THE
Personal Math Trainer

Name _____

✓ Chapter 1 Review/Test

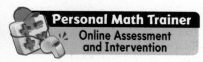

1. Use the numbers to complete the factor tree. You may use a number more than once.

Write the prime factorization of 54.

_____

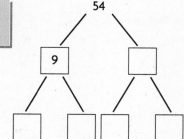

2. For numbers 2a–2d, choose Yes or No to indicate whether the LCM of the two numbers is 15.

2a. 5, 3   ○ Yes   ○ No

2b. 5, 10   ○ Yes   ○ No

2c. 5, 15   ○ Yes   ○ No

2d. 5, 20   ○ Yes   ○ No

3. Select two numbers that have 9 as their greatest common factor. Mark all that apply.

(A) 3, 9

(B) 3, 18

(C) 9, 18

(D) 9, 36

(E) 18, 27

 Assessment Options
Chapter Test

4. The prime factorization of each number is shown.

$$15 = 3 \times 5$$
$$18 = 2 \times 3 \times 3$$

Part A

Using the prime factorization, complete the Venn diagram.

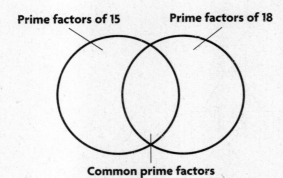

Prime factors of 15   Prime factors of 18

Common prime factors

Part B

Find the GCF of 15 and 18.

_____

5. For numbers 5a–5d, choose Yes or No to indicate whether each equation is correct.

5a. $222.2 \div 11 = 22.2$ ○ Yes   ○ No

5b. $400 \div 50 = 8$ ○ Yes   ○ No

5c. $1{,}440 \div 36 = 40$ ○ Yes   ○ No

5d. $7{,}236 \div 9 = 804$ ○ Yes   ○ No

6. For numbers 6a–6d, select True or False for each equation.

6a. $1.7 + 4.03 = 6$　　　　　○ True　　　　○ False

6b. $2.58 + 3.5 = 6.08$　　　○ True　　　　○ False

6c. $3.21 - 0.98 = 2.23$　　　○ True　　　　○ False

6d. $14 - 1.3 = 0.01$　　　　○ True　　　　○ False

Personal Math Trainer

7. **THINK SMARTER +** Four friends went shopping at a music store. The table shows the number of CDs each friend bought and the total cost. Complete the table to show the average cost of the CDs each friend bought.

Friend	Number of CDs Purchased	Total Cost (in dollars)	Average Cost (in dollars)
Lana	4	$36.68	
Troy	5	$40.55	
Juanita	5	$47.15	
Alex	6	$54.42	

What is the average cost of all the CDs that the four friends bought? Show your work.

_____

_____

8. The table shows the earnings and the number of hours worked for five employees. Complete the table by finding the missing values.

Employee	Total Money Earned (in dollars)	Number of Hours Worked	Earnings per Hour (in dollars)
1	$23.75		$9.50
2	$28.38	3.3	
3	$38.50		$8.75
4	$55.00	5.5	
5	$60.00	2.5	

9. The distance around the outside of Cedar Park is 0.8 mile. Joanie ran 0.25 of the distance during her lunch break. How far did she run? Show your work.

10. A one-celled organism measures 32 millimeters in length in a photograph. If the photo has been enlarged by a factor of 100, what is the actual length of the organism? Show your work.

11. GO DEEPER You can buy 5 T-shirts at Baxter's for the same price that you can buy 4 T-shirts at Bixby's. If one T-shirt costs $11.80 at Bixby's, how much does one T-shirt cost at Baxter's? Use numbers and words to explain your answer.

12. Crackers come in packages of 24. Cheese slices come in packages of 18. Andy wants one cheese slice for each cracker. Patrick made the statement shown.

> If Andy doesn't want any crackers or cheese slices left over, he needs to buy at least 432 of each.

Is Patrick's statement correct? Use numbers and words to explain why or why not. If Patrick's statement is incorrect, what should he do to correct it?

13. There are 16 sixth graders and 20 seventh graders in the Robotics Club. For the first project, the club sponsor wants to organize the club members into equal-size groups. Each group will have only sixth graders or only seventh graders.

Part A

How many students will be in each group if each group has the greatest possible number of club members? Show your work.

Part B

If each group has the greatest possible number of club members, how many groups of sixth graders and how many groups of seventh graders will there be? Use numbers and words to explain your answer.

14. The Hernandez family is going to the beach. They buy sun block for $9.99, 5 snacks for $1.89 each, and 3 beach toys for $1.49 each. Before they leave, they fill up the car with 13.1 gallons of gasoline at a cost of $3.70 per gallon.

Part A

Complete the table by calculating the total cost for each item.

Item	Calculation	Total Cost
Gasoline	13.1 × $3.70	
Snacks	5 × $1.89	
Beach toys	3 × $1.49	
Sun block	1 × $9.99	

Part B

What is the total cost for everything before tax? Show your work.

Part C

Mr. Hernandez calculates the total cost for everything before tax using this equation.

Total cost = 13.1 + 3.70 × 5 + 1.89 × 3 + 1.49 × 9.99

Do you agree with his equation? Use numbers and words to explain why or why not. If the equation is not correct, write a correct equation.

Chapter 2 Fractions

✓ Show What You Know

Personal Math Trainer
Online Assessment and Intervention

Check your understanding of important skills.

Name _____

▶ **Compare and Order Whole Numbers** **Compare.** (4.NBT.A.2)
Write <, >, or = for the ◯.

1. 289 ◯ 291

2. 476,225 ◯ 476,225

3. 5,823 ◯ 5,286

4. 30,189 ◯ 30,201

▶ **Benchmark Fractions** **Write whether the fraction is closest to 0, $\frac{1}{2}$ or 1.** (4.NF.A.2)

5. $\frac{3}{5}$ _____

6. $\frac{6}{7}$ _____

7. $\frac{1}{6}$ _____

8. $\frac{1}{3}$ _____

▶ **Multiply Fractions and Whole Numbers** **Find the product.**
Write it in simplest form. (4.NF.B.4b)

9. $\frac{2}{3} \times 21$

_____

10. $\frac{1}{4} \times 10$

_____

11. $6 \times \frac{2}{9}$

_____

12. $\frac{3}{4} \times 14$

_____

13. $35 \times \frac{2}{5}$

_____

14. $\frac{3}{8} \times 12$

_____

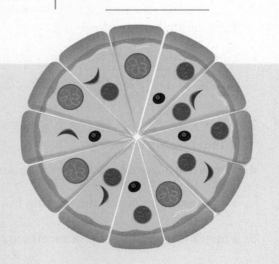

Cyndi bought an extra large pizza, cut into 12 pieces, for today's meeting of the Mystery Club. She ate $\frac{1}{6}$ of the pizza yesterday afternoon. Her brother ate $\frac{1}{5}$ of what was left last night. Cyndi knows that she needs 8 pieces of pizza for the club meeting. Help Cyndi figure out if she has enough pizza left for the meeting.

© Houghton Mifflin Harcourt Publishing Company

▶ **Visualize It** •

Complete the Bubble Map using review words that are related to fractions.

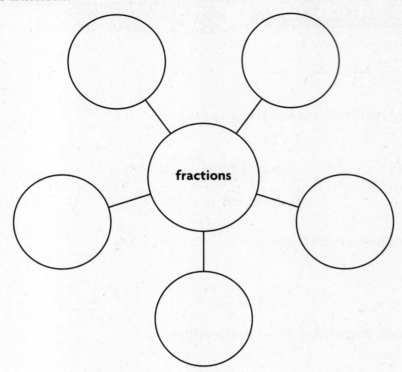

fractions

Review Words

✓ benchmark

✓ compatible numbers

  denominator

✓ equivalent fractions

  fractions

  mixed numbers

  numerator

✓ simplest form

Preview Words

✓ multiplicative inverse

✓ reciprocal

▶ **Understand Vocabulary** •

Complete the sentences using the checked words.

1. _____ are numbers that are easy to compute with mentally.

2. One of two numbers whose product is 1 is a

   _____ or a _____.

3. A _____ is a reference point that is used for estimating fractions.

4. When the numerator and denominator of a fraction have only

   1 as a common factor, the fraction is in _____.

5. Fractions that name the same amount are _____.

• **Interactive Student Edition**
• **Multimedia eGlossary**

Chapter 2 Vocabulary

common denominator

denominador común

11

compatible numbers

números compatibles

13

equivalent fractions

fracciones equivalentes

29

fraction

fracción

35

mixed number

número mixto

60

multiplicative inverse

inverso multiplicativo

63

reciprocal

recíproco

89

simplest form

mínima expresión

92

Numbers that are easy to compute with mentally

Example: $14\frac{3}{4} \div 4\frac{5}{6}$

$15 \div 5 = 3$

A common multiple of two or more denominators

Example: $\frac{3}{8}$ ← common denominator → $\frac{7}{8}$

A number that names a part of a whole or a part of a group

Examples:

$\frac{2}{3}$

$\frac{2}{5}$

Fractions that name the same amount or part

Example:

$\frac{2}{3}$

$\frac{4}{6}$

A reciprocal of a number that is multiplied by that number resulting in a product of 1

Example: $\frac{2}{3} \times \frac{3}{2} = 1$

A number that is made up of a whole number and a fraction

Example: $3\frac{2}{5}$

A fraction is in simplest form when the numerator and denominator have only 1 as a common factor

Example: $\frac{6 \div 2}{8 \div 2} = \frac{3}{4}$

Two numbers are reciprocals of each other if their product equals 1.

Example: $\frac{2}{3} \times \frac{3}{2} = 1$

Guess the Word

For 3 to 4 players

Materials

- timer

How to Play

1. Take turns to play.

2. Choose a math term, but do not say it aloud.

3. Set the timer for 1 minute.

4. Give a one-word clue about your term. Give each player one chance to guess the term.

5. If nobody guesses correctly, repeat Step 4 with a different clue. Repeat until a player guesses the term or time runs out.

6. The player who guesses the term gets 1 point. If he or she can use the term in a sentence, he or she gets 1 more point. Then that player gets a turn.

7. The first player to score 10 points wins.

Word Box

common denominator
compatible numbers
equivalent fractions
fraction
mixed number
multiplicative inverse
reciprocal
simplest form

The Write Way

Reflect

Choose one idea. Write about it.

- How can you determine if a fraction is greater than, less than, or equal to another fraction? Write 2–3 sentences to explain.

- Is this fraction in simplest form? Tell how you know.
$\frac{4}{12}$

- Explain how to estimate an answer to this problem using compatible numbers.
$7\frac{5}{8} \div \frac{3}{5} = $ _____.

- Write step-by-step instructions for how to divide two mixed numbers. Be sure to use the word *reciprocal* in your instructions.

Name _____

Fractions and Decimals

Essential Question How can you convert between fractions and decimals?

Common Core The Number System—
6.NS.C.6c
MATHEMATICAL PRACTICES
MP5, MP6, MP7

CONNECT You can use place value to write a decimal as a fraction or a mixed number.

Place Value

Ones	Tenths	Hundredths	Thousandths
1	2	3	4

🔑 Unlock the Problem

The African pygmy hedgehog is a popular pet in North America. The average African pygmy hedgehog weighs between 0.5 lb and 1.25 lb. How can these weights be written as fractions or mixed numbers?

🔑 **Write 0.5 as a fraction and 1.25 as a mixed number in simplest form.**

Ⓐ 0.5

0.5 is five _____.

$$0.5 = \frac{5}{\boxed{}}$$

Simplify using the GCF.

The GCF of 5 and 10 is _____.

$$\frac{5}{\boxed{}} = \frac{5 \div \boxed{}}{\boxed{} \div \boxed{}} = \frac{\boxed{}}{\boxed{}}$$

Divide the numerator and

the denominator by _____.

Ⓑ 1.25

1.25 is one and

_____.

$$1.25 = 1\frac{\boxed{}}{\boxed{}}$$

Simplify using the GCF.

The GCF of 25 and 100 is _____.

$$1\frac{\boxed{}}{\boxed{}} = 1\frac{\boxed{} \div \boxed{}}{\boxed{} \div \boxed{}} = 1\frac{\boxed{}}{\boxed{}}$$

Divide the numerator and

the denominator by _____.

So, the average African pygmy hedgehog weighs between

_____ lb and _____ lb.

* How do you know if a fraction is in simplest form?

_____

_____

_____

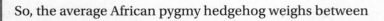

Math Talk

MATHEMATICAL PRACTICES ⑦

Look for Structure Explain how you can use place value to write 0.05 and 0.005 as fractions. Then write the fractions in simplest form.

You can use division to write a fraction or a mixed number as a decimal.

Example 1 Write $6\frac{3}{8}$ as a decimal.

STEP 1

Use division to rename the fraction part as a decimal.

The quotient has _____ decimal places.

_____

STEP 2

Add the whole number to the decimal.

6 + _____ = _____

So, $6\frac{3}{8}$ = _____ .

$$8\overline{)3.000}$$

Math Talk

MATHEMATICAL PRACTICES ⑥

Explain why zeros were placed after the decimal point in the dividend.

Sometimes you can use a number line to convert between fractions and decimals.

Example 2 Graph $3\frac{3}{5}$ on the number line and write it as a decimal.

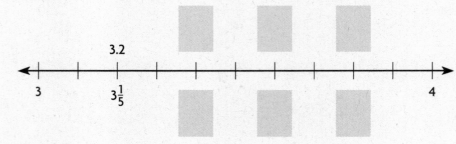

So, $3\frac{3}{5}$ = _____ .

---

1. **THINK SMARTER** On the number line below, write decimals for the fractions $\frac{1}{50}$ and $\frac{2}{25}$.

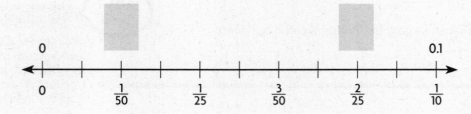

Name _____

Write as a fraction or as a mixed number in simplest form.

1. $95.5 = 95\dfrac{5}{} = $ ☐

2. 0.6

✓ 3. 5.75

_____   _____   _____

Write as a decimal.

4. $\dfrac{7}{8}$

✓ 5. $\dfrac{13}{20}$

6. $\dfrac{3}{25}$

_____   _____   _____

Math Talk   MATHEMATICAL PRACTICES ⑥

Explain how you can find the decimal that is equivalent to $\dfrac{7}{8}$.

On Your Own

Write as a fraction or as a mixed number in simplest form.

7. 0.27

8. 0.055

9. 2.45

_____   _____   _____

Write as a decimal.

10. $\dfrac{3}{8}$

11. $3\dfrac{1}{5}$

12. $2\dfrac{11}{20}$

_____   _____   _____

Identify a decimal and a fraction in simplest form for the point.

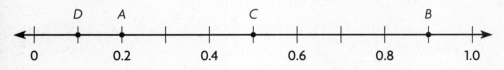

13. Point *A*

14. Point *B*

15. Point *C*

16. Point *D*

_____   _____   _____   _____

Problem Solving • Applications

Ozark Trail Hiking Club

Hiker	June	July
Maria	2.95	$2\frac{5}{8}$
Devin	3.25	$3\frac{1}{8}$
Kelsey	3.15	$2\frac{7}{8}$
Zoey	2.85	$3\frac{3}{8}$

Use the table for 17 and 18.

17. Members of the Ozark Trail Hiking Club hiked a steep section of the trail in June and July. The table shows the distances club members hiked in miles. Write Maria's July distance as a decimal.

_____

18. **GO DEEPER** How much farther did Zoey hike in June and July than Maria hiked in June and July? Explain how you found your answer.

_____

_____

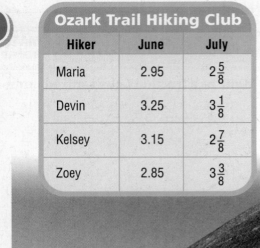

19. **THINK SMARTER** What's the Error? Tabitha's hiking distance in July was $2\frac{1}{5}$ miles. She wrote the distance as 2.02 miles. What error did she make?

_____

_____

20. **MATHEMATICAL PRACTICE ⑤ Use Patterns** Write $\frac{3}{8}$, $\frac{4}{8}$, and $\frac{5}{8}$ as decimals. What pattern do you see? Use the pattern to predict the decimal form of $\frac{6}{8}$ and $\frac{7}{8}$.

_____

_____

21. **THINK SMARTER** Identify a decimal and a fraction in simplest form for the point.

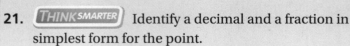

Point A [ ]   Point B [ ]

Point C [ ]   Point D [ ]

Fractions and Decimals

Common Core

COMMON CORE STANDARD—6.NS.C.6c
Apply and extend previous understandings of
numbers to the system of rational numbers.

Write as a fraction or as a mixed number in simplest form.

1. 0.52

$$0.52 = \frac{52}{100}$$

$$= \frac{52 \div 4}{100 \div 4} = \frac{13}{25}$$

2. 0.02

_____

3. 4.8

_____

4. 6.025

_____

Write as a decimal.

5. $\frac{17}{25}$

_____

6. $\frac{11}{20}$

_____

7. $4\frac{13}{20}$

_____

8. $7\frac{3}{8}$

_____

Identify a decimal and a fraction or mixed number in simplest form for each point.

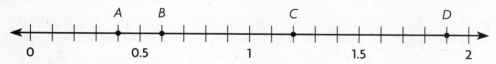

9. Point A

10. Point D

11. Point C

12. Point B

_____   _____   _____   _____

Problem Solving · Real World

13. Grace sold $\frac{5}{8}$ of her stamp collection. What is this amount as a decimal?

14. What if you scored an 0.80 on a test? What fraction of the test, in simplest form, did you answer correctly?

_____   _____

15. **WRITE** ▸ Math What fraction in simplest form is equivalent to 0.45? What decimal is equivalent to $\frac{17}{20}$? Explain how you found your answers.

_____

_____

Lesson Check (6.NS.C.6c)

1. After a storm, Michael measured $6\frac{7}{8}$ inches of snow. What is this amount as a decimal?

2. A recipe calls for 3.75 cups of flour. What is this amount as a mixed number in simplest form?

Spiral Review (6.NS.B.2, 6.NS.B.3, 6.NS.B.4)

3. Gina bought 2.3 pounds of red apples and 2.42 pounds of green apples. They were on sale for $0.75 a pound. How much did the apples cost altogether?

4. Ken has 4.66 pounds of walnuts, 2.1 pounds of cashews, and 8 pounds of peanuts. He mixes them together and divides them equally among 18 bags. How many pounds of nuts are in each bag?

5. Mia needs to separate 270 blue pens and 180 red pens into packs. Each pack will have the same number of blue pens and the same number of red pens. What is the greatest number of packs she can make? How many red pens and how many blue pens will be in each pack?

6. Evan buys 19 tubes of watercolor paint for $50.35. What is the cost of each tube of paint?

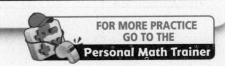

FOR MORE PRACTICE
GO TO THE
Personal Math Trainer

Compare and Order Fractions and Decimals

Essential Question How can you compare and order fractions and decimals?

Common Core

The Number System—
6.NS.C.7a

MATHEMATICAL PRACTICES
MP3, MP6, MP8

To compare fractions with the same denominators, compare the numerators. To compare fractions with the same numerators, compare the denominators.

Same Denominators

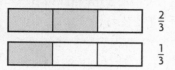

$\frac{2}{3}$

$\frac{1}{3}$

Two of three equal parts is greater than one of three equal parts.

So, $\frac{2}{3} > \frac{1}{3}$.

Same Numerators

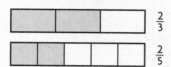

$\frac{2}{3}$

$\frac{2}{5}$

Two of three equal parts is greater than two of five equal parts.

So, $\frac{2}{3} > \frac{2}{5}$.

Unlock the Problem

Three new flowering dogwood trees were planted in a park in Springfield, Missouri. The trees were $6\frac{1}{2}$ ft, $5\frac{2}{3}$ ft, and $5\frac{5}{8}$ ft tall. Order the plant heights from least to greatest.

To compare and order fractions with unlike denominators, write equivalent fractions with common denominators.

Remember

- Equivalent fractions are fractions that name the same amount or part.
- A common denominator is a denominator that is the same in two or more fractions.

One Way Order $6\frac{1}{2}$, $5\frac{2}{3}$, and $5\frac{5}{8}$ from least to greatest.

STEP 1

Compare the whole numbers first.

$6\frac{1}{2}$ $5\frac{2}{3}$ $5\frac{5}{8}$

5 ◯ 6

STEP 2

If the whole numbers are the same, compare the fractions.

Use common denominators to write equivalent fractions.

Think: _____ is a multiple of 3 and 8,

so _____ is a common denominator.

$5\frac{2 \times 8}{3 \times 8} = 5\frac{}{}$

$5\frac{5 \times}{8 \times} = 5\frac{}{}$

STEP 3

Compare the numerators.

Order the fractions from least to greatest.

$5\frac{}{} < 5\frac{}{} < 6\frac{1}{2}$

So, from least to greatest, the order is _____ ft,

_____ ft, _____ ft.

MATHEMATICAL PRACTICES ③

Apply Explain a simple method to compare $3\frac{3}{4}$ and $3\frac{3}{7}$.

Fractions and Decimals You can compare fractions and decimals.

🔑 One Way Compare to $\frac{1}{2}$.

Compare 0.92 and $\frac{2}{7}$. Write <, >, or =.

STEP 1 Compare 0.92 to $\frac{1}{2}$.

0.92 ◯ $\frac{1}{2}$

STEP 2 Compare $\frac{2}{7}$ to $\frac{1}{2}$.

$\frac{2}{7}$ ◯ $\frac{1}{2}$

So, 0.92 ◯ $\frac{2}{7}$.

Math Talk

MATHEMATICAL PRACTICES ⑧

Generalize Explain how to compare a fraction such as $\frac{2}{7}$ to $\frac{1}{2}$.

🔑 Another Way Rewrite the fraction as a decimal.

Compare 0.8 and $\frac{3}{4}$. Write <, >, or =.

STEP 1 Write $\frac{3}{4}$ as a decimal.

$4\overline{)3.00}$

$\frac{3}{4} =$ _____

STEP 2 Use <, >, or = to compare the decimals.

0.80 ◯ _____

So, 0.8 ◯ $\frac{3}{4}$.

You can use a number line to order fractions and decimals.

🔑 Example Use a number line to order 0.95, $\frac{3}{10}$, $\frac{1}{4}$, and 0.45 from least to greatest.

STEP 1 Write each fraction as a decimal.

$\frac{3}{10} \rightarrow 10\overline{)3.00}$ $\frac{1}{4} \rightarrow 4\overline{)1.00}$

Math Idea

- Numbers read from left to right on a number line are in order from least to greatest.
- Numbers read from right to left are in order from greatest to least.

STEP 2 Locate each decimal on a number line.

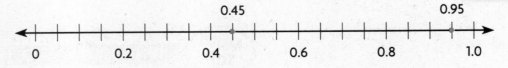

So, from least to greatest, the order is _____, _____, _____, _____.

Name _____

Order from least to greatest.

1. $3\frac{3}{6}, 3\frac{5}{8}, 2\frac{9}{10}$

Think: Compare the whole numbers first.

$3\frac{3 \times}{6 \times}\,\rule{1cm}{0.4pt} = 3\,\rule{1cm}{0.4pt}$ $3\frac{5 \times}{8 \times}\,\rule{1cm}{0.4pt} = 3\,\rule{1cm}{0.4pt}$

_____, _____, _____

Write <, >, or =.

2. $0.8 \bigcirc \frac{4}{12}$

3. $0.22 \bigcirc \frac{1}{4}$

4. $\frac{1}{20} \bigcirc 0.06$

Use a number line to order from least to greatest.

5. $1\frac{4}{5}, 1.25, 1\frac{1}{10}$

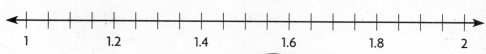

_____

Math Talk

MATHEMATICAL PRACTICES 6

Explain how to compare $\frac{3}{5}$ and 0.37 by comparing to $\frac{1}{2}$.

On Your Own

Order from least to greatest.

6. $0.6, \frac{4}{5}, 0.75$

7. $\frac{1}{2}, \frac{2}{5}, \frac{7}{15}$

8. $5\frac{1}{2}, 5.05, 5\frac{5}{9}$

9. $\frac{5}{7}, \frac{5}{6}, \frac{5}{12}$

Write <, >, or =.

10. $\frac{7}{15} \bigcirc \frac{7}{10}$

11. $\frac{1}{8} \bigcirc 0.125$

12. $7\frac{1}{3} \bigcirc 6\frac{2}{3}$

13. $1\frac{2}{5} \bigcirc 1\frac{7}{15}$

14. **THINK SMARTER** Darrell spent $3\frac{2}{5}$ hours on a project for school. Jan spent $3\frac{1}{4}$ hours and Maeve spent 3.7 hours on the project. Who spent the least amount of time? Show how you found your answer. Then describe another possible method.

_____

_____

_____

Problem Solving • Applications

Use the table for 15–18.

15. **GO DEEPER** In one week, Altoona, PA, and Bethlehem, PA, received snowfall every day, Monday through Friday. On which days did Altoona receive over 0.1 inch more snow than Bethlehem?

_____

16. **THINK SMARTER** What if Altoona received an additional 0.3 inch of snow on Thursday? How would the total amount of snow in Altoona compare to the amount received in Bethlehem that day?

_____

_____

Altoona and Bethlehem Snowfall (inches)		
Day	Altoona	Bethlehem
Monday	$2\frac{1}{4}$	2.6
Tuesday	$3\frac{1}{4}$	3.2
Wednesday	$2\frac{5}{8}$	2.5
Thursday	$4\frac{3}{5}$	4.8
Friday	$4\frac{3}{4}$	2.7

17. **MATHEMATICAL PRACTICE ⑥** Explain two ways you could compare the snowfall amounts in Altoona and Bethlehem on Monday.

_____

_____

_____

_____

18. **WRITE ▶ Math** Explain how you could compare the snowfall amounts in Altoona on Thursday and Friday.

_____

_____

_____

19. **THINK SMARTER** Write the values in order from least to greatest.

$\frac{1}{3}$	0.45	0.39	$\frac{2}{5}$

_____   _____   _____   _____

Compare and Order Fractions and Decimals

COMMON CORE STANDARD—6.NS.C.7a
Apply and extend previous understandings of numbers to the system of rational numbers.

Common
Core

Write <, >, or =.

1. $0.64 \; \boxed{<} \; \frac{7}{10}$

$0.64 < 0.7$

2. $0.48 \; \bigcirc \; \frac{6}{15}$

3. $0.75 \; \bigcirc \; \frac{7}{8}$

4. $7\frac{1}{8} \; \bigcirc \; 7.025$

Order from least to greatest.

5. $\frac{7}{12}, 0.75, \frac{5}{6}$

6. $0.5, 0.41, \frac{3}{5}$

7. $3.25, 3\frac{2}{5}, 3\frac{3}{8}$

8. $0.9, \frac{8}{9}, 0.86$

_____

_____

_____

_____

Order from greatest to least.

9. $0.7, \frac{7}{9}, \frac{7}{8}$

10. $0.2, 0.19, \frac{3}{5}$

11. $6\frac{1}{20}, 6.1, 6.07$

12. $2\frac{1}{2}, 2.4, 2.35, 2\frac{1}{8}$

_____

_____

_____

_____

Problem Solving (Real World)

13. One day it snowed $3\frac{3}{8}$ inches in Altoona and 3.45 inches in Bethlehem. Which city received less snow that day?

14. Malia and John each bought 2 pounds of sunflower seeds. Each ate some seeds. Malia has $1\frac{1}{3}$ pounds left, and John has $1\frac{2}{5}$ pounds left. Who ate more sunflower seeds?

_____

_____

15. **WRITE** ▶*Math* Explain how you would compare the numbers 0.4 and $\frac{3}{8}$.

_____

_____

1. Andrea has $3\frac{7}{8}$ yards of purple ribbon, 3.7 yards of pink ribbon, and $3\frac{4}{5}$ yards of blue ribbon. List the numbers in order from least to greatest.

2. Nassim completed $\frac{18}{25}$ of the math homework. Kara completed 0.7 of it. Debbie completed $\frac{5}{8}$ of it. List the numbers in order from greatest to least.

Spiral Review (6.NS.C.6c, 6.NS.B.3, 6.NS.B.4)

3. Tyler bought $3\frac{2}{5}$ pounds of oranges. Graph $3\frac{2}{5}$ on a number line and write this amount using a decimal.

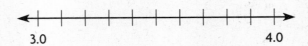

3.0   4.0

4. At the factory, a baseball card is placed in every 9th package of cereal. A football card is placed in every 25th package of the cereal. What is the first package that gets both a baseball card and a football card?

5. $15.30 is divided among 15 students. How much does each student receive?

6. Carrie buys 4.16 pounds of apples for $5.20. How much does 1 pound cost?

FOR MORE PRACTICE
GO TO THE
Personal Math Trainer

Multiply Fractions

Essential Question How do you multiply fractions?

 Common Core The Number System—
6.NS.B.4

MATHEMATICAL PRACTICES
MP2, MP6, MP8

Unlock the Problem

Sasha still has $\frac{4}{5}$ of a scarf left to knit. If she finishes $\frac{1}{2}$ of the remaining part of the scarf today, how much of the scarf will Sasha knit today?

Multiply $\frac{1}{2} \times \frac{4}{5}$. Write the product in simplest form.

Multiply the numerators.
Multiply the denominators.

$$\frac{1}{2} \times \frac{4}{5} = \frac{1 \times \boxed{}}{2 \times \boxed{}} = \underline{}$$

Simplify using the GCF.

The GCF of 4 and 10 is _____.

Divide the numerator and the

denominator by _____.

$$= \frac{\boxed{} \div \boxed{}}{10 \div \boxed{}} = \underline{}$$

$\frac{1}{2} \times \frac{4}{5} = $ _____, so Sasha will knit _____ of the scarf today.

> **Remember**
> You can find the product of two fractions by multiplying the numerators and multiplying the denominators.
> $$\frac{1}{3} \times \frac{2}{5} = \frac{1 \times 2}{3 \times 5} = \frac{2}{15}$$

Example 1

Multiply $1\frac{1}{4} \times 1\frac{2}{3}$. Write the product in simplest form.

Estimate. $1 \times$ _____ = _____

Write the mixed numbers as fractions greater than 1.

$$1\frac{1}{4} \times 1\frac{2}{3} = \frac{5}{4} \times \frac{\boxed{}}{3}$$

Multiply the fractions.

$$= \frac{5 \times \boxed{}}{4 \times 3} = \underline{}, \text{ or } \underline{}$$

Write the product as a fraction or mixed number in simplest form.

Since the estimate is _____, the answer is reasonable.

So, $1\frac{1}{4} \times 1\frac{2}{3} = $ _____, or _____.

 Math Talk MATHEMATICAL PRACTICES ⑧

Generalize Without multiplying, how do you know that $\frac{1}{3} \times \frac{3}{4} < \frac{3}{4}$?

🔓 Example 2

Evaluate $\frac{4}{5} + \left(6 \times \frac{3}{8}\right)$ using the order of operations.

STEP 1

Estimate using benchmarks.

$$\boxed{} + \left(6 \times \frac{1}{2}\right) = \boxed{} + 3 = \boxed{}$$

STEP 2

Perform operations in parentheses.

$$\frac{4}{5} + \left(6 \times \frac{3}{8}\right) = \frac{4}{5} + \left(\frac{6 \times 3}{\boxed{} \times 8}\right)$$

$$= \frac{4}{5} + \frac{\boxed{}}{\boxed{}}$$

STEP 3

Write equivalent fractions using a common denominator.

Then add.

$$= \frac{4 \times 8}{5 \times 8} + \frac{\boxed{} \times 5}{\boxed{} \times 5}$$

$$= \frac{32}{40} + \frac{\boxed{}}{\boxed{}} = \frac{\boxed{}}{\boxed{}}$$

STEP 4

Simplify using the GCF.

$$= \frac{122 \div \boxed{}}{40 \div \boxed{}}$$

$$= \frac{\boxed{}}{\boxed{}}, \text{ or } \underline{}$$

Since the estimate is _____, the answer is reasonable.

So, $\frac{4}{5} + \left(6 \times \frac{3}{8}\right) =$ _____, or _____.

---

1. **MATHEMATICAL PRACTICE ②** **Use Reasoning** What if you did not follow the order of operations and instead worked from left to right? How would that affect your answer?

_____

_____

2. **MATHEMATICAL PRACTICE ⑥** **Explain** how you used benchmarks to estimate the answer.

_____

_____

Name _____

Share and Show MATH BOARD

Find the product. Write it in simplest form.

1. $6 \times \frac{3}{8}$

$\frac{6}{1} \times \frac{3}{8} = $ _____

$\frac{ \div }{8 \div } = $ _____

or _____

2. $\frac{3}{8} \times \frac{8}{9}$

3. Sam and his friends ate $3\frac{3}{4}$ bags of fruit snacks. If each bag contained $2\frac{1}{2}$ ounces, how many ounces of fruit snacks did Sam and his friends eat?

MATHEMATICAL PRACTICE 6 Attend to Precision **Algebra** Evaluate using the order of operations.
Write the answer in simplest form.

4. $\left(\frac{3}{4} - \frac{1}{2}\right) \times \frac{3}{5}$

5. $\frac{1}{3} + \frac{4}{9} \times 12$

6. $\frac{5}{8} \times \frac{7}{10} - \frac{1}{4}$

7. $3 \times \left(\frac{5}{18} + \frac{1}{6}\right) + \frac{2}{5}$

On Your Own

Math Talk

MATHEMATICAL PRACTICES 6

Explain why the product of two fractions has the same value before and after dividing the numerator and denominator by the GCF.

Practice: Copy and Solve **Find the product. Write it in simplest form.**

8. $1\frac{2}{3} \times 2\frac{5}{8}$

9. $\frac{4}{9} \times \frac{4}{5}$

10. $\frac{1}{6} \times \frac{2}{3}$

11. $4\frac{1}{7} \times 3\frac{1}{9}$

12. **GO DEEPER** $\frac{5}{6}$ of the 90 pets in the pet show are cats. $\frac{4}{5}$ of the cats are calico cats. What fraction of the pets are calico cats? How many of the pets are calico cats?

13. **GO DEEPER** Five cats each ate $\frac{1}{4}$ cup of cat food. Four other cats each ate $\frac{1}{3}$ cup of cat food. How much food did the nine cats eat?

MATHEMATICAL PRACTICE 6 Attend to Precision **Algebra** Evaluate using the order of operations.
Write the answer in simplest form.

14. $\frac{1}{4} \times \left(\frac{3}{9} + 5\right)$

15. $\frac{9}{10} - \frac{3}{5} \times \frac{1}{2}$

16. $\frac{4}{5} + \left(\frac{1}{2} - \frac{3}{7}\right) \times 2$

17. $15 \times \frac{3}{10} + \frac{7}{8}$

18. **THINK SMARTER** Write and solve a word problem for the

expression $\frac{1}{4} \times \frac{2}{3}$. Show your work.

_____

_____

_____

Connect to Health

Changing Recipes

You can make a lot of recipes more healthful by reducing the amounts of fat, sugar, and salt.

Kelly has a recipe for muffins that asks for $1\frac{1}{2}$ cups of sugar. She wants to use $\frac{1}{2}$ that amount of sugar and more cinnamon and vanilla. How much sugar will she use?

Find $\frac{1}{2}$ of $1\frac{1}{2}$ cups to find the amount of sugar to use.

Write the mixed number as a
fraction greater than 1.

$$\frac{1}{2} \times 1\frac{1}{2} = \frac{1}{2} \times \frac{\boxed{}}{2}$$

Multiply.

$$= \frac{\boxed{}}{\boxed{}}$$

So, Kelly will use _____ cup of sugar.

19. **GO DEEPER** Michelle has a recipe that asks for $2\frac{1}{2}$ cups of vegetable oil. She wants to use $\frac{2}{3}$ that amount of oil and use applesauce to replace the rest. How much applesauce will she use?

_____

20. **THINK SMARTER** Cara's muffin recipe asks for $1\frac{1}{2}$ cups of flour for the muffins and $\frac{1}{4}$ cup of flour for the topping. If she makes $\frac{1}{2}$ of the original recipe, how much flour will she use for the muffins and topping?

_____

Multiply Fractions

COMMON CORE STANDARD—6.NS.B.4
*Compute fluently with multi-digit numbers
and find common factors and multiples.*

Find the product. Write it in simplest form.

1. $\frac{4}{5} \times \frac{7}{8} = \frac{28}{40}$

    $= \frac{7}{10}$

2. $\frac{1}{8} \times 20$

3. $\frac{4}{5} \times \frac{3}{8}$

4. $1\frac{1}{8} \times \frac{1}{9}$

5. $\frac{3}{4} \times \frac{1}{3} \times \frac{2}{5}$

6. Karen raked $\frac{3}{5}$ of the yard. Minni raked $\frac{1}{3}$ of the amount Karen raked. How much of the yard did Minni rake?

7. $\frac{3}{8}$ of the pets in the pet show are dogs. $\frac{2}{3}$ of the dogs have long hair. What fraction of the pets are dogs with long hair?

Evaluate using the order of operations.

8. $\left(\frac{1}{2} + \frac{3}{8}\right) \times 8$

9. $\frac{3}{4} \times \left(1 - \frac{1}{9}\right)$

10. $4 \times \frac{1}{8} \times \frac{3}{10}$

11. $6 \times \left(\frac{4}{5} + \frac{2}{10}\right) \times \frac{2}{3}$

Problem Solving · Real World

12. Jason ran $\frac{5}{7}$ of the distance around the school track. Sara ran $\frac{4}{5}$ of Jason's distance. What fraction of the total distance around the track did Sara run?

13. A group of students attend a math club. Half of the students are boys and $\frac{4}{9}$ of the boys have brown eyes. What fraction of the group are boys with brown eyes?

14. **WRITE** *Math* Write and solve a word problem that involves multiplying by a fraction.

_____

_____

_____

Lesson Check (6.NS.B.4)

1. Veronica's mom left $\frac{3}{4}$ of a cake on the table. Her brothers ate $\frac{1}{2}$ of it. What fraction of the cake did they eat?

2. One lap around the school track is $\frac{5}{8}$ mile. Carin ran $3\frac{1}{2}$ laps. How far did she run?

Spiral Review (6.NS.B.3, 6.NS.B.4, 6.NS.C.7a)

3. Tom bought $2\frac{5}{16}$ pounds of peanuts and 2.45 pounds of cashews. Which did he buy more of? Explain.

4. Eve has 24 stamps each valued at $24.75. What is the total value of her stamps?

5. Naomi went on a 6.5-mile hike. In the morning, she hiked 1.75 miles, rested, and then hiked 2.4 more miles. She completed the hike in the afternoon. How much farther did she hike in the morning than in the afternoon?

6. A bookstore owner has 48 science fiction books and 30 mysteries he wants to sell quickly. He will make discount packages with one type of book in each. He wants the most books possible in each package, but all packages must contain the same number of books. How many packages can he make? How many packages of each type of book does he have?

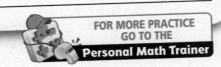

FOR MORE PRACTICE
GO TO THE
Personal Math Trainer

Simplify Factors

Essential Question How do you simplify fractional factors by using the greatest common factor?

 The Number System—6.NS.B.4

MATHEMATICAL PRACTICES
MP3, MP6

Unlock the Problem

Some of the corn grown in the United States is used for making fuel. Suppose $\frac{7}{10}$ of a farmer's total crop is corn. He sells $\frac{2}{5}$ of the corn for fuel production. What fraction of the farmer's total crop does he sell for fuel production?

Multiply $\frac{2}{5} \times \frac{7}{10}$.

One Way Simplify the product.

Multiply the numerators.
Multiply the denominators.

$$\frac{2}{5} \times \frac{7}{10} = \frac{2 \times 7}{5 \times 10} = \frac{}{}$$

Write the product as a fraction in simplest form.

$$= \frac{ \div 2}{50 \div } = \frac{}{}$$

So, $\frac{2}{5} \times \frac{7}{10} =$ _____.

Another Way Simplify before multiplying.

Write the problem as a single fraction.

$$\frac{2}{5} \times \frac{7}{10} = \frac{2 \times 7}{5 \times 10}$$

Think: Do any numbers in the numerator have common factors with numbers in the denominator?

2 in the numerator and _____ in the denominator have a common factor other than 1.

Divide the numerator and the denominator by the GCF.

The GCF of 2 and 10 is _____.

$2 \div 2 =$ _____ $10 \div 2 =$ _____

$$\frac{\overset{1}{\cancel{2}} \times 7}{5 \times \cancel{10}}$$

Multiply the numerators.
Multiply the denominators.

$$\frac{1 \times 7}{5 \times } = \frac{}{}$$

 MATHEMATICAL PRACTICES ③

Compare When you multiply two fractions, will the product be the same whether you multiply first or simplify first? Explain.

$\frac{2}{5} \times \frac{7}{10} =$ _____, so the farmer sells _____ of his crop for fuel production.

🔑 Example

Find $\frac{5}{8} \times \frac{14}{15}$. **Simplify before multiplying.**

Divide a numerator and a denominator by their GCF.

The GCF of 5 and 15 is _____.

$$\overset{1}{\cancel{5}} \over 8 \times \frac{14}{\cancel{15}}$$

The GCF of 8 and 14 is _____.

$$\overset{1}{\cancel{5}} \over \cancel{8} \times \frac{14}{\cancel{15}}_{\,3}$$

Multiply the numerators.
Multiply the denominators.

$$\frac{1}{\Box} \times \frac{\Box}{3} = \frac{\Box}{\Box}$$

So, $\frac{5}{8} \times \frac{14}{15} =$ _____.

> **! ERROR Alert**
>
> Be sure to divide both a numerator and a denominator by a common factor to write a fraction in simplest form.

Try This! Find the product. Simplify before multiplying.

A $\frac{3}{8} \times \frac{2}{9}$

The GCF of 3 and 9 is _____.

The GCF of 2 and 8 is _____.

$$\frac{\cancel{3}}{\cancel{8}} \times \frac{\cancel{2}}{\cancel{9}} = \frac{\Box}{\Box}$$

B $\frac{4}{7} \times \frac{7}{12}$

The GCF of 4 and 12 is _____.

The GCF of 7 and 7 is _____.

$$\frac{\cancel{4}}{7} \times \frac{\cancel{7}}{\cancel{12}} = \frac{\Box}{\Box}$$

1. **MATHEMATICAL PRACTICE 6** **Explain** why you cannot simplify before multiplying when finding $\frac{3}{5} \times \frac{6}{7}$.

_____

_____

2. **MATHEMATICAL PRACTICE 3** **Compare Strategies** What if you divided by a common factor other than the GCF before you multiplied? How would that affect your answer?

_____

_____

88

Name _____

Find the product. Simplify before multiplying.

1. $\frac{5}{6} \times \frac{3}{10}$

$$\frac{\cancel{5}}{\cancel{6}} \times \frac{\cancel{3}}{\cancel{10}} = \frac{\quad}{\quad}$$

_____

2. $\frac{3}{4} \times \frac{5}{9}$

_____

3. $\frac{2}{3} \times \frac{9}{10}$

_____

4. After a picnic, $\frac{5}{12}$ of the cornbread is left over. Val eats $\frac{3}{5}$ of the leftover cornbread. What fraction of the cornbread does Val eat?

_____

5. The reptile house at the zoo has an iguana that is $\frac{5}{6}$ yd long. It has a Gila monster that is $\frac{4}{5}$ of the length of the iguana. How long is the Gila monster?

_____

On Your Own

Math Talk MATHEMATICAL PRACTICES ⑥

Explain two ways to find the product $\frac{1}{6} \times \frac{2}{3}$ in simplest form.

Find the product. Simplify before multiplying.

6. $\frac{3}{4} \times \frac{1}{6}$

_____

7. $\frac{7}{10} \times \frac{2}{3}$

_____

8. $\frac{5}{8} \times \frac{2}{5}$

_____

9. $\frac{9}{10} \times \frac{5}{6}$

_____

10. $\frac{11}{12} \times \frac{3}{7}$

_____

11. Shelley's basketball team won $\frac{3}{4}$ of their games last season. In $\frac{1}{6}$ of the games they won, they outscored their opponents by more than 10 points. What fraction of their games did Shelley's team win by more than 10 points?

_____

12. **GO DEEPER** Mr. Ortiz has $\frac{3}{4}$ pound of oatmeal. He uses $\frac{2}{3}$ of the oatmeal to bake muffins. How much oatmeal does Mr. Ortiz have left?

_____

13. **MATHEMATICAL PRACTICE ③** **Compare Strategies** To find $\frac{16}{27} \times \frac{3}{4}$, you can multiply the fractions and then simplify the product or you can simplify the fractions and then multiply. Which method do you prefer? Explain.

_____

_____

Problem Solving • Applications (Real World)

14. Three students each popped $\frac{3}{4}$ cup of popcorn kernels. The table shows the fraction of each student's kernels that did not pop. Which student had $\frac{1}{16}$ cup unpopped kernels?

_____

15. **GO DEEPER** The jogging track at Francine's school is $\frac{3}{4}$ mile long. Yesterday Francine completed two laps on the track. If she ran $\frac{1}{3}$ of the distance and walked the remainder of the way, how far did she walk?

_____

16. **THINK SMARTER** At a snack store, $\frac{7}{12}$ of the customers bought pretzels and $\frac{3}{10}$ of those customers bought low-salt pretzels. Bill states that $\frac{7}{30}$ of the customers bought low-salt pretzels. Does Bill's statement make sense? Explain.

_____

_____

_____

Popcorn Popping

Student	Fraction of Kernels not Popped
Katie	$\frac{1}{10}$
Mirza	$\frac{1}{12}$
Jawan	$\frac{1}{9}$

Math on the Spot

17. **THINK SMARTER** The table shows Tonya's homework assignment. Tonya's teacher instructed the class to simplify each expression by dividing the numerator and denominator by the GCF. Complete the table by simplifying each expression and then finding the value.

Problem	Expression	Simplified Expression	Value
a	$\frac{2}{7} \times \frac{3}{4}$		
b	$\frac{3}{7} \times \frac{7}{9}$		
c	$\frac{5}{7} \times \frac{2}{3}$		
d	$\frac{4}{15} \times \frac{3}{8}$		

Simplify Factors

Common Core

COMMON CORE STANDARD—6.NS.B.4
*Compute fluently with multi-digit numbers
and find common factors and multiples.*

Find the product. Simplify before multiplying.

1. $\frac{8}{9} \times \frac{5}{12} = \frac{2 \cancel{8} \times 5}{9 \times \cancel{12}_3}$

       $= \frac{10}{27}$

2. $\frac{3}{4} \times \frac{16}{21}$

_____

3. $\frac{15}{20} \times \frac{2}{5}$

_____

4. $\frac{9}{18} \times \frac{2}{3}$

_____

5. $\frac{3}{4} \times \frac{7}{30}$

6. $\frac{8}{15} \times \frac{15}{32}$

7. $\frac{12}{21} \times \frac{7}{9}$

8. $\frac{18}{22} \times \frac{8}{9}$

_____   _____   _____   _____

Problem Solving *Real World*

9. Amber has a $\frac{4}{5}$-pound bag of colored sand. She uses $\frac{1}{2}$ of the bag for an art project. How much sand does she use for the project?

10. Tyler has $\frac{3}{4}$ month to write a book report. He finished the report in $\frac{2}{3}$ that time. How much time did it take Tyler to write the report?

_____   _____

11. **WRITE** *Math* Show two ways to multiply $\frac{2}{15} \times \frac{3}{20}$. Then tell which way is easier and justify your choice.

_____

_____

_____

Lesson Check (6.NS.B.4)

Find each product. Simplify before multiplying.

1. At Susie's school, $\frac{5}{8}$ of all students play sports. Of the students who play sports, $\frac{2}{5}$ play soccer. What fraction of the students in Susie's school play soccer?

2. A box of popcorn weighs $\frac{15}{16}$ pounds. The box contains $\frac{1}{3}$ buttered popcorn and $\frac{2}{3}$ cheesy popcorn. How much does the cheesy popcorn weigh?

Spiral Review (6.NS.B.3, 6.NS.C.7a)

3. Ramòn bought a dozen ears of corn for $1.80. What was the cost of each ear of corn?

4. A 1.8-ounce jar of cinnamon costs $4.05. What is the cost per ounce?

5. Rose bought $\frac{7}{20}$ kilogram of ginger candy and 0.4 kilogram of cinnamon candy. Which did she buy more of? Explain how you know.

6. Don walked $3\frac{3}{5}$ miles on Friday, 3.7 miles on Saturday, and $3\frac{5}{8}$ miles on Sunday. List the distances from least to greatest.

FOR MORE PRACTICE
GO TO THE
Personal Math Trainer

Name _____

✓ Mid-Chapter Checkpoint

Vocabulary

Choose the best term from the box to complete the sentence.

Vocabulary
common denominator
equivalent fractions
mixed number

1. The fractions $\frac{1}{2}$ and $\frac{5}{10}$ are _____. (p. 75)

2. A _____ is a denominator that is the same in two or more fractions. (p. 75)

Concepts and Skills

Write as a decimal. Tell whether you used division, a number line, or some other method. (6.NS.C.6c)

3. $\frac{7}{20}$

4. $8\frac{39}{40}$

5. $1\frac{5}{8}$

6. $\frac{19}{25}$

_____ | _____ | _____ | _____

Order from least to greatest. (6.NS.C.7a)

7. $\frac{4}{5}, \frac{3}{4}, 0.88$

8. $0.65, 0.59, \frac{3}{5}$

9. $1\frac{1}{4}, 1\frac{2}{3}, \frac{11}{12}$

10. $0.9, \frac{7}{8}, 0.86$

_____ | _____ | _____ | _____

Find the product. Write it in simplest form. (6.NS.B.4)

11. $\frac{2}{3} \times \frac{1}{8}$

12. $\frac{4}{5} \times \frac{2}{5}$

13. $12 \times \frac{3}{4}$

14. Mia climbs $\frac{5}{8}$ of the height of the rock wall. Lee climbs $\frac{4}{5}$ of Mia's distance. What fraction of the wall does Lee climb?

_____ | _____ | _____ | _____

15. **GO DEEPER** In Zoe's class, $\frac{4}{5}$ of the students have pets. Of the students who have pets, $\frac{1}{8}$ have rodents. What fraction of the students in Zoe's class have pets that are rodents? What fraction of the students in Zoe's class have pets that are not rodents? (6.NS.B.4)

_____

16. A recipe calls for $2\frac{2}{3}$ cups of flour. Terell wants to make $\frac{3}{4}$ of the recipe. How much flour should he use? (6.NS.B.4)

_____

17. Following the Baltimore Running Festival in 2009, volunteers collected and recycled 3.75 tons of trash. Graph 3.75 on a number line and write the weight as a mixed number. (6.NS.C.6c)

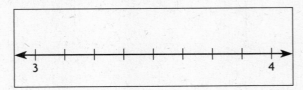

_____

18. **GO DEEPER** Four students took an exam. The fraction of the total possible points that each received is given. Which student had the highest score? If students receive a whole number of points on every exam item, can the exam be worth a total of 80 points? Explain. (6.NS.C.7a)

Student	Score
Monica	$\frac{22}{25}$
Lily	$\frac{17}{20}$
Nikki	$\frac{4}{5}$
Sydney	$\frac{3}{4}$

_____

_____

_____

Name _____

Model Fraction Division

Essential Question How can you use a model to show division of fractions?

Common Core The Number System—
6.NS.A.1
MATHEMATICAL PRACTICES
MP1, MP3, MP4

CONNECT There are two types of division problems. In one type you find how many or how much in each group, and in the other you find how many groups.

Investigate

Hands On

Materials ■ fraction strips

A class is working on a community project to clear a path near the lake. They are working in teams on sections of the path.

A. Four students clear a section that is $\frac{2}{3}$ mi long. If each student clears an equal part, what fraction of a mile will each clear?

Divide $\frac{2}{3} \div 4$.

- Use fraction strips to model the division. Draw your model.

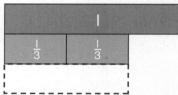

- What are you trying to find?

_____

_____

$\frac{2}{3} \div 4 =$ _____ , so each student will clear _____ of a mile.

B. Another team clears a section of the path that is $\frac{3}{4}$ mi long. If each student clears $\frac{1}{8}$ of a mile, how many students are on the team?

Divide $\frac{3}{4} \div \frac{1}{8}$.

- Use fraction strips to model the division. Draw your model.

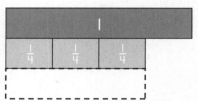

- What are you trying to find?

_____

$\frac{3}{4} \div \frac{1}{8} =$ _____ , so there are _____ students on the team.

Draw Conclusions

1. **MATHEMATICAL PRACTICE 4** **Use Models** Explain how the model in problem A shows a related multiplication fact.

_____

2. **MATHEMATICAL PRACTICE 1** **Analyze** Suppose a whole number is divided by a fraction between 0 and 1. Is the quotient greater than or less than the dividend? Explain and give an example.

_____

_____

_____

Make Connections

You can draw a model to help you solve a fraction division problem.

Jessica is making a recipe that calls for $\frac{3}{4}$ cup of flour. Suppose she only has a $\frac{1}{2}$ cup-size measuring scoop. How many $\frac{1}{2}$ cup scoops of flour does she need?

Divide $\frac{3}{4} \div \frac{1}{2}$.

STEP 1 Draw a model that represents the total amount of flour.

Think: Divide a whole into _____.

Jessica needs _____ cup.

STEP 2 Draw fraction parts that represent the scoops of flour.

Think: What are you trying to find?

_____

There is _____ full group of $\frac{1}{2}$ and _____ of a group of $\frac{1}{2}$.

So, there are _____ groups of $\frac{1}{2}$ in $\frac{3}{4}$.

$\frac{3}{4} \div \frac{1}{2} =$ _____, so Jessica will need _____ scoops of flour.

- **What if** Jessica's recipe calls for $\frac{1}{4}$ cup flour? How many $\frac{1}{2}$ cup scoops of flour does she need?

_____

Math Talk

MATHEMATICAL PRACTICES 1

Describe how you used the model to determine the number of groups of $\frac{1}{2}$ in $\frac{3}{4}$.

Name _____

 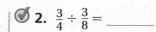
Use the model to find the quotient.

1. $\frac{1}{2} \div 3 =$ _____

Think: $\frac{1}{2}$ is shared among 3 groups.

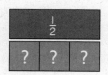

2. $\frac{3}{4} \div \frac{3}{8} =$ _____

Use fraction strips to find the quotient. Then draw the model.

3. $\frac{1}{3} \div 4 =$ _____

4. $\frac{3}{5} \div \frac{3}{10} =$ _____

Draw a model to solve. Then write an equation for the model. Interpret the result.

5. How many $\frac{1}{4}$ cup servings of raisins are in $\frac{3}{8}$ cup of raisins?

_____

_____

6. How many $\frac{1}{3}$ lb bags of trail mix can Josh make from $\frac{5}{6}$ lb of trail mix?

_____

_____

7. **WRITE** *Math* **Pose a Problem** Write and solve a problem for $\frac{3}{4} \div 3$ that represents how much in each of 3 groups.

_____

_____

Problem Solving • Applications (Real World)

The table shows the amount of each material that students in a sewing class need for one purse.

Use the table for 8–10. Use models to solve.

8. **GO DEEPER** Mrs. Brown has $\frac{1}{3}$ yd of blue denim and $\frac{1}{2}$ yd of black denim. How many purses can be made using denim as the main fabric?

_____

9. **THINK SMARTER** One student brings $\frac{1}{2}$ yd of ribbon. If 3 students receive an equal length of the ribbon, how much ribbon will each student receive? Will each of them have enough ribbon for a purse? Explain.

_____

Purse Materials (yd)	
Ribbon	$\frac{1}{4}$
Main fabric	$\frac{1}{6}$
Trim fabric	$\frac{1}{12}$

10. **MATHEMATICAL PRACTICE ③ Make Arguments** There was $\frac{1}{2}$ yd of purple and pink striped fabric. Jessie said she could only make $\frac{1}{24}$ of a purse using that fabric as the trim. Is she correct? Use what you know about the meanings of multiplication and division to defend your answer.

_____

_____

_____

• • • • • • • | **WRITE** ► *Math* • **Show Your Work** • • •

11. **THINK SMARTER** Draw a model to find the quotient.

$$\frac{1}{2} \div 4 = \boxed{}$$

Model Fraction Division

COMMON CORE STANDARD—6.NS.A.1
Apply and extend previous understandings of
multiplication and division to divide fractions
by fractions.

Use the model to find the quotient.

1. $\frac{1}{4} \div 3 = \frac{1}{12}$

2. $\frac{1}{2} \div \frac{2}{12} =$ _____

Use fraction strips to find the quotient.

3. $\frac{5}{6} \div \frac{1}{2}$

4. $\frac{2}{3} \div 4$

5. $\frac{1}{2} \div 6$

6. $\frac{1}{3} \div \frac{1}{12}$

_____   _____   _____   _____

**Draw a model to solve. Then write an equation
for the model. Interpret the result.**

7. If Jerry runs $\frac{1}{10}$ mile each day, how many days
will it take for him to run $\frac{4}{5}$ mile?

_____

Problem Solving · Real World

8. Mrs. Jennings has $\frac{3}{4}$ gallon of paint for an art
project. She plans to divide the paint equally into
jars. If she puts $\frac{1}{8}$ gallon of paint into each jar,
how many jars will she use?

9. If one jar of glue weighs $\frac{1}{12}$ pound, how
many jars can Rickie get from $\frac{2}{3}$ pound
of glue?

_____   _____

10. **WRITE** ▸*Math* Explain how to use a model to show $\frac{2}{6} \div \frac{1}{12}$ and $\frac{2}{6} \div 4$.

_____

_____

Lesson Check (6.NS.A.1)

Draw a model to find the quotient.

1. Darcy needs $\frac{1}{4}$ yard of fabric to make a banner. She has 2 yards of fabric. How many banners can she make?

2. Lorenzo bought $\frac{15}{16}$ pounds of ground beef. He wants to make hamburgers that weigh $\frac{3}{16}$ pound each. How many hamburgers can he make?

Spiral Review (6.NS.B.2, 6.NS.B.4)

3. Letisha wants to read 22 pages a night. At that rate, how long will it take her to read a book with 300 pages?

4. A principal wants to order enough notebooks for 624 students. The notebooks come in boxes of 28. How many boxes should he order?

5. Each block in Ton's neighborhood is $\frac{2}{3}$ mile long. If he walks $4\frac{1}{2}$ blocks, how far does he walk?

6. In Cathy's garden, $\frac{5}{6}$ of the area is planted with flowers. Of the flowers, $\frac{3}{10}$ of them are red. What fraction of Cathy's garden is planted with red flowers?

FOR MORE PRACTICE
GO TO THE
Personal Math Trainer

Estimate Quotients

Essential Question How can you use compatible numbers to estimate quotients of fractions and mixed numbers?

The Number System—
6.NS.A.1

MATHEMATICAL PRACTICES
MP1, MP2, MP3, MP6

Remember
Compatible numbers are pairs of numbers that are easy to compute mentally.

CONNECT You have used compatible numbers to estimate quotients of whole numbers and decimals. You can also use compatible numbers to estimate quotients of fractions and mixed numbers.

Unlock the Problem

Humpback whales have "songs" that they repeat continuously over periods of several hours. Eric is using an underwater microphone to record a $3\frac{5}{6}$ minute humpback song. He has $15\frac{3}{4}$ minutes of battery power left. About how many times will he be able to record the song?

- Which operation should you use to solve the problem? Why?

  _____

  _____

- How do you know that the problem calls for an estimate?

  _____

One Way Estimate $15\frac{3}{4} \div 3\frac{5}{6}$ using compatible numbers.

Think: What whole numbers close to $15\frac{3}{4}$ and $3\frac{5}{6}$ are easy to divide mentally?

$15\frac{3}{4}$ is close to _____.

$3\frac{5}{6}$ is close to _____.

Rewrite the problem using compatible numbers.

$$15\frac{3}{4} \div 3\frac{5}{6}$$
$$\downarrow \qquad \downarrow$$

Divide.

$$16 \div 4 = \text{_____}$$

So, Eric will be able to record the complete whale song

about _____ times.

1. 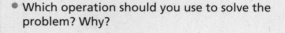 **Compare Strategies** To estimate $15\frac{3}{4} \div 3\frac{5}{6}$, Martin used 15 and 3 as compatible numbers. Tina used 15 and 4. Were their choices good ones? Explain why or why not.

_____

_____

_____

🔑 Example Estimate using compatible numbers.

A $5\frac{2}{3} \div \frac{5}{8}$

Rewrite the problem using compatible numbers.

$$5\frac{2}{3} \qquad \div \qquad \frac{5}{8}$$
$$\downarrow \qquad\qquad \downarrow$$
$$\underline{\qquad\quad} \div \underline{\qquad\quad}$$

Think: How many halves are there in 6?

$6 \div \frac{1}{2} = \underline{\qquad\quad}$

So, $5\frac{2}{3} \div \frac{5}{8}$ is about $\underline{\qquad\quad}$.

B $\frac{7}{8} \div \frac{1}{4}$

Rewrite the problem using compatible numbers.

$$\frac{7}{8} \qquad \div \qquad \frac{1}{4}$$
$$\downarrow \qquad\qquad \downarrow$$
$$\underline{\qquad\quad} \div \quad \frac{1}{4}$$

Think: How many fourths are there in 1?

$1 \div \frac{1}{4} = \underline{\qquad\quad}$

So, $\frac{7}{8} \div \frac{1}{4}$ is about $\underline{\qquad\quad}$.

2. **MATHEMATICAL PRACTICE ②** **Use Reasoning** Will the actual quotient $5\frac{2}{3} \div \frac{5}{8}$ be greater than or less than the estimated quotient? Explain.

_____

_____

_____

3. Will the actual quotient $\frac{7}{8} \div \frac{1}{4}$ be greater than or less than the estimated quotient? Explain.

_____

_____

_____

4. **MATHEMATICAL PRACTICE ⑥** **Explain** how you would estimate the quotient $14\frac{3}{4} \div 3\frac{9}{10}$ using compatible numbers.

_____

Name _____

Estimate using compatible numbers.

1. $22\frac{4}{5}$ ÷ $6\frac{1}{4}$

↓   ↓

_____ ÷ _____ = _____

2. $12 ÷ 3\frac{3}{4}$

_____

☑3. $33\frac{7}{8} ÷ 5\frac{1}{3}$

_____

☑4. $3\frac{7}{8} ÷ \frac{5}{9}$

_____

5. $34\frac{7}{12} ÷ 7\frac{3}{8}$

_____

6. $1\frac{2}{9} ÷ \frac{1}{6}$

_____

Math Talk | MATHEMATICAL PRACTICES ⑥

Explain how using compatible numbers is different than rounding to estimate $35\frac{1}{2} ÷ 6\frac{5}{6}$.

On Your Own

Estimate using compatible numbers.

7. $44\frac{1}{4} ÷ 11\frac{7}{9}$

_____

8. $71\frac{11}{12} ÷ 8\frac{3}{4}$

_____

9. $1\frac{1}{6} ÷ \frac{1}{8}$

_____

THINK SMARTER **Estimate to compare. Write <, >, or =.**

10. $21\frac{3}{10} ÷ 2\frac{5}{6}$ ◯ $35\frac{7}{9} ÷ 3\frac{2}{3}$

11. $29\frac{4}{5} ÷ 5\frac{1}{6}$ ◯ $27\frac{8}{9} ÷ 6\frac{5}{8}$

12. $55\frac{5}{6} ÷ 6\frac{7}{10}$ ◯ $11\frac{5}{7} ÷ \frac{5}{8}$

13. Marion is making school flags. Each flag uses $2\frac{3}{4}$ yards of felt. Marion has $24\frac{1}{8}$ yards of felt. About how many flags can he make?

_____

14. **GO DEEPER** A garden snail travels about $2\frac{3}{5}$ feet in 1 minute. At that speed, about how many hours would it take the snail to travel 350 feet?

_____

Problem Solving • Applications Real World

What's the Error?

15. Megan is making pennants from a piece of butcher paper that is $10\frac{3}{8}$ yards long. Each pennant requires $\frac{3}{8}$ yard of paper. To estimate the number of pennants she could make, Megan estimated the quotient $10\frac{3}{8} \div \frac{3}{8}$.

Look at how Megan solved the problem. Find her error.

Correct the error. Estimate the quotient.

Estimate:

$$10\frac{3}{8} \div \frac{3}{8}$$

$$\downarrow \quad \downarrow$$

$$10 \div \frac{1}{2} = 5$$

So, Megan can make about _____ pennants.

- **MATHEMATICAL PRACTICE ①** **Describe** the error that Megan made.

_____

_____

- **MATHEMATICAL PRACTICE ⑥** **Explain** Tell which compatible numbers you used to estimate $10\frac{3}{8} \div \frac{3}{8}$. Explain why you chose those numbers.

_____

16. **THINK SMARTER** For numbers 16a–16c, estimate to compare. Choose $<$, $>$, or $=$.

16a. $18\frac{3}{10} \div 2\frac{5}{6}$ $\boxed{\begin{array}{c}<\\>\\=\end{array}}$ $30\frac{7}{9} \div 3\frac{1}{3}$

16b. $17\frac{4}{5} \div 6\frac{1}{6}$ $\boxed{\begin{array}{c}<\\>\\=\end{array}}$ $19\frac{8}{9} \div 4\frac{5}{8}$

16c. $35\frac{5}{6} \div 6\frac{1}{4}$ $\boxed{\begin{array}{c}<\\>\\=\end{array}}$ $11\frac{5}{7} \div 2\frac{3}{4}$

Estimate Quotients

Common Core

COMMON CORE STANDARD—6.NS.A.1
Apply and extend previous understandings of multiplication and division to divide fractions by fractions.

Estimate using compatible numbers.

1. $12\frac{3}{16} \div 3\frac{9}{10}$

↓ ↓

$12 \div 4 = 3$

2. $15\frac{3}{8} \div \frac{1}{2}$

3. $22\frac{1}{5} \div 1\frac{5}{6}$

4. $7\frac{7}{9} \div \frac{4}{7}$

5. $18\frac{1}{4} \div 2\frac{4}{5}$

6. $\frac{15}{16} \div \frac{1}{7}$

7. $14\frac{7}{8} \div \frac{5}{11}$

8. $53\frac{7}{12} \div 8\frac{11}{12}$

9. $1\frac{1}{6} \div \frac{1}{9}$

Problem Solving · Real World

10. Estimate the number of pieces Sharon will have if she divides $15\frac{1}{3}$ yards of fabric into $4\frac{4}{5}$ yard lengths.

11. Estimate the number of $\frac{1}{2}$ quart containers Ethan can fill from a container with $8\frac{7}{8}$ quarts of water.

12. **WRITE** ▸ *Math* How is estimating quotients different from estimating products?

_____

_____

Lesson Check (6.NS.A.1)

1. Each loaf of pumpkin bread calls for $1\frac{3}{4}$ cups of raisins. About how many loaves can be made from 10 cups of raisins?

_____

_____

2. Perry's goal is to run $2\frac{1}{4}$ miles each day. One lap around the school track is $\frac{1}{3}$ mile. About how many laps must he run to reach his goal?

_____

_____

Spiral Review (6.NS.B.3, 6.NS.B.4)

3. A recipe calls for $\frac{3}{4}$ teaspoon of red pepper. Uri wants to use $\frac{1}{3}$ of that amount. How much red pepper should he use?

_____

4. A recipe calls for $2\frac{2}{3}$ cups of apple slices. Zoe wants to use $1\frac{1}{2}$ times this amount. How many cups of apples should Zoe use?

_____

5. Edgar has 2.8 meters of rope. If he cuts it into 7 equal parts, how long will each piece be?

_____

6. Kami has 7 liters of water to fill water bottles that each hold 2.8 liters. How many bottles can she fill?

_____

FOR MORE PRACTICE
GO TO THE
Personal Math Trainer

Name _____

Divide Fractions

Essential Question How do you divide fractions?

Common Core The Number System—
6.NS.A.1

MATHEMATICAL PRACTICES
MP2, MP5, MP6, MP8

Unlock the Problem

Toby and his dad are building a doghouse. They need to cut a board that is $\frac{2}{3}$ yard long into $\frac{1}{6}$ yard pieces. How many $\frac{1}{6}$ yard pieces can they cut?

One Way Divide $\frac{2}{3} \div \frac{1}{6}$ by using a number line.

STEP 1 Draw a number line, and shade it to represent the total length of the board.

Think: Divide a whole into thirds.

Toby and his dad have $\frac{2}{3}$ yard, so shade $\frac{2}{3}$.

STEP 2 Show fraction parts that represent the pieces of board.

Think: Find the number of groups of $\frac{1}{6}$ in $\frac{2}{3}$.

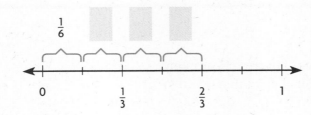

So, there are _____ $\frac{1}{6}$ yard pieces in $\frac{2}{3}$ yard.

Another Way Divide $\frac{2}{3} \div \frac{1}{6}$ by using a common denominator.

STEP 1 Write equivalent fractions using a common denominator.

Think: _____ is a multiple of 3 and 6,

so _____ is a common denominator.

$$\frac{2}{3} \div \frac{1}{6} = \frac{2 \times \boxed{}}{3 \times \boxed{}} \div \frac{1}{6} = \frac{\boxed{}}{6} \div \frac{1}{6}$$

STEP 2 Divide.

Think: There are _____ groups of $\frac{1}{6}$ in $\frac{4}{6}$.

$$\frac{4}{6} \div \frac{1}{6} = \underline{\hspace{1cm}}$$

So, $\frac{2}{3} \div \frac{1}{6} = \underline{\hspace{1cm}}$. Toby and his dad can cut _____ $\frac{1}{6}$ yard pieces.

Math Talk

MATHEMATICAL PRACTICES ②

Reasoning How can you find the quotient $\frac{2}{3} \div \frac{2}{9}$ by using a common denominator?

You can use reciprocals and inverse operations to divide fractions.

Two numbers whose product is 1 are **reciprocals** or **multiplicative inverses**.

$\frac{2}{3} \times \frac{3}{2} = 1$ $\frac{2}{3}$ and $\frac{3}{2}$ are reciprocals.

🔑 Activity Find a pattern.

- Complete the table by finding the products.

- How are each pair of division and multiplication problems the same, and how are they different?

_____

_____

_____

Division	Multiplication
$\frac{4}{7} \div \frac{2}{7} = 2$	$\frac{4}{7} \times \frac{7}{2} =$
$\frac{5}{6} \div \frac{4}{6} = \frac{5}{4}$	$\frac{5}{6} \times \frac{6}{4} =$
$\frac{1}{3} \div \frac{5}{9} = \frac{3}{5}$	$\frac{1}{3} \times \frac{9}{5} =$

- How could you use the pattern in the table to rewrite a division problem involving fractions as a multiplication problem?

_____

_____

🔑 Example

Winnie needs pieces of string for a craft project. How many $\frac{1}{12}$ yd pieces of string can she cut from a piece that is $\frac{3}{4}$ yd long?

Divide $\frac{3}{4} \div \frac{1}{12}$.

Estimate. _____ $\div \frac{1}{12} =$ _____

Use the reciprocal of the divisor to write a multiplication problem.

$$\frac{3}{4} \div \frac{1}{12} = \frac{3}{4} \times \frac{\quad}{\quad}$$

Simplify the factors.

$$= \frac{3}{\cancel{4}} \times \frac{\cancel{12}}{1}$$

Multiply.

$$= \underline{\quad\quad}$$

Check your answer.

$$\frac{1}{12} \times \underline{\quad\quad} = \underline{\quad\quad} = \underline{\quad\quad}$$

Since the estimate is _____, the answer is reasonable.

So, Winnie can cut _____ $\frac{1}{12}$ yd pieces of string.

© Houghton Mifflin Harcourt Publishing Company

MATHEMATICAL PRACTICES ⑥

Explain how you used multiplication to check your answer.

Name _____

Estimate. Then find the quotient.

1. $\dfrac{5}{6} \div 3$

Write the whole number as a fraction.

Use the reciprocal of the divisor to write a multiplication problem.

Estimate. _____ $\div 3 =$ _____

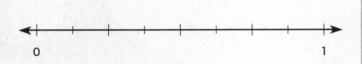

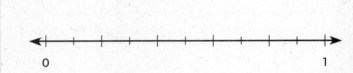

Use a number line to find the quotient.

2. $\dfrac{3}{4} \div \dfrac{1}{8} =$ _____

⊘ 3. $\dfrac{3}{5} \div \dfrac{3}{10} =$ _____

0   1

0   1

Estimate. Then write the quotient in simplest form.

⊘ 4. $\dfrac{3}{4} \div \dfrac{5}{6}$

5. $3 \div \dfrac{3}{4}$

6. $\dfrac{1}{2} \div \dfrac{3}{4}$

7. $\dfrac{5}{12} \div 3$

Math Talk MATHEMATICAL PRACTICES ⑤

Use Tools Explain how to find a reasonable estimate for $\dfrac{11}{12} \div \dfrac{1}{4}$.

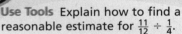

On Your Own

Practice: Copy and Solve Estimate. Then write the quotient in simplest form.

8. $2 \div \dfrac{1}{8}$

9. $\dfrac{3}{4} \div \dfrac{3}{5}$

10. $\dfrac{2}{5} \div 5$

11. $4 \div \dfrac{1}{7}$

Practice: Copy and Solve Evaluate using the order of operations. Write the answer in simplest form.

12. $\left(\dfrac{3}{5} + \dfrac{1}{10}\right) \div 2$

13. $\dfrac{3}{5} + \dfrac{1}{10} \div 2$

14. $\dfrac{3}{5} + 2 \div \dfrac{1}{10}$

15. MATHEMATICAL PRACTICE ⑧ **Generalize** Suppose the divisor and the dividend of a division problem are both fractions between 0 and 1, and the divisor is greater than the dividend. Is the quotient less than, equal to, or greater than 1?

_____

Problem Solving • Applications Real World

Use the table for 16–19.

Tree House Measurements	
Item	**Board Length**
Ladder rung	$\frac{3}{4}$ ft
"Keep Out" sign	$\frac{5}{8}$ yd
Windowsill	$\frac{1}{2}$ yd

16. Kristen wants to cut ladder rungs from a 6 ft board. How many ladder rungs can she cut?

_____

17. **THINK SMARTER** **Pose a Problem** Look back at Problem 16. Write and solve a new problem by changing the length of the board Kristen is cutting for ladder rungs.

_____

_____

_____

_____

18. Dan paints a design that has 8 equal parts along the entire length of the windowsill. How long is each part of the design?

_____

19. **GO DEEPER** Dan has a board that is $\frac{15}{16}$ yd. How many "Keep Out" signs can he make if the length of the sign is changed to half of the original length?

_____

WRITE *Math* • **Show Your Work**

Personal Math Trainer

20. **THINK SMARTER +**  Lauren has $\frac{3}{4}$ cup of dried fruit. She puts the dried fruit into bags, each holding $\frac{1}{8}$ cup. How many bags will Lauren use? Explain your answer using words and numbers.

_____

_____

_____

Divide Fractions

Common Core

COMMON CORE STANDARD—6.NS.A.1
Apply and extend previous understandings of multiplication and division to divide fractions by fractions.

Estimate. Then write the quotient in simplest form.

1. $5 \div \frac{1}{6}$

Estimate: 30

$= 5 \times \frac{6}{1}$

$= \frac{30}{1}$

$= 30$

2. $\frac{1}{2} \div \frac{1}{4}$

3. $\frac{4}{5} \div \frac{2}{3}$

4. $\frac{14}{15} \div 7$

5. $8 \div \frac{1}{3}$

6. $\frac{12}{21} \div \frac{2}{3}$

7. $\frac{5}{6} \div \frac{5}{12}$

8. $\frac{5}{8} \div \frac{1}{2}$

9. Joy ate $\frac{1}{4}$ of a pizza. If she divides the rest of the pizza into pieces equal to $\frac{1}{8}$ pizza for her family, how many pieces will her family get?

10. Hideko has $\frac{3}{5}$ yard of ribbon to tie on balloons for the festival. Each balloon will need $\frac{3}{10}$ yard of ribbon. How many balloons can Hideko tie with ribbon?

Problem Solving Real World

11. Rick knows that 1 cup of glue weighs $\frac{1}{18}$ pound. He has $\frac{2}{3}$ pound of glue. How many cups of glue does he have?

12. Mrs. Jennings had $\frac{5}{7}$ gallon of paint. She gave $\frac{1}{7}$ gallon each to some students. How many students received paint if Mrs. Jennings gave away all the paint?

13. **WRITE** *Math* Write a word problem that involves two fractions. Include the solution.

Lesson Check (6.NS.A.1)

1. There was $\frac{2}{3}$ of a pizza for 6 friends to share equally. What fraction of the pizza did each person get?

2. Rashad needs $\frac{2}{3}$ pound of wax to make a candle. How many candles can he make with 6 pounds of wax?

Spiral Review (6.NS.A.1, 6.NS.B.3, 6.NS.B.4)

3. Jeremy had $\frac{3}{4}$ of a submarine sandwich and gave his friend $\frac{1}{3}$ of it. What fraction of the sandwich did the friend receive?

4. Ebony walked at a rate of $3\frac{1}{2}$ miles per hour for $1\frac{1}{3}$ hours. How far did she walk?

5. Penny uses $\frac{3}{4}$ yard of fabric for each pillow she makes. How many pillows can she make using 6 yards of fabric?

6. During track practice, Chris ran 2.5 laps in 81 seconds. What was his average time per lap?

FOR MORE PRACTICE
GO TO THE
Personal Math Trainer

Lesson **2.8**

Model Mixed Number Division

Essential Question How can you use a model to show division of mixed numbers?

Common Core — The Number System—
6.NS.A.1

MATHEMATICAL PRACTICES
MP1, MP4, MP5, MP8

Investigate

Materials ■ pattern blocks

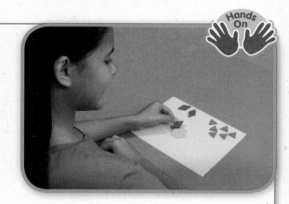

A science teacher has $1\frac{2}{3}$ cups of baking soda. She performs an experiment for her students by mixing $\frac{1}{6}$ cup of baking soda with vinegar. If the teacher uses the same amount of baking soda for each experiment, how many times can she perform the experiment?

A. Which operation should you use to find the answer? Why?

_____

_____

B. Use pattern blocks to show $1\frac{2}{3}$.

Draw your model.

Think: A hexagon block is one whole, and a rhombus is

_____ of a whole.

• What type and number of blocks did you use to model $1\frac{2}{3}$?

_____

C. Cover $1\frac{2}{3}$ with blocks that represent $\frac{1}{6}$ to show dividing by $\frac{1}{6}$. Draw your model.

Think: One _____

block represents _____ of a whole.

_____ triangle blocks cover $1\frac{2}{3}$.

$1\frac{2}{3} \div \frac{1}{6} =$ _____

So, the teacher can perform the experiment _____ times.

Math Talk

MATHEMATICAL PRACTICES ⑤

Use Tools How can you check that your answer is reasonable?

Draw Conclusions

1. **MATHEMATICAL PRACTICE 5** **Communicate** Tell how your model shows a related multiplication problem.

   _____

2. **MATHEMATICAL PRACTICE 1** **Describe Relationships** Suppose a mixed number is divided by a fraction between 0 and 1. Is the quotient greater than or less than the dividend? Explain and give an example.

   _____

   _____

   _____

   _____

Make Connections

You can use a model to divide a mixed number by a whole number.

Naomi has $2\frac{1}{4}$ quarts of lemonade. She wants to divide the lemonade equally between 2 pitchers. How many quarts of lemonade should she pour into each pitcher?

Divide $2\frac{1}{4} \div 2$.

STEP 1 Draw a model that represents the total amount of lemonade.

Think: Divide 3 wholes into _____.

Shade _____.

STEP 2 Draw parts that represent the amount in each pitcher.

Think: What are you trying to find?

_____

Think: In each of the two equal groups there is _____ whole and _____ of $\frac{1}{4}$.

$\frac{1}{2}$ of $\frac{1}{4}$ is _____.

So, $2\frac{1}{4} \div 2 =$ _____. Naomi should pour _____ quarts of lemonade into each pitcher.

MATHEMATICAL PRACTICES 8

Generalize Explain how the quotient compares to the dividend when dividing a mixed number by a whole number greater than 1.

Name _____

Use the model to find the quotient.

1. $3\frac{1}{3} \div \frac{1}{3} =$ _____

2. $2\frac{1}{2} \div \frac{1}{6} =$ _____

Use pattern blocks to find the quotient. Then draw the model.

3. $2\frac{2}{3} \div \frac{1}{6} =$ _____

4. $3\frac{1}{2} \div \frac{1}{2} =$ _____

Draw a model to find the quotient.

5. $3\frac{1}{2} \div 3 =$ _____

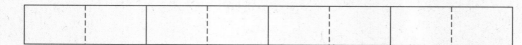

6. $1\frac{1}{4} \div 2 =$ _____

7. **MATHEMATICAL PRACTICE ⑤ Use Appropriate Tools** Explain how models can be used to divide mixed numbers by fractions or whole numbers.

_____

_____

_____

_____

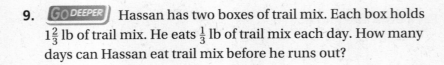

Problem Solving • Applications

Use a model to solve. Then write an equation for the model.

8. **MATHEMATICAL PRACTICE 4 Use Models** Eliza opens a box of bead kits. The box weighs $2\frac{2}{3}$ lb. Each bead kit weighs $\frac{1}{6}$ lb. How many kits are in the box? What does the answer mean?

_____

_____

9. **GO DEEPER** Hassan has two boxes of trail mix. Each box holds $1\frac{2}{3}$ lb of trail mix. He eats $\frac{1}{3}$ lb of trail mix each day. How many days can Hassan eat trail mix before he runs out?

_____

10. **THINK SMARTER** **Sense or Nonsense?** Steve made this model to show $2\frac{1}{3} \div \frac{1}{6}$. He says that the quotient is 7. Is his answer sense or nonsense? Explain your reasoning.

_____

_____

_____

11. **THINK SMARTER** Eva is making muffins to sell at a fundraiser. She has $2\frac{1}{4}$ cups of flour, and the recipe calls for $\frac{3}{4}$ cup of flour for each batch of muffins. Explain how to use a model to find the number of batches of muffins Eva can make.

_____

_____

_____

_____

_____

WRITE ▸ Math
Show Your Work

Model Mixed Number Division

Common Core

COMMON CORE STANDARD—6.NS.A.1
Apply and extend previous understandings of multiplication and division to divide fractions by fractions.

Use the model to find the quotient.

1. $4\frac{1}{2} \div \frac{1}{2} =$ _____9_____

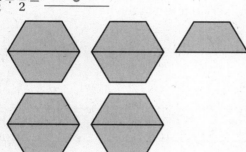

2. $3\frac{1}{3} \div \frac{1}{6} =$ _____

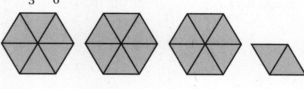

Use pattern blocks or another model to find the quotient. Then draw the model.

3. $2\frac{1}{2} \div \frac{1}{6} =$ _____

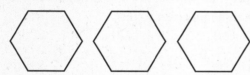

4. $2\frac{3}{4} \div 2 =$ _____

Problem Solving (Real World)

5. Marty has $2\frac{4}{5}$ quarts of juice. He pours the same amount of juice into 2 bottles. How much does he pour into each bottle?

6. How many $\frac{1}{3}$ pound servings are in $4\frac{2}{3}$ pounds of cheese?

_____

7. **WRITE** ▸*Math* Write a word problem that involves dividing a mixed number by a whole number. Solve the problem and describe how you found the answer.

_____

_____

_____

Lesson Check (6.NS.A.1)

Sketch a model to find the quotient.

1. Emma has $4\frac{1}{2}$ pounds of birdseed. She wants to divide it evenly among 3 bird feeders. How much birdseed should she put in each?

2. A box of crackers weighs $11\frac{1}{4}$ ounces. Kaden estimates that one serving is $\frac{3}{4}$ ounce. How many servings are in the box?

Spiral Review (6.NS.B.3, 6.NS.B.4, 6.NS.C.6c)

3. The Ecology Club has volunteered to clean up 4.8 kilometers of highway. The members are organized into 16 teams. Each team will clean the same amount of highway. How much highway will each team clean?

4. Tyrone has $8.06. How many bagels can he buy if each bagel costs $0.65?

5. A nail is 0.1875 inch thick. What is its thickness as a fraction? Is 0.1875 inch closer to $\frac{1}{8}$ inch or $\frac{1}{4}$ inch on a number line?

6. Maria wants to find the product of $5\frac{3}{20} \times 3\frac{4}{25}$ using decimals instead of fractions. How can she rewrite the problem using decimals?

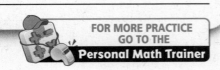

FOR MORE PRACTICE
GO TO THE
Personal Math Trainer

Name _____

Divide Mixed Numbers

Essential Question How do you divide mixed numbers?

Common Core The Number System—
6.NS.A.1
MATHEMATICAL PRACTICES
MP1, MP6, MP7

Unlock the Problem Real World

A box weighing $9\frac{1}{3}$ lb contains robot kits weighing $1\frac{1}{6}$ lb apiece. How many robot kits are in the box?

- Underline the sentence that tells you what you are trying to find.
- Circle the numbers you need to use to solve the problem.

Divide $9\frac{1}{3} \div 1\frac{1}{6}$.

Estimate the quotient. _____ ÷ _____ = _____

Write the mixed numbers
as fractions.

$$9\frac{1}{3} \div 1\frac{1}{6} = \frac{\boxed{}}{3} \div \frac{\boxed{}}{6}$$

Use the reciprocal of
the divisor to write a
multiplication problem.

$$= \frac{28}{3} \times \frac{\boxed{}}{\boxed{}}$$

Simplify.

$$= \frac{28}{\cancel{3}} \times \frac{\cancel{6}}{\cancel{7}}$$

Multiply.

$$= \frac{\boxed{}}{\boxed{}}, \text{ or } _____$$

Compare your estimate with the quotient. Since the estimate, _____,

is close to _____, the answer is reasonable.

So, there are _____ robot kits in the box.

Try This! **Estimate. Then write the quotient in simplest form.**

Think: Write the mixed numbers as fractions.

Ⓐ $2\frac{1}{3} \div \frac{1}{6}$

_____

Ⓑ $5\frac{3}{4} \div \frac{3}{8}$

_____

🔑 Example
Four hikers shared $3\frac{1}{3}$ qt of water equally. How much did each hiker receive?

Divide $3\frac{1}{3} \div 4$. Check.

Estimate. _____ ÷ 4 = 1

Write the mixed number and the whole number as fractions.

$$3\frac{1}{3} \div 4 = \frac{\boxed{}}{3} \div \frac{\boxed{}}{\boxed{}}$$

Use the reciprocal of the divisor to write a multiplication problem.

$$= \frac{10}{3} \times \frac{\boxed{}}{\boxed{}}$$

Simplify.

$$= \frac{\overset{\boxed{}}{\cancel{10}}}{3} \times \frac{1}{\cancel{4}}_{\boxed{}}$$

Multiply.

$$= \underline{}$$

Check your answer.

$$4 \times \underline{} = \frac{\boxed{}}{\boxed{}} = \underline{}$$

So, each hiker received _____ qt.

Math Talk

MATHEMATICAL PRACTICES ①

Evaluate whether your answer is reasonable using the information in the problem.

1. Describe what you are trying to find in the Example above.

_____

2. **MATHEMATICAL PRACTICE ⑥ Compare** Explain how dividing mixed numbers is similar to multiplying mixed numbers. How are they different?

_____

_____

_____

_____

3. **THINK SMARTER** The divisor in a division problem is between 0 and 1 and the dividend is greater than 0. Will the quotient be greater than or less than the dividend? Explain.

_____

_____

Name _____

Estimate. Then write the quotient in simplest form.

1. Estimate: _____

$$4\frac{1}{3} \div \frac{3}{4} = \frac{\boxed{}}{3} \div \frac{3}{4}$$

$$= \frac{13}{3} \times \frac{\boxed{}}{\boxed{}}$$

$$= \frac{\boxed{}}{\boxed{}}, \text{ or } 5\frac{\boxed{}}{9}$$

2. Six hikers shared $4\frac{1}{2}$ lb of trail mix. How much trail mix did each hiker receive?

_____

3. $5\frac{2}{3} \div 3$

_____

4. $7\frac{1}{2} \div 2\frac{1}{2}$

_____

Math Talk

MATHEMATICAL PRACTICES ⑥

Explain why you write a mixed number as a fraction before using it as a dividend or divisor.

On Your Own

Estimate. Then write the quotient in simplest form.

5. $5\frac{3}{4} \div 4\frac{1}{2}$

6. $5 \div 1\frac{1}{3}$

7. $6\frac{3}{4} \div 2$

8. $2\frac{2}{9} \div 1\frac{3}{7}$

_____

9. How many $3\frac{1}{3}$ yd pieces can Amanda get from a $13\frac{1}{3}$ yd ribbon?

_____

10. **THINK SMARTER** Samantha cut $6\frac{3}{4}$ yd of yarn into 3 equal pieces. Explain how she could use mental math to find the length of each piece.

_____

MATHEMATICAL PRACTICE ① **Evaluate Algebra** **Evaluate using the order of operations. Write the answer in simplest form.**

11. $1\frac{1}{2} \times 2 \div 1\frac{1}{3}$

12. $1\frac{2}{5} \div 1\frac{13}{15} + \frac{5}{8}$

13. $3\frac{1}{2} - 1\frac{5}{6} \div 1\frac{2}{9}$

_____

14. **MATHEMATICAL PRACTICE ⑦** **Look for a Pattern** Find these quotients: $20 \div 4\frac{4}{5}$, $10 \div 4\frac{4}{5}$, $5 \div 4\frac{4}{5}$. Describe a pattern you see.

_____

Unlock the Problem

15. **GO DEEPER** Dina hikes $\frac{1}{2}$ of the easy trail and stops for a break every $3\frac{1}{4}$ miles. How many breaks will she take?

Hiking Trails			
Park	**Trail**	**Length (mi)**	**Difficulty**
Cuyahoga Valley National Park, Ohio	Ohio and Erie Canal Towpath	$19\frac{1}{2}$	easy
	Brandywine Gorge	$1\frac{1}{4}$	moderate
	Buckeye Trail (Jaite to Boston)	$5\frac{3}{5}$	difficult

a. What problem are you asked to solve?

_____

_____

b. How will you use the information in the table to solve the problem?

_____

_____

c. How can you find the distance Dina hikes? How far does she hike?

_____

_____

d. What operation will you use to find how many breaks Dina takes?

_____

_____

e. How many breaks will Dina take?

_____

---

16. **THINK SMARTER** Carlo packs $15\frac{3}{4}$ lb of books in 2 boxes. Each book weighs $1\frac{1}{8}$ lb. There are 4 more books in Box A than in Box B. How many books are in Box A? Explain your work.

_____

_____

_____

---

17. **THINK SMARTER** Rex's goal is to run $13\frac{3}{4}$ miles over 5 days. He wants to run the same distance each day. Jordan said that Rex would have to run $3\frac{3}{4}$ miles each day to reach his goal. Do you agree with Jordan? Explain your answer using words and numbers.

_____

_____

_____

Divide Mixed Numbers

Common Core COMMON CORE STANDARD—6.NS.A.1
Apply and extend previous understandings of
multiplication and division to divide fractions
by fractions.

Estimate. Then write the quotient in simplest form.

1. $2\frac{1}{2} \div 2\frac{1}{3}$

Estimate: $2 \div 2 = 1$

$2\frac{1}{2} \div 2\frac{1}{3} = \frac{5}{2} \div \frac{7}{3}$

$= \frac{5}{2} \times \frac{3}{7}$

$= \frac{15}{14} \text{ or } 1\frac{1}{14}$

2. $2\frac{2}{3} \div 1\frac{1}{3}$

3. $2 \div 3\frac{5}{8}$

4. $1\frac{13}{15} \div 1\frac{2}{5}$

5. $10 \div 6\frac{2}{3}$

6. $2\frac{3}{5} \div 1\frac{1}{25}$

7. $2\frac{1}{5} \div 2$

8. Sid and Jill hiked $4\frac{1}{8}$ miles in the morning
and $1\frac{7}{8}$ miles in the afternoon. How many
times as far did they hike in the morning
as in the afternoon?

Problem Solving · Real World

9. It takes Nim $2\frac{2}{3}$ hours to weave a basket. He
worked Monday through Friday, 8 hours a day.
How many baskets did he make?

10. A tree grows $1\frac{3}{4}$ feet per year. How long will it
take the tree to grow from a height of $21\frac{1}{4}$ feet to a
height of 37 feet?

11. **WRITE** ▸Math Explain how you would find how many $1\frac{1}{2}$ cup
servings there are in a pot that contains $22\frac{1}{2}$ cups of soup.

Lesson Check (6.NS.A.1)

1. Tom has a can of paint that covers $37\frac{1}{2}$ square meters. Each board on the fence has an area of $\frac{3}{16}$ square meters. How many boards can he paint?

2. A baker wants to put $3\frac{3}{4}$ pounds of apples in each pie she makes. She purchased $52\frac{1}{2}$ pounds of apples. How many pies can she make?

Spiral Review (6.NS.A.1, 6.NS.B.3)

3. The three sides of a triangle measure 9.97 meters, 10.1 meters, and 0.53 meter. What is the distance around the triangle?

4. Selena bought 3.75 pounds of meat for $4.64 per pound. What was the total cost of the meat?

5. Melanie prepared $7\frac{1}{2}$ tablespoons of a spice mixture. She uses $\frac{1}{4}$ tablespoon to make a batch of barbecue sauce. Estimate the number of batches of barbecue sauce she can make using the spice mixture.

6. Arturo mixed together 1.24 pounds of pretzels, 0.78 pounds of nuts, 0.3 pounds of candy, and 2 pounds of popcorn. He then packaged it in bags that each contained 0.27 pounds. How many bags could he fill?

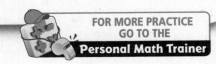

FOR MORE PRACTICE
GO TO THE
Personal Math Trainer

Name _____

Problem Solving • Fraction Operations

Essential Question How can you use the strategy *use a model* to help you solve a division problem?

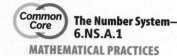

Common Core The Number System—
6.NS.A.1

MATHEMATICAL PRACTICES
MP1, MP2, MP4, MP6

Unlock the Problem

Sam had $\frac{3}{4}$ lb of granola. Each day he took $\frac{1}{8}$ lb to school for a snack. If he had $\frac{1}{4}$ lb left over, how many days did Sam take granola to school?

Use the graphic organizer below to help you solve the problem.

Read the Problem

What do I need to find?

I need to find _____

_____

_____.

What information do I need to use?

Sam started with _____ lb of

granola and took _____ lb

each day. He had _____ lb

left over.

How will I use the information?

I will draw a bar model to find

how much _____

_____

_____.

Solve the Problem

$\frac{3}{4}$ lb

$\frac{1}{8}$			
used		left	

The model shows that Sam used _____ lb of granola.

_____ groups of $\frac{1}{8}$ are equivalent to $\frac{1}{2}$

so $\frac{1}{2} \div \frac{1}{8} =$ _____ .

MATHEMATICAL PRACTICES ②

Reasoning Justify your answer by using a different representation for the problem.

So, Sam took granola to school for _____ days.

🔐 Try Another Problem

For a science experiment, Mr. Barrows divides $\frac{2}{3}$ cup of salt into small jars, each containing $\frac{1}{12}$ cup. If he has $\frac{1}{6}$ cup of salt left over, how many jars does he fill?

Read the Problem

What do I need to find?	What information do I need to use?	How will I use the information?

Solve the Problem

So, Mr. Barrows fills _____ jars.

1. **MATHEMATICAL PRACTICE ④ Write an Expression** you could use to solve the problem.

   _____

2. **MATHEMATICAL PRACTICE ⑥ Explain a Method** Suppose that Mr. Barrows starts with $1\frac{2}{3}$ cups of salt. Explain how you could find how many jars he fills.

   _____

   _____

   _____

Name _____

Unlock the Problem

- Underline the question.
- Circle important information.
- Check to make sure you answered the question.

1. There is $\frac{4}{5}$ lb of sand in the class science supplies. If one scoop of sand weighs $\frac{1}{20}$ lb, how many scoops of sand can Maria get from the class supplies and still leave $\frac{1}{2}$ lb in the supplies?

First, draw a bar model.

$\frac{4}{5}$ lb

WRITE *Math* · **Show Your Work**

Next, find how much sand Maria gets.

Maria will get $\frac{}{10}$ lb of sand.

Finally, find the number of scoops.

_____ groups of $\frac{1}{20}$ are equivalent to $\frac{}{10}$

so $\frac{}{10} \div \frac{1}{20} =$ _____.

So, Maria will get _____ scoops of sand.

2. **THINK SMARTER** **What if** Maria leaves $\frac{2}{5}$ lb of sand in the supplies? How many scoops of sand can she get?

_____

3. There are 6 gallons of distilled water in the science supplies. If 10 students each use an equal amount of the distilled water and there is 1 gal left in the supplies, how much will each student get?

_____

On Your Own

4. **THINK SMARTER** The total weight of the fish in a tank of tropical fish at Fish 'n' Fur was $\frac{7}{8}$ lb. Each fish weighed $\frac{1}{64}$ lb. After Eric bought some fish, the total weight of the fish remaining in the tank was $\frac{1}{2}$ lb. How many fish did Eric buy?

_____

5. **GO DEEPER** Fish 'n' Fur had a bin containing $2\frac{1}{2}$ lb of gerbil food. After selling bags of gerbil food that each held $\frac{3}{4}$ lb, $\frac{1}{4}$ lb of food was left in the bin. If each bag of gerbil food sold for $3.25, how much did the store earn?

_____

6. **MATHEMATICAL PRACTICE ①** **Describe** Niko bought 2 lb of dog treats. He gave his dog $\frac{3}{5}$ lb of treats one week and $\frac{7}{10}$ lb of treats the next week. Describe how Niko can find how much is left.

_____

_____

_____

_____

WRITE *Math* · **Show Your Work**

Personal Math Trainer

7. **THINK SMARTER +** There were $14\frac{1}{4}$ cups of apple juice in a container. Each day, Elise drank $1\frac{1}{2}$ cups of apple juice. Today, there is $\frac{3}{4}$ cup of apple juice left.

Derek said that Elise drank apple juice on nine days. Do you agree with Derek? Use words and numbers to explain your answer.

_____

_____

_____

_____

Problem Solving • Fraction Operations

Common Core

COMMON CORE STANDARD—6.NS.A.1
Apply and extend previous understandings of multiplication and division to divide fractions by fractions.

Read each problem and solve.

1. $\frac{2}{3}$ of a pizza was left over. A group of friends divided the leftover pizza into pieces each equal to $\frac{1}{18}$ of the original pizza. After each friend took one piece, $\frac{1}{6}$ of the original pizza remained. How many friends were in the group?

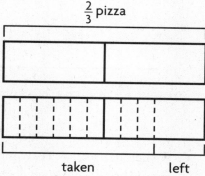

$\frac{2}{3}$ pizza

taken   left

_____ 9

2. Sarah's craft project uses pieces of yarn that are $\frac{1}{8}$ yard long. She has a piece of yarn that is 3 yards long. How many $\frac{1}{8}$-yard pieces can she cut and still have $1\frac{1}{4}$ yards left?

_____

3. Alex opens a 1-pint container of orange butter. He spreads $\frac{1}{16}$ of the butter on his bread. Then he divides the rest of the butter into $\frac{3}{4}$-pint containers. How many $\frac{3}{4}$-pint containers is he able to fill?

_____

4. Kaitlin buys $\frac{9}{10}$ pound of orange slices. She eats $\frac{1}{3}$ of them and divides the rest equally into 3 bags. How much is in each bag?

_____

5. **WRITE** ▸*Math* Explain how to draw a model that represents $\left(1\frac{1}{4} - \frac{1}{2}\right) \div \frac{1}{8}$.

_____

_____

Lesson Check (6.NS.A.1)

1. Eva wanted to fill bags with $\frac{3}{4}$ pounds of trail mix. She started with $11\frac{3}{8}$ pounds but ate $\frac{1}{8}$ pound before she started filling the bags. How many bags could she fill?

2. John has a roll containing $24\frac{2}{3}$ feet of wrapping paper. He wants to divide it into 11 pieces. First, though, he must cut off $\frac{5}{6}$ foot because it was torn. How long will each piece be?

Spiral Review (6.NS.A.1, 6.NS.B.3, 6.NS.B.4)

3. Alexis has $32\frac{2}{5}$ ounces of beads. How many necklaces can she make if each uses $2\frac{7}{10}$ ounces of beads?

4. Joseph has $32.40. He wants to buy several comic books that each cost $2.70. How many comic books can he buy?

5. A rectangle is $2\frac{4}{5}$ meters wide and $3\frac{1}{2}$ meters long. What is its area?

6. A rectangle is 2.8 meters wide and 3.5 meters long. What is its area?

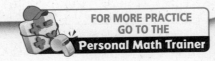

FOR MORE PRACTICE
GO TO THE
Personal Math Trainer

✓ Chapter 2 Review/Test

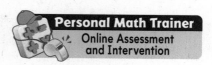

Personal Math Trainer
Online Assessment
and Intervention

1. Write the values in order from least to greatest.

| 0.45 | $\frac{3}{4}$ | $\frac{5}{8}$ | 0.5 |

_____ _____ _____ _____

2. For numbers 2a–2d, compare. Choose <, >, or =.

2a. 0.75 $\boxed{\begin{array}{c} < \\ > \\ = \end{array}}$ $\frac{3}{4}$

2c. $1\frac{3}{5}$ $\boxed{\begin{array}{c} < \\ > \\ = \end{array}}$ 1.9

2b. $\frac{4}{5}$ $\boxed{\begin{array}{c} < \\ > \\ = \end{array}}$ 0.325

2d. 7.4 $\boxed{\begin{array}{c} < \\ > \\ = \end{array}}$ $7\frac{2}{5}$

3. The table lists the heights of 4 trees.

Type of Tree	Height (feet)
Sycamore	$15\frac{2}{3}$
Oak	$14\frac{3}{4}$
Maple	$15\frac{3}{4}$
Birch	15.72

For numbers 3a–3d, select True or False for each statement.

3a. The oak tree is the shortest. ○ True ○ False

3b. The birch tree is the tallest. ○ True ○ False

3c. Two of the trees are the same height. ○ True ○ False

3d. The sycamore tree is taller than the maple tree. ○ True ○ False

GO DIGITAL Assessment Options
Chapter Test

4. For numbers 4a–4d, choose Yes or No to indicate whether the statement is correct.

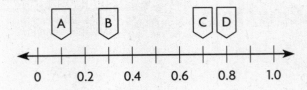

4a. Point *A* represents 1.0. ○ Yes ○ No

4b. Point *B* represents $\frac{3}{10}$. ○ Yes ○ No

4c. Point *C* represents 6.5. ○ Yes ○ No

4d. Point *D* represents $\frac{4}{5}$. ○ Yes ○ No

5. Select the values that are equivalent to one twenty-fifth. Mark all that apply.

Ⓐ $\frac{1}{25}$

Ⓑ 25

Ⓒ 0.04

Ⓓ 0.025

6. The table shows Lily's homework assignment. Lily's teacher instructed the class to simplify each expression by dividing the numerator and denominator by the GCF. Complete the table by simplifying each expression and then finding the product.

Problem	Expression	Simplified Expression	Product
a	$\frac{2}{5} \times \frac{1}{4}$		
b	$\frac{4}{5} \times \frac{5}{8}$		
c	$\frac{3}{7} \times \frac{5}{8}$		
d	$\frac{4}{9} \times \frac{3}{16}$		

Name _____

7.  Two-fifths of the fish in Gary's fish tank are guppies. One-fourth of the guppies are red. What fraction of the fish in Gary's tank are red guppies? What fraction of the fish in Gary's tank are not red guppies? Show your work.

8. One-third of the students at Finley High School play sports. Two-fifths of the students who play sports are girls. What fraction of all students are girls who play sports? Use numbers and words to explain your answer.

9. Draw a model to find the quotient.

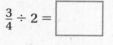

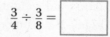

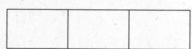

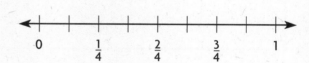

How are your models alike? How are they different?

10. Explain how to use a model to find the quotient.

$2\frac{1}{2} \div 2 =$ ☐

Divide. Show your work.

11. $\frac{7}{8} \div \frac{3}{5} =$ [ ]

12. $2\frac{1}{10} \div 1\frac{1}{5} =$ [ ]

13. Sophie has $\frac{3}{4}$ quart of lemonade. If she divides the lemonade into glasses that hold $\frac{1}{16}$ quart, how many glasses can Sophie fill? Show your work.

14. Ink cartridges weigh $\frac{1}{8}$ pound. The total weight of the cartridges in a box is $4\frac{1}{2}$ pounds. How many cartridges does the box contain? Show your work and explain why you chose the operation you did.

15. THINK SMARTER + Beth had 1 yard of ribbon. She used $\frac{1}{3}$ yard for a project. She wants to divide the rest of the ribbon into pieces $\frac{1}{6}$ yard long. How many $\frac{1}{6}$ yard pieces of ribbon can she make? Explain your solution.

16. Complete the table by finding the products. Then answer the questions in Part A and Part B.

Division	Multiplication
$\frac{1}{5} \div \frac{3}{4} = \frac{4}{15}$	$\frac{1}{5} \times \frac{4}{3} =$
$\frac{2}{13} \div \frac{1}{5} = \frac{10}{13}$	$\frac{2}{13} \times \frac{5}{1} =$
$\frac{4}{5} \div \frac{3}{5} = \frac{4}{3}$	$\frac{4}{5} \times \frac{5}{3} =$

Part A

Explain how each pair of division and multiplication problems are the same, and how they are different.

Part B

Explain how to use the pattern in the table to rewrite a division problem involving fractions as a multiplication problem.

17. Margie hiked a $17\frac{7}{8}$ mile trail. She stopped every $3\frac{2}{5}$ miles to take a picture. Martin and Tina estimated how many times Margie stopped.

Martin's Estimate

$17\frac{7}{8} \div 3\frac{2}{5}$
$\downarrow \qquad \downarrow$
$16 \div 4 = 4$

Tina's Estimate

$17\frac{7}{8} \div 3\frac{2}{5}$
$\downarrow \qquad \downarrow$
$18 \div 3 = 6$

Who made the better estimate? Use numbers and words to explain your answer.

18. Brad and Wes are building a tree house. They cut a $12\frac{1}{2}$ foot piece of wood into 5 of the same length pieces. How long is each piece of wood? Show your work.

Rational Numbers

✓ Show What You Know

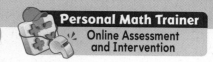
Personal Math Trainer
Online Assessment and Intervention

Check your understanding of important skills.

Name _____

▶ **Compare Fractions** Compare. Write <, >, or =. (4.NF.A.2)

1. $\frac{3}{5}$ ◯ $\frac{1}{3}$

2. $\frac{3}{7}$ ◯ $\frac{1}{2}$

3. $\frac{3}{3}$ ◯ $\frac{5}{5}$

4. $\frac{6}{8}$ ◯ $\frac{2}{4}$

▶ **Equivalent Fractions** Write an equivalent fraction. (4.NF.A.1)

5. $\frac{3}{8}$ _____

6. $\frac{2}{5}$ _____

7. $\frac{10}{12}$ _____

8. $\frac{6}{9}$ _____

▶ **Compare Decimals** Compare. Write <, >, or =. (5.NBT.A.3b)

9. 0.3 ◯ 0.30

10. 4 ◯ 3.8

11. 0.4 ◯ 0.51

12. $2.61 ◯ $6.21

Angie finds a treasure map. Use the clues to find the location of the treasure. Write the location as an ordered pair.

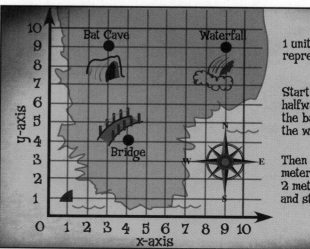

1 unit on the map represents 1 meter.

Start at the point halfway between the bat cave and the waterfall.

Then walk 7 meters south and 2 meters west, and start digging.

Vocabulary Builder

▶ Visualize It •

Use the checked words to complete the flow map.

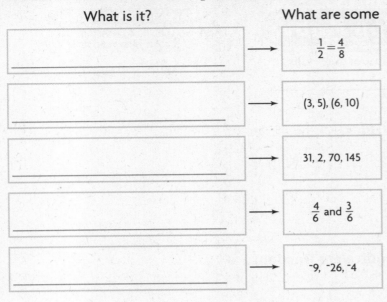

What is it?		What are some
_____	→	$\frac{1}{2} = \frac{4}{8}$
_____	→	(3, 5), (6, 10)
_____	→	31, 2, 70, 145
_____	→	$\frac{4}{6}$ and $\frac{3}{6}$
_____	→	⁻9, ⁻26, ⁻4

Review Words

compare
✓ common denominator
✓ equivalent fractions
order
✓ whole numbers

Preview Words

absolute value
coordinate plane
integers
✓ negative number
opposite
✓ ordered pair
origin
positive number
quadrants
rational number

▶ Understand Vocabulary •

Complete the sentences using the preview words.

1. The _____ are the set of whole numbers and their opposites.

2. The distance of a number from 0 on a number line is the number's _____.

3. Two numbers that are the same distance from zero on the number line, but on different sides of zero, are called _____.

4. A _____ is any number that can be written as $\frac{a}{b}$, where a and b are integers and $b \neq 0$.

5. The four regions of the coordinate plane that are separated by the x- and y-axes are called _____.

GO DIGITAL
• Interactive Student Edition
• Multimedia eGlossary

Chapter 3 Vocabulary

absolute value

valor absoluto

1

coordinate plane

plano cartesiano

17

integers

enteros

44

line of symmetry

eje de simetría

51

line symmetry

simetría axial

52

negative integer

entero negativo

64

opposites

opuestos

68

ordered pair

par ordenado

70

A plane formed by a horizontal line called the *x*-axis and a vertical line called the *y*-axis

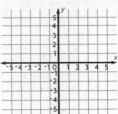

The distance of an integer from zero on a number line

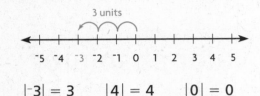

$|{}^-3| = 3$ $|4| = 4$ $|0| = 0$

A line that divides a figure into two halves that are reflections of each other

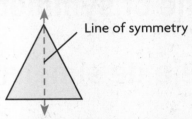

Line of symmetry

The set of whole numbers and their opposites

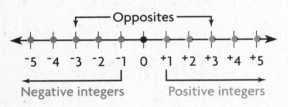

Any integer less than zero

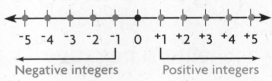

A figure has line symmetry if it can be folded about a line so that its two parts match exactly

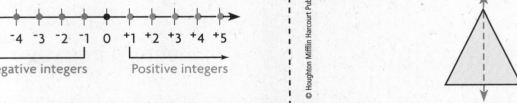

A pair of numbers used to locate a point on a grid.

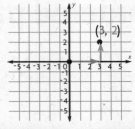

Two numbers that are the same distance, but in opposite directions, from zero on a number line

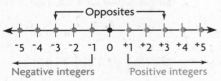

${}^-3$ and 3 are opposites

origin

origen

71

positive integer

entero positivo

76

quadrants

cuadrantes

82

rational number

número racional

88

***x*-axis**

eje de la *x*

108

***x*-coordinate**

coordenada *x*

109

***y*-axis**

eje de la *y*

110

***y*-coordinate**

coordenada *y*

111

Any integer greater than zero

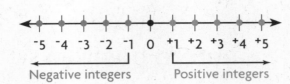

Negative integers   Positive integers

The point where the two axes of a coordinate plane intersect; (0,0)

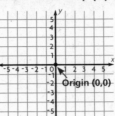

Origin (0,0)

Any number that can be written as a ratio $\frac{a}{b}$ where a and b are integers and $b \neq 0$.

Examples: $6 = \frac{6}{1}$, $0.75 = \frac{3}{4}$, and $^-2\frac{1}{3} = \frac{^-7}{3}$

The four regions of the coordinate plane separated by the x- and y-axes

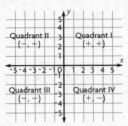

The first number in an ordered pair; tells the distance to move right or left from (0,0)

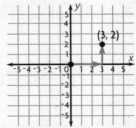

(3, 2)

The horizontal number line on a coordinate plane

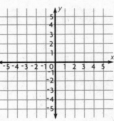

The second number in an ordered pair; tells the distance to move up or down from (0,0)

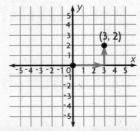

(3, 2)

The vertical number line on a coordinate plane

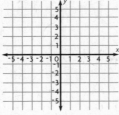

Picture It

For 3 to 4 players

Materials

- timer
- sketch pad

How to Play

1. Take turns to play.
2. To take a turn, choose a math term from the Word Box. Do not say the term.
3. Set the timer for 1 minute.
4. Draw pictures and numbers to give clues about the term.
5. The first player to guess the term before time runs out gets 1 point. If he or she can use the term in a sentence, they get 1 more point. Then that player gets a turn.
6. The first player to score 10 points wins.

Word Box

- absolute value
- coordinate plane
- integers
- line of symmetry
- line symmetry
- negative integer
- opposites
- ordered pair
- origin
- positive integer
- quadrants
- rational number
- x-axis
- x-coordinate
- y-axis
- y-coordinate

The Write Way

Reflect

Choose one idea. Write about it.

- Which two numbers are opposites? Tell how you know.

  4 and ⁻4   ⁻4 and 0   ⁻4 and 4   4 and 0   4 and 4

- Describe a situation in which you might record both positive and negative integers.

- Define the term *absolute value* in your own words. Give an example.

- Write a paragraph that uses at least **three** of these words.

  coordinate plane   origin   quadrants   *x*-axis   *y*-axis

_____

_____

_____

_____

_____

_____

_____

_____

_____

_____

_____

_____

_____

_____

_____

Understand Positive and Negative Numbers

Essential Question How can you use positive and negative numbers to represent real-world quantities?

Common Core — The Number System—6.NS.C.5, 6.NS.C.6a, 6.NS.C.6c
MATHEMATICAL PRACTICES
MP2, MP6, MP7

Integers are the set of all whole numbers and their opposites. Two numbers are **opposites** if they are the same distance from 0 on the number line, but on different sides of 0. For example, the integers $^{+}3$ and $^{-}3$ are opposites. Zero is its own opposite.

Math Idea
You do not need to write the + symbol for positive integers, so $^{+}3$ can also be written as 3.

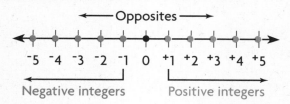

Positive numbers are located to the right of 0 on the number line, and negative numbers are located to the left of 0.

Unlock the Problem

The temperature at the start of a 2009 Major League Baseball playoff game between the Colorado Rockies and the Philadelphia Phillies was 2°C. The temperature at the end of the game was $^{-}4$°C. What is the opposite of each temperature?

- What are you asked to find?

  _____

- Where can you find the opposite of a number on the number line?

  _____

  _____

Graph each integer and its opposite on a number line.

A 2

The integer 2 is on the _____ side of 0.

Graph the opposite of 2 at _____.

So, the opposite of 2°C is _____.

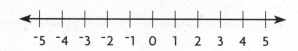

B $^{-}4$

The integer $^{-}4$ is on the _____ side of 0.

Graph the opposite of $^{-}4$ at _____.

So, the opposite of $^{-}4$°C is _____.

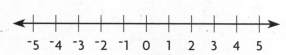

Math Talk

MATHEMATICAL PRACTICES ⑥

Explain how to find the opposite of $^{-}8$ on a number line.

🔑 Example 1 Name the integer that represents the situation, and tell what 0 represents in that situation.

Situation	Integer	What Does 0 Represent?
A team loses 10 yards on a football play.	⁻10	the team neither gains nor loses yardage
A point in Yuma, Arizona, is 70 feet above sea level.		
A temperature of 40 degrees below zero was recorded in Missouri.		
Larry withdraws $30 from his bank account.		
Tricia's golf score was 7 strokes below par.		
A chlorine ion has one more electron than proton.		

🔑 Example 2 Use a number line to find ⁻(⁻3), the opposite of the opposite of 3.

STEP 1

Graph 3 on the number line.

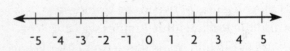

STEP 2

Use the number line to graph the opposite of 3.

STEP 3

Use the number line to graph the opposite of the number you graphed in Step 2.

So, ⁻(⁻3), or the opposite of the opposite of 3, equals _____.

Try This! Write the opposite of the opposite of the integer.

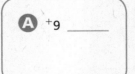

A ⁺9 _____

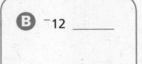

B ⁻12 _____

C 0 _____

Math Talk

MATHEMATICAL PRACTICES ⑦

Look for a Pattern Describe the pattern you see when finding the opposite of the opposite of a number.

• **MATHEMATICAL PRACTICE** ⑥ **Explain** A plane's altitude changes by ⁻1,000 feet. Is the plane going up or down? Explain.

_____

_____

Name _____

Share and Show MATH BOARD

Graph the integer and its opposite on a number line.

1. ⁻7   opposite: _____

<-+---+---+---+---+---+---+---+---+---+---+->
⁻10 ⁻8 ⁻6 ⁻4 ⁻2 0 2 4 6 8 10

2. 9   opposite: _____

<-+---+---+---+---+---+---+---+---+---+---+->
⁻10 ⁻8 ⁻6 ⁻4 ⁻2 0 2 4 6 8 10

Name the integer that represents the situation, and tell what 0 represents in that situation.

Situation	Integer	What Does 0 Represent?
3. Kerri gained 24 points during a round of a game show.		
4. Ben lost 5 pounds during the summer.		
5. Marcy deposited $35 in her savings account.		

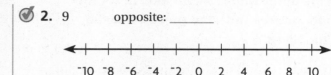

Math Talk

MATHEMATICAL PRACTICES 2

Reason Abstractly Identify a real-world situation involving an integer and its opposite.

On Your Own

Write the opposite of the integer.

6. ⁻98 _____ | **7.** 0 _____ | **8.** ⁻53 _____

Name the integer that represents the situation, and tell what 0 represents in that situation.

Situation	Integer	What Does 0 Represent?
9. Desmond made $850 at his summer job.		
10. Miguel withdraws $300 from his checking account.		
11. A barium ion has two more protons than electrons		

Write the opposite of the opposite of the integer.

12. ⁻23 _____ | **13.** 17 _____ | **14.** ⁻125 _____

15. GO DEEPER Suppose you know a certain number's distance from zero on the number line. Explain how you could find the number's distance from its opposite.

Problem Solving • Applications Real World

Wind makes the air temperature seem colder. The chart gives the wind chill temperature (what the temperature *seems* like) at several air temperatures and wind speeds. Use the chart for 16–18.

Wind Chill Chart				
Air Temperature (°F)				
	30	25	20	15
25	16	9	3	⁻4
35	14	7	0	⁻7
45	12	5	⁻2	⁻9
55	11	3	⁻4	⁻11

Wind (mi/hr)

16. At 6 A.M., the air temperature was 20°F and the wind speed was 55 mi/hr. What was the wind chill temperature at 6 A.M.?

_____

17. **GO DEEPER** At noon, the air temperature was 15°F and the wind speed was 45 mi/hr. At what air temperature and wind speed would the wind chill temperature be the opposite of what it was at noon?

_____

18. **THINK SMARTER** The wind was blowing 35 mi/hr in both Ashton and Fenton. The wind chill temperatures in the two towns were opposites. If the air temperature in Ashton was 25°F, what was the air temperature in Fenton?

_____

19. **Sense or Nonsense?** Claudia states that the opposite of any integer is always a different number than the integer. Is Claudia's statement sense or nonsense? Explain.

_____

20. **THINK SMARTER** For numbers 20a–20d, choose Yes or No to indicate whether the situation can be represented by a negative number.

20a. Death Valley is located 282 feet below sea level. ○ Yes ○ No

20b. Austin's golf score was 3 strokes below par. ○ Yes ○ No

20c. The average temperature in Santa Monica in August is 75°F. ○ Yes ○ No

20d. Janai withdraws $20 from her bank account. ○ Yes ○ No

Understand Positive and Negative Numbers

 COMMON CORE STANDARDS—6.NS.C.5, 6.NS.C.6a, 6.NS.C.6c *Apply and extend previous understandings of numbers to the system of rational numbers.*

Graph the integer and its opposite on a number line.

1. ⁻6   opposite: ___⁺6___

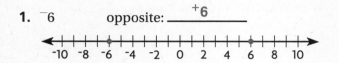

2. 3   opposite: _____

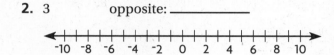

3. 10   opposite: _____

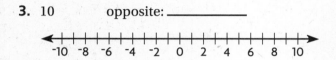

4. ⁻8   opposite: _____

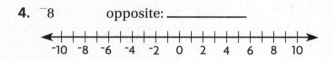

Name the integer that represents the situation, and tell what 0 represents in that situation.

Situation	Integer	What Does 0 Represent?
5. Michael withdrew $60 from his checking account.		
6. Raquel gained 12 points while playing a video game.		

Write the opposite of the opposite of the integer.

7. ⁻20 _____   **8.** 4 _____   **9.** 95 _____   **10.** ⁻63 _____

Problem Solving *Real World*

11. Dakshesh won a game by scoring 25 points. Randy scored the opposite number of points as Dakshesh. What is Randy's score?

12. When Dakshesh and Randy played the game again, Dakshesh scored the opposite of the opposite of his first score. What is his score?

_____

_____

13. **WRITE** *Math*   Give three examples of when negative numbers are used in daily life.

_____

_____

Lesson Check (6.NS.C.5, 6.NS.C.6a)

Name the integers that represent each situation.

1. During their first round of golf, Imani was 7 strokes over par and Peter was 8 strokes below par.

2. Wyatt earned $15 baby-sitting on Saturday. Wilson spent $12 at the movies.

Spiral Review (6.NS.A.1, 6.NS.B.3, 6.NS.B.4)

3. Mr. Nolan's code for his ATM card is a 4-digit number. The digits of the code are the prime factors of 84 listed from least to greatest. What is the code for Mr. Nolan's ATM card?

4. Over a four-year period, a tree grew 2.62 feet. If the tree grows at a constant rate, how many feet did the tree grow each year?

5. Omarion has $\frac{9}{10}$ of the pages in a book remaining to read for school. He reads $\frac{2}{3}$ of the remaining pages over the weekend. What fraction of the book does Omarion read over the weekend?

6. Marianne has $\frac{5}{8}$ pound of peas. She cooks $\frac{2}{3}$ of those peas for 5 people. If each person is served an equal amount, how much peas did each person get?

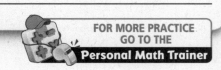

FOR MORE PRACTICE GO TO THE Personal Math Trainer

Compare and Order Integers

Essential Question How can you compare and order integers?

You can use a number line to compare integers.

The Number System—6.NS.C.7a, 6.NS.C.7b

MATHEMATICAL PRACTICES
MP1, MP4, MP7, MP8

Unlock the Problem · Real World

On one play of a football game, the ball changed position by ⁻7 yards. On the next play, the ball changed position by ⁻4 yards. Compare ⁻7 and ⁻4.

Use a number line to compare the numbers.

STEP 1 Graph ⁻7 and ⁻4 on the number line.

```
←—+——+——+——+——+——+——+——+——+——+——+——+——+——+——+——+→
  ⁻10 ⁻9 ⁻8 ⁻7 ⁻6 ⁻5 ⁻4 ⁻3 ⁻2 ⁻1  0  1  2  3  4  5
```

STEP 2 Note the locations of the numbers.

⁻7 is to the _____ of ⁻4 on the number

line, so ⁻7 is _____ ⁻4.

Math Idea

As you move to the right on a horizontal number line, the values become greater. As you move to the left, values become less.

Try This! Use the number line to compare the numbers.

A 5 and ⁻9

```
←—+——+——+——+——+——+——+——+——+——+——+——+——+——+——+——+——+——+——+——+→
 ⁻10 ⁻9 ⁻8 ⁻7 ⁻6 ⁻5 ⁻4 ⁻3 ⁻2 ⁻1  0  1  2  3  4  5  6  7  8  9 10
```

5 is to the _____ of ⁻9 on the number line, so 5 is _____ ⁻9.

B ⁻2 and 0

```
←—+——+——+——+——+——+——+——+——+——+——+——+——+——+——+——+——+——+——+——+→
 ⁻10 ⁻9 ⁻8 ⁻7 ⁻6 ⁻5 ⁻4 ⁻3 ⁻2 ⁻1  0  1  2  3  4  5  6  7  8  9 10
```

_____ is to the left of _____ on the number line, so ⁻2 is _____ 0.

Math Talk

MATHEMATICAL PRACTICES ①

Analyze Relationships If $r < ⁻4$, where on a number line is r compared to ⁻4?

You can also use a vertical number line to order integers.

Example The table gives the coldest temperatures recorded in seven cities in 2007.

Record Coldest Temperatures for 2007 (°F)					
Anchorage, AK ⁻17	Boise, ID 7	Duluth, MN ⁻25	Los Angeles, CA 35	Memphis, TN 18	Pittsburgh, PA ⁻5

A Order the temperatures from least to greatest.

STEP 1 Draw a dot on the number line to represent the record temperature of each city. Write the first letter of the city beside the dot.

_____

STEP 2 Write the record temperatures in order from least to greatest. Explain how you determined the order.

_____

_____

_____

Record Coldest Temperatures (°F) for 2007

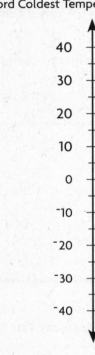

B Use the table and the number line to answer each question.

* Which city had the colder record temperature, Memphis or Pittsburgh? How do you know?

_____

_____

* Which city had the warmest record temperature? How do you know?

_____

_____

* What are the record temperatures for Boise, Memphis, and Pittsburgh in order from least to greatest?

_____ < _____ < _____

* What are the record temperatures for Anchorage, Duluth, and Los Angeles in order from greatest to least?

_____ > _____ > _____

Remember

The symbol < means *less than*.
The symbol > means *greater than*.

Math Talk   MATHEMATICAL PRACTICES ⑧

Generalize What rule can you use to compare numbers on a vertical number line?

Name _____

Compare the numbers. Write < or >.

1. ⁻8 ◯ 6   Think: ⁻8 is to the _____ of 6 on the number line, so ⁻8 is _____ 6.

✓ 2. 1 ◯ ⁻8

3. ⁻4 ◯ 0

4. 3 ◯ ⁻7

Order the numbers from least to greatest.

✓ 5. 4, ⁻3, ⁻7

_____ < _____ < _____

6. 0, ⁻1, 3

_____ < _____ < _____

7. ⁻5, ⁻3, ⁻9

_____ < _____ < _____

Order the numbers from greatest to least.

8. ⁻1, ⁻4, 2

_____ > _____ > _____

9. 5, 0, 10

_____ > _____ > _____

10. ⁻5, ⁻4, ⁻3

_____ > _____ > _____

On Your Own

> **Math Talk**
>
> **MATHEMATICAL PRACTICES ⑦**
>
> Look for Structure Explain how you can use a number line to compare numbers.

Order the numbers from least to greatest.

11. 2, 1, ⁻1

_____ < _____ < _____

12. ⁻6, ⁻12, 30

_____ < _____ < _____

13. 15, ⁻9, ⁻20

_____ < _____ < _____

Order the numbers from greatest to least.

14. ⁻13, 14, ⁻14

_____ > _____ > _____

15. ⁻20, ⁻30, ⁻40

_____ > _____ > _____

16. 9, ⁻37, 0

_____ > _____ > _____

17. **GO DEEPER** Saturday's low temperature was ⁻6°F. Sunday's low temperature was 3°F. Monday's low temperature was ⁻2°F. Tuesday's low temperature was 5°F. Which day's low temperature was closest to 0°F?

_____

18. **MATHEMATICAL PRACTICE ④** **Use Symbols** Write a comparison using < or > to show that South America's Valdes Peninsula (elevation ⁻131 ft) is lower than Europe's Caspian Sea (elevation ⁻92 ft).

_____

Problem Solving • Applications

What's the Error?

19. In the game of golf, the player with the lowest score wins. Raheem, Erin, and Blake played a game of miniature golf. The table shows their scores compared to par.

Raheem	Erin	Blake
0	⁻5	⁻1

At the end of the game, they wanted to know who had won.

Look at how they solved the problem. Find their error.

Correct the error by ordering the scores from least to greatest.

STEP 1: 0 is greater than both ⁻1 and ⁻5. Since Raheem had the highest score, he did not win.

STEP 2: ⁻1 is less than ⁻5, so Blake's score was less than Erin's score. Since Blake had the lowest score, he won the game.

So, _____ won. _____ came in second. _____ came in third.

- Describe the error that the players made.

_____

_____

20.   Jasmine recorded the low temperatures for 3 cities.

City	Temperature (°F)
A	6
B	−4
C	2

Draw a dot on the number line to represent the low temperature of each city. Write the letter of the city above the dot.

Name _____

Compare and Order Integers

 COMMON CORE STANDARDS—6.NS.C.7a, 6.NS.C.7b *Apply and extend previous understandings of numbers to the system of rational numbers.*

Compare the numbers. Write < or >.

1. $^-4 \bigcirc\!\!\!> \,^-5$ Think: $^-4$ is to the ____right____ of $^-5$ on the number line,

   so $^-4$ is _____greater than_____ $^-5$.

2. $0 \bigcirc \,^-1$

3. $4 \bigcirc \,^-6$

4. $^-9 \bigcirc \,^-8$

5. $2 \bigcirc \,^-10$

6. $^-12 \bigcirc \,^-11$

7. $1 \bigcirc \,^-10$

Order the numbers from least to greatest.

8. $3, \,^-2, \,^-7$

9. $0, 2, \,^-5$

10. $^-9, \,^-12, \,^-10$

____ < ____ < ____   ____ < ____ < ____   ____ < ____ < ____

11. $^-2, \,^-3, \,^-4$

12. $1, \,^-6, \,^-13$

13. $5, 7, 0$

____ < ____ < ____   ____ < ____ < ____   ____ < ____ < ____

Order the numbers from greatest to least.

14. $0, 13, \,^-13$

15. $^-11, 7, \,^-5$

16. $^-9, \,^-8, 1$

____ > ____ > ____   ____ > ____ > ____   ____ > ____ > ____

Problem Solving

17. Meg and Derek played a game. Meg scored $^-11$ points, and Derek scored 4 points. Write a comparison to show that Meg's score is less than Derek's score.

18. Misha is thinking of a negative integer greater than $^-4$. What number could she be thinking of?

_____

_____

19. **WRITE** ▸*Math* Explain how to use a number line to compare two negative integers. Give an example.

_____

_____

Lesson Check (6.NS.C.7a, 6.NS.C.7b)

The chart shows the high temperatures for seven cities on one day in January.

Chama	Chicago	Denver	Fargo	Glen Spey	Helena	Lansing
$^-5°$	2°	$^-8°$	$^-10°$	6°	$^-1°$	3°

1. Which city had the lower temperature, Helena or Chicago?

2. Write the temperatures of the following cities in order from greatest to least: Denver, Helena, Lansing

Spiral Review (6.NS.A.1, 6.NS.B.3, 6.NS.B.4)

3. Fiona starts at the beginning of a hiking trail and walks $\frac{4}{5}$ mile. She counts the mileage markers that are placed every $\frac{1}{10}$ mile along the trail. How many markers does she count?

4. If Amanda hikes at an average speed of 2.72 miles per hour, how long will it take her to hike 6.8 miles?

5. The area of a rectangle is $5\frac{4}{5}$ square meters. The width of the rectangle is $2\frac{1}{4}$ meter. Which is the best estimate for the length of the rectangle?

6. Lillian bought 2.52 pounds of tomatoes and 1.26 pounds of lettuce to make a salad for 18 people. If each person got the same amount of salad, how much salad did each person get?

**FOR MORE PRACTICE
GO TO THE
Personal Math Trainer**

Rational Numbers and the Number Line

Essential Question How can you plot rational numbers on a number line?

Common Core **The Number System—6.NS.C.6a, 6.NS.C.6c** Also 6.NS.C.5
MATHEMATICAL PRACTICES
MP2, MP4, MP6, MP7, MP8

CONNECT A **rational number** is any number that can be written as $\frac{a}{b}$, where a and b are integers and $b \neq 0$. Decimals, fractions, and integers are all rational numbers.

Unlock the Problem Real World

The freezing point of a liquid is the temperature at which the liquid turns into a solid when it is cooled. The table shows the approximate freezing points of various liquids. Graph each temperature on a number line.

Liquid Freezing Points	
Liquid	Freezing Point (°C)
Carbonated water	⁻0.3
Fizzy lemonade	⁻0.5
Hydrazine	1.4

 Graph the values in the table.

STEP 1 Locate each number in relation to the nearest integers.

Think: ⁻0.3 is the opposite of _____.

0.3 is between the integers _____ and _____.
So, ⁻0.3 is between the opposites of these integers. ⁻0.3 is between _____ and _____.

⁻0.5 is between _____ and _____.   1.4 is between _____ and _____.

STEP 2 Graph each temperature.

Think: ⁻0.3 is 3 tenths below 0 on the number line.

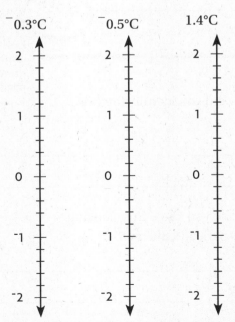

Math Talk MATHEMATICAL PRACTICES ⑧

Draw Conclusions How can you tell which number ⁻0.3 is closer to, 0 or ⁻1? Explain.

🔒 Example

City Hall is located at point 0 on a map of Maple Avenue. Other points of interest on Maple Avenue are located on the map based on their distances in miles to the east of City Hall (positive numbers) or to the west of City Hall (negative numbers). Graph each location on a number line.

Points of Interest	
Name	**Location**
City Park	$-\frac{3}{8}$
Fountain	$^-1\frac{1}{2}$
Library	$1\frac{1}{4}$
Mall	$\frac{3}{4}$

STEP 1 Locate the numbers in relation to the nearest integers.

$-\frac{3}{8}$ is between _____ and _____.

$^-1\frac{1}{2}$ is between _____ and _____.

Think: $^-\frac{3}{8}$ is the opposite of _____.

$1\frac{1}{4}$ is between _____ and _____.

$\frac{3}{4}$ is between _____ and _____.

STEP 2 Graph each location on the number line.

City Park: $-\frac{3}{8}$ **Think:** $^-\frac{3}{8}$ is three eighths to the left of 0 on the number line.

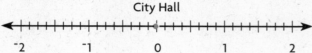

Fountain: $^-1\frac{1}{2}$

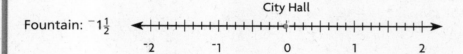

Library: $1\frac{1}{4}$

Mall: $\frac{3}{4}$

Math Talk

MATHEMATICAL PRACTICES ⑥

Explain how you can use a horizontal or vertical number line to graph a rational number.

1. **MATHEMATICAL PRACTICE ②** **Reason Quantitatively** How did you identify the two integers that $^-1\frac{1}{2}$ is between?

_____

_____

2. **MATHEMATICAL PRACTICE ⑦** **Identify Relationships** How do you know from looking at the table that City Hall is between the city park and the mall?

_____

_____

_____

Name _____

Math Talk MATHEMATICAL PRACTICES ②

Reason Abstractly Two numbers are opposites. Zero is not one of the numbers. Are the numbers on the same side or opposite sides of zero on a number line? Explain.

Graph the number on the horizontal number line.

1. ‾2.25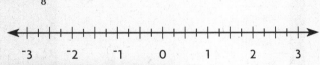
   ‾3   ‾2   ‾1   0   1   2   3

   The number is between the integers _____ and _____.

   It is closer to the integer _____.

2. ‾1$\frac{5}{8}$

   ‾3   ‾2   ‾1   0   1   2   3

3. $\frac{1}{2}$

   ‾3   ‾2   ‾1   0   1   2   3

On Your Own

Practice: Copy and Solve Graph the number on a vertical number line.

4. 0.6   5. ‾1.25   6. ‾1$\frac{1}{2}$ 7. 0.3

8. ‾0.7   9. 1.4   10. ‾0.5   11. ‾$\frac{1}{4}$

State whether the numbers are on the same or opposite sides of zero.

12. ‾1.38 and 2.9   13. ‾3$\frac{9}{10}$ and ‾0.99   14. $\frac{5}{6}$ and ‾4.713

_____   _____   _____

Identify a decimal and a fraction in simplest form for the point.

       D A   C   B
   ‾1.5   ‾1.0   ‾0.5   0   0.5   1   1.5

15. Point *A*   16. Point *B*   17. Point *C*   18. Point *D*

19. **GoDEEPER** The roots of 6 corn plants grew to ‾3.54 feet, ‾2$\frac{4}{5}$ feet, ‾3.86 feet, ‾4$\frac{1}{8}$ feet, ‾4.25 feet, and ‾3$\frac{2}{5}$ feet. How many corn plants had roots between 3 and 4 feet deep?

_____

Problem Solving • Applications Real World

A star's *magnitude* is a number that measures the star's brightness. Use the table of star magnitudes for 20–22.

20. Between what two integers is the magnitude of Canopus?

_____

21. **MATHEMATICAL PRACTICE ④ Model Mathematics**
Graph the magnitude of Betelgeuse on the number line.

```
←—+—+—+—+—+—+—+—+—+—+—+—+—→
  ⁻1     ⁻0.5      0      0.5      1
```

22. **THINK SMARTER** **What's the Error?**
Jacob graphed the magnitude of Sirius on the number line. Explain his error. Then graph the magnitude correctly.

```
←—+—+—+—+—+—+—+—•—+—+—+—+—→
    ⁻2            ⁻1            0
```

Magnitudes of Stars	
Star	**Magnitude**
Arcturus	⁻0.04
Betelgeuse	0.7
Canopus	⁻0.72
Deneb	1.25
Rigel Kentaurus A	⁻0.01
Sirius	⁻1.46

Personal Math Trainer

23. **THINK SMARTER +** The flag pole is located at point 0 on a map of Orange Avenue. Other points of interest on Orange Avenue are located on the number line based on their distances, in miles to the right of the flag pole (positive numbers) or to the left of the flag pole (negative numbers). Graph and label each location on the number line.

Name	Location
School	0.4
Post Office	1.8
Library	⁻1
Fire Station	⁻1.3

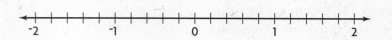

```
←—+—+—+—+—+—+—+—+—+—+—+—+—+—+—+—+—→
  -2        -1         0         1         2
```

154

Rational Numbers and the Number Line

COMMON CORE STANDARDS—
6.NS.C.6a, 6.NS.C.6c *Apply and extend previous understandings of numbers to the system of rational numbers. Also 6.NS.C.5*

Graph the number on the number line.

1. $-2\frac{3}{4}$

The number is between the integers ___-3___ and ___-2___.

It is closer to the integer ___-3___.

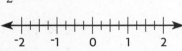

2. $-\frac{1}{4}$

3. -0.5

4. 1.75

5. $1\frac{1}{2}$

State whether the numbers are on the same or opposite sides of zero.

6. -2.4 and 2.3

7. $-2\frac{1}{5}$ and -1

8. -0.3 and 0.3

9. 0.44 and $-\frac{2}{3}$

_____   _____   _____   _____

Write the opposite of the number.

10. -5.23

11. $\frac{4}{5}$

12. -5

13. $-2\frac{2}{3}$

_____   _____   _____   _____

Problem Solving · Real World

14. The outdoor temperature yesterday reached a low of $-4.5°$ F. Between what two integers was the temperature?

15. Jacob needs to graph $-6\frac{2}{5}$ on a horizontal number line. Should he graph it to the left or right of -6?

_____   _____

16. **WRITE** ▸*Math* Describe how to plot $-3\frac{3}{4}$ on a number line.

_____

_____

Lesson Check (6.NS.C.6a, 6.NS.C.6c)

1. What number is the opposite of 0.2?

2. Between which two integers would you locate ⁻3.4 on a number line?

Spiral Review (6.NS.A.1, 6.NS.C.6c, 6.NS.C.7a)

3. Yemi used these pattern blocks to solve a division problem. He found a quotient of 7. Which division problem was he solving?

4. Eric had 2 liters of water. He gave 0.42 liter to his friend and then drank 0.32 liter. How much water does he have left?

5. To pass a math test, students must correctly answer at least 0.6 of the questions. Donald's score is $\frac{5}{8}$, Karen's score is 0.88, Gino's score is $\frac{3}{5}$ and Sierra's score is $\frac{4}{5}$. How many of the students passed the test?

6. Jonna mixes $\frac{1}{4}$ gallon of orange juice and $\frac{1}{2}$ gallon of pineapple juice to make punch. Each serving is $\frac{1}{16}$ gallon. How many servings can Jonna make?

FOR MORE PRACTICE GO TO THE
Personal Math Trainer

Name _____

Compare and Order Rational Numbers

Essential Question How can you compare and order rational numbers?

Common Core The Number System—6.NS.C.7a, 6.NS.C.7b
MATHEMATICAL PRACTICES
MP1, MP2, MP4, MP5

CONNECT You have used a number line to compare and order integers. You can also use a number line to compare other rational numbers, including decimals and fractions.

Unlock the Problem (Real World)

The table shows the average December temperatures in five U.S. cities. Which city has the greater average December temperature, Indianapolis or Boise?

Average December Temperatures	
City	Temperature (°C)
Boise, ID	⁻1
Boston, MA	0.9
Indianapolis, IN	⁻0.6
Philadelphia, PA	2.1
Syracuse, NY	⁻2

One Way Use a number line.

Graph the temperatures for Indianapolis and Boise.

Think: As you move to the _____ on a horizontal number line, the numbers become greater.

⁻0.6 is to the _____ of ⁻1.

So, the city whose temperature is farther to the right is _____.

Another Way Use place value to compare the decimals.

STEP 1 Write the temperatures with their decimal points lined up.

Indianapolis: _____

Boise: _____

STEP 2 Compare the digits in the ones place. If the number is negative, include a negative sign with the digit.

Think: 0 is _____ than ⁻1.

⁻0.6 is _____ than ⁻1.

⁻0.6°C is _____ than ⁻1°C, so _____ has a greater average December temperature than _____.

Math Talk MATHEMATICAL PRACTICES ⑤

Use Appropriate Tools How can you order the average December temperatures of Boston, Philadelphia, and Syracuse from greatest to least?

🔑 Example 1

The elevations of objects found at a dig site are recorded in the table. Which object was found at a lower elevation, the fossil of the shell or the fossil of the fish?

🔑 One Way Use a number line.

Graph the elevations for the fossil of the shell and the fossil of the fish.

Think: As you move _____ on a vertical number line, the numbers become less.

$^-3\frac{1}{2}$ is _____ $^-3\frac{1}{4}$ on the number line.

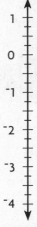

Fossils	
Object	**Elevation (ft)**
Shell	$^-3\frac{1}{2}$
Fern	$\frac{1}{4}$
Fish	$^-3\frac{1}{4}$

Number line (vertical):
1
0
$^-1$
$^-2$
$^-3$
$^-4$

🔑 Another Way Use common denominators to compare fractions.

STEP 1 Write the elevations with a common denominator.

$$^-3\frac{1}{2} = {}^-3\frac{}{} \qquad ^-3\frac{1}{4} = {}^-3\frac{}{}$$

STEP 2 Since the whole numbers are the same, you only need to compare the fractions. If the number is negative, include a negative sign with the fraction.

$^-\frac{2}{4}$ is _____ than $^-\frac{1}{4}$, so

$^-3\frac{1}{2}$ is _____ than $^-3\frac{1}{4}$.

So, the fossil of the _____ was found at a lower

elevation than the fossil of the _____.

🔑 Example 2 Compare $^-0.1$ and $^-\frac{4}{5}$.

Convert to all fractions or all decimals.

fractions $\quad ^-0.1 = {}^-\frac{}{10} \qquad ^-\frac{4}{5} = {}^-\frac{}{10}$

$^-8$ is _____ than $^-1$, so $^-\frac{4}{5}$ is less than $^-0.1$.

decimals $\quad ^-0.1 = {}^-0.1 \qquad ^-\frac{4}{5} = {}^-0.$

$^-0.8$ is _____ than $^-0.1$, so $^-\frac{4}{5}$ is less than $^-0.1$.

Use a number line to check your answer.

$^-\frac{4}{5}$ $^-0.1$

$^-1$ 0

MATHEMATICAL PRACTICES ①

Describe Relationships
Explain how you could use number sense to compare $^-0.1$ and $^-\frac{4}{5}$.

Name _____

Compare the numbers. Write < or >.

1. ⁻0.3 ◯ 0.2   Think: ⁻0.3 is to the _____ of 0.2 on the number line, so ⁻0.3 is _____ than 0.2.

2. $\frac{1}{3}$ ◯ $\frac{-2}{5}$

3. ⁻0.8 ◯ ⁻0.5

4. $\frac{-3}{4}$ ◯ ⁻0.7

Order the numbers from least to greatest.

5. 3.6, ⁻7.1, ⁻5.9

_____ < _____ < _____

6. $\frac{-6}{7}$, $\frac{1}{9}$, $\frac{-2}{3}$

_____ < _____ < _____

7. ⁻5$\frac{1}{4}$, ⁻6.5, ⁻5.3

_____ < _____ < _____

MATHEMATICAL PRACTICES ②

Connect Symbols and Words
Tell what the statement $\frac{-1}{3} > \frac{-1}{2}$ means. Explain how you know that the statement is true.

On Your Own

Compare the numbers. Write < or >.

8. $\frac{-1}{2}$ ◯ $\frac{-3}{7}$

9. ⁻23.7 ◯ ⁻18.8

10. ⁻3$\frac{1}{4}$ ◯ ⁻4.3

Order the numbers from greatest to least.

11. ⁻2.4, 1.9, ⁻7.6

_____ > _____ > _____

12. $\frac{-2}{5}$, $\frac{-3}{4}$, $\frac{-1}{2}$

_____ > _____ > _____

13. 3, ⁻6$\frac{4}{5}$, ⁻3$\frac{2}{3}$

_____ > _____ > _____

14. **GO DEEPER** Last week, Wednesday's low temperature was ⁻4.5°F, Thursday's low temperature was ⁻1.2°F, Friday's low temperature was ⁻2.7°F, and Saturday's low temperature was 0.5°F. The average low temperature for the week was ⁻1.5°F. How many of these days had low temperatures less than the average low temperature for the week?

_____

15. **MATHEMATICAL PRACTICE ④** **Use Symbols** Write a comparison using < or > to show the relationship between an elevation of ⁻12$\frac{1}{2}$ ft and an elevation of ⁻16$\frac{5}{8}$ ft.

_____

Problem Solving • Applications (Real World)

Elevations, in miles, are given for the lowest points below sea level for 4 bodies of water. Use the table for 16–19.

16. The lowest point of which has the greater elevation, the Arctic Ocean or Lake Tanganyika?

_____

17. Which has a lower elevation, the lowest point of Lake Superior or a point at an elevation of $-\frac{2}{5}$ mi?

_____

18. List the elevations in order from least to greatest.

_____

_____

Lowest Points	
Location	**Elevation (mi)**
Arctic Ocean	$^-0.8$
Lake Superior	$-\frac{1}{4}$
Lake Tanganyika	$^-0.9$
Red Sea	$-\frac{1}{3}$

19. THINK SMARTER A shipwreck is found at an elevation of $^-0.75$ mile. In which bodies of water could the shipwreck have been found?

_____

· · · · WRITE ▸ Math · **Show Your Work** · · · · ·

20. THINK SMARTER Circle $<$, $>$, or $=$.

20a. $-\frac{3}{5}$ ⬚ $\begin{array}{c}<\\>\\=\end{array}$ $-\frac{4}{5}$

20b. $-\frac{2}{5}$ ⬚ $\begin{array}{c}<\\>\\=\end{array}$ $-\frac{3}{4}$

20c. $^-6.5$ ⬚ $\begin{array}{c}<\\>\\=\end{array}$ $^-4.2$

20d. $^-2.4$ ⬚ $\begin{array}{c}<\\>\\=\end{array}$ $^-3.7$

Compare and Order Rational Numbers

 COMMON CORE STANDARDS—6.NS.C.7a,
6.NS.C.7b *Apply and extend previous
understandings of numbers to the system of
rational numbers.*

Compare the numbers. Write < or >.

1. $^-1\frac{1}{2}$ ⬅< $^-\frac{1}{2}$ Think: $^-1\frac{1}{2}$ is to the ____**left**____ of $^-\frac{1}{2}$ on the number line,

so $^-1\frac{1}{2}$ is _____**less than**_____ $^-\frac{1}{2}$.

2. 0.1 ◯ $^-1.9$

3. 0.4 ◯ $^-\frac{1}{2}$

4. $\frac{2}{5}$ ◯ 0.5

Order the numbers from least to greatest.

5. $0.2, \ ^-1.7, \ ^-1$

6. $^-2\frac{3}{4}, \ ^-\frac{3}{5}, \ ^-1\frac{3}{4}$

7. $^-0.5, \ ^-1\frac{2}{3}, \ ^-2.7$

_____ < _____ < _____

_____ < _____ < _____

_____ < _____ < _____

Order the numbers from greatest to least.

8. $^-1, \ \frac{^-5}{6}, \ 0$

9. $1.82, \ ^-\frac{2}{5}, \ \frac{4}{5}$

10. $^-2.19, \ ^-2.5, \ 1.1$

_____ > _____ < _____

_____ > _____ > _____

_____ > _____ > _____

**Write a comparison using < or > to show the relationship
between the two values.**

11. an elevation of $^-15$ m and an
elevation of $^-20.5$ m

12. a balance of $78 and a balance
of $^-$42

13. a score of $^-31$ points and a
score of $^-30$ points

_____

_____

_____

Problem Solving Real World

14. The temperature in Cold Town on Monday was
1°C. The temperature in Frosty Town on
Monday was $^-2$°C. Which town was colder
on Monday?

15. Stan's bank account balance is less than $^-$20.00
but greater than $^-$21.00. What could Stan's
account balance be?

_____

_____

16. **WRITE** ▸*Math* Describe two situations in which it would be helpful to
compare or order positive and negative rational numbers.

_____

Lesson Check (6.NS.C.7a, 6.NS.C.7b)

1. The low temperature was ⁻1.8 °C yesterday and ⁻2.1 °C today. Use the symbols < or > to show the relationship between the temperatures.

2. The scores at the end of a game are shown. List the scores in order from greatest to least.

Vince: ⁻0.5, Allison: $\frac{3}{8}$, Mariah: $\frac{^-7}{20}$

_____

_____

Spiral Review (6.NS.A.1, 6.NS.B.3, 6.NS.B.4)

3. Simone bought 3.42 pounds of green apples and 2.19 pounds of red apples. She used 3 pounds to make a pie. How many pounds of apples are left?

4. Kwan bought three rolls of regular wrapping paper with 6.7 square meters of paper each. He also bought a roll of fancy wrapping paper containing 4.18 square meters. How much paper did he have altogether?

_____

_____

5. Eddie needs $2\frac{2}{3}$ cups of flour for one batch of pancakes. How much flour does he need for $2\frac{1}{2}$ batches?

6. Tommy notices that he reads $\frac{2}{3}$ page in a minute. At that rate, how long will it take him to read 12 pages?

_____

_____

FOR MORE PRACTICE GO TO THE Personal Math Trainer

Name _____

Vocabulary

Vocabulary
integers
opposites
rational number

Choose the best term from the box to complete the sentence.

1. Any number that can be written as $\frac{a}{b}$, where a and b are integers

   and $b \neq 0$ is called a(n) _____. (p. 151)

2. The set of whole numbers and their opposites is the set of

   _____. (p. 139)

Concepts and Skills

Write the opposite of the integer. (6.NS.C.6a)

3. ⁻72

4. 0

5. ⁻31

6. 27

Name the integer that represents the situation, and tell what 0 represents in that situation. (6.NS.C.5)

Situation	Integer	What Does 0 Represent?
7. Greg scored 278 points during his turn in the video game.		
8. The temperature was 8 degrees below zero.		

Compare the numbers. Write < or >. (6.NS.C.7a)

9. 3 ◯ ⁻4

10. ⁻6 ◯ ⁻5

11. 5 ◯ ⁻6

12. $\frac{1}{3}$ ◯ $\frac{-1}{2}$

13. ⁻3.1 ◯ ⁻4.3

14. $1\frac{3}{4}$ ◯ $-2\frac{1}{2}$

Order the numbers. (6.NS.7a)

15. 5, ⁻2, ⁻8

   _____ < _____ < _____

16. 0, ⁻3, 1

   _____ < _____ < _____

17. ⁻7, ⁻6, ⁻11

   _____ > _____ > _____

18. 2.5, ⁻1.7, ⁻4.3

   _____ < _____ < _____

19. $\frac{2}{3}$, $\frac{-1}{4}$, $\frac{5}{12}$

   _____ < _____ < _____

20. ⁻5.2, ⁻3.8, ⁻9.4

   _____ > _____ > _____

21. Judy is scuba diving at ⁻7 meters, Nelda is scuba diving at ⁻9 meters, and Rod is scuba diving at ⁻3 meters. List the divers in order from the deepest diver to the diver who is closest to the surface. (6.NS.C.7b)

_____

22. A football team gains 8 yards on their first play. They lose 12 yards on the next play. What two integers represent the two plays? (6.NS.C.5)

_____

23. **GO DEEPER** The player who scores the closest to 0 points wins the game. The scores of four players are given in the table. Who won the game? (6.NS.C.7b)

Game Scores	
Player	**Points**
Myra	⁻1.93
Amari	⁻1$\frac{2}{3}$
Justine	⁻1.8
Donovan	⁻1$\frac{1}{2}$

_____

24. Which point on the graph represents ⁻3$\frac{3}{4}$? What number does point *C* represent? (6.NS.C.6c)

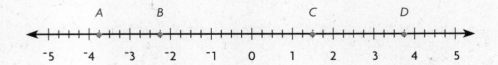

_____

Absolute Value

Essential Question How can you find and interpret the absolute value of rational numbers?

Common Core   The Number System—
6.NS.C.7c

MATHEMATICAL PRACTICES
MP2, MP3, MP4, MP6

The **absolute value** or magnitude of a number is the number's distance from 0 on a number line. The absolute value of ⁻3 is 3.

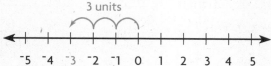

3 units

⁻5 ⁻4 ⁻3 ⁻2 ⁻1 0 1 2 3 4 5

The absolute value of ⁻3 is written symbolically as |⁻3|.

🔑 Unlock the Problem Real World

In 1934, a cargo ship called the *Mohican* sank off the coast of Florida. Divers today can visit the ship at an elevation of ⁻32 feet. Use a number line to find |⁻32|.

 Graph ⁻32. Then find its absolute value.

Graph ⁻32 on the number line.

Think: The distance from 0 to the point I graphed

is _____ units.

So, |⁻32| = _____.

10
0
⁻10
⁻20
⁻30
⁻40
⁻50

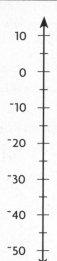

Math Idea
Since distance can never be negative, the absolute value of a number can never be negative.

Math Talk   MATHEMATICAL PRACTICES ⑥

Compare the absolute values of two numbers that are opposites. Explain your reasoning.

1. The depth of a diver is her distance below sea level. Because depth represents a distance, it is never negative. Find the depth of a diver visiting the *Mohican*, and explain how her depth is related to the ship's elevation of ⁻32 ft.

_____

_____

2. Explain how the expression |⁻32| relates to the diver's depth.

_____

_____

_____

You can find the absolute values of decimals, fractions, and other rational numbers just as you found the absolute values of integers.

🔒 Example 1

A food scientist tested a new dog food on five dogs. Each dog's weight was monitored during the course of the test. The results are shown in the table. Positive values indicate weight gains in pounds. Negative values indicate weight losses in pounds.

Food Test Results	
Name	**Weight Change (lb)**
Buck	$\frac{3}{4}$
Goldie	$\frac{-5}{8}$
Mackerel	$^-1\frac{7}{16}$
Paloma	$2\frac{1}{8}$
Spike	$\frac{-3}{8}$

Graph the weight changes on the number line. Then find their absolute values.

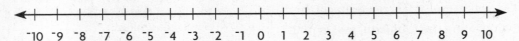

Think: The distance from 0 to the point I graphed is $\frac{3}{4}$. $\left|\frac{3}{4}\right| = \frac{3}{4}$

$\left|\frac{-5}{8}\right| = $ _____ $\left|^-1\frac{7}{16}\right| = $ _____ $\left|2\frac{1}{8}\right| = $ _____ $\left|\frac{-3}{8}\right| = $ _____

---

3. **MATHEMATICAL PRACTICE 4** **Interpret a Result** Explain how the absolute values of the positive and negative weight changes relate to the starting weights of the dogs.

_____

_____

_____

🔒 Example 2 Find all integers with an absolute value of 7.

Number line from -10 to 10.

Think: The distance from 0 to integers with an absolute value of 7 is _____ units.

Graph integers located 7 units from 0 on the number line.

|_____| = 7 and |_____| = 7

So, both _____ and _____ have an absolute value of 7.

---

4. **MATHEMATICAL PRACTICE 3** **Use Counterexamples** Paula says that there are always two numbers that have a given absolute value. Is she correct? Explain.

_____

Name _____

Find the absolute value.

1. $|^-2|$ Graph $^-2$ on the number line.

$^-2$ is _____ units from 0.

$|^-2| =$ _____

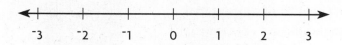

$^-3 \quad ^-2 \quad ^-1 \quad 0 \quad 1 \quad 2 \quad 3$

2. $|6|$ **3.** $|^-5|$ **4.** $|^-11|$ ✓**5.** $|9|$ **6.** $|^-15|$

_____ | _____ | _____ | _____ | _____

Math Talk

MATHEMATICAL PRACTICES ②

Use Reasoning Can a number have a negative absolute value? Explain.

On Your Own

Find the absolute value.

7. $|^-37|$ **8.** $|1.8|$ **9.** $\left|\dfrac{-2}{3}\right|$ **10.** $|^-6.39|$ **11.** $\left|^-5\dfrac{7}{8}\right|$

_____ | _____ | _____ | _____ | _____

Find all numbers with the given absolute value.

12. 13 **13.** $\dfrac{5}{6}$ **14.** 14.03 **15.** 0.59 **16.** $3\dfrac{1}{7}$

_____ | _____ | _____ | _____ | _____

MATHEMATICAL PRACTICE ② **Use Reasoning** **Algebra** Find the missing number or numbers to make the statement true.

17. $|\blacksquare| = 10$ **18.** $|\blacksquare| = 1.78$ **19.** $|\blacksquare| = 0$ **20.** $|\blacksquare| = \dfrac{15}{16}$

_____ | _____ | _____ | _____

21. **GO DEEPER** Find all of the integers whose absolute value is less than $|^-4|$.

_____

Unlock the Problem Real World

22. The Blue Ridge Trail starts at Park Headquarters in Big Bear Park and goes up the mountain. The Green Creek Trail starts at Park Headquarters and goes down the mountain. The table gives elevations of various points of interest in relation to Park Headquarters. How many points of interest are less than 1 kilometer above or below Park Headquarters?

Point of Interest	Elevation Compared to Park Headquarters (km)
A	1.9
B	1.1
C	0.7
D	0.3
E	⁻0.2
F	⁻0.5
G	⁻0.9
H	⁻1.6

a. How can you find how far above or below Park Headquarters a given point of interest is located?

_____

_____

b. How can you find the number of points of interest that are less than 1 km above or below Park Headquarters?

_____

_____

c. Find how far above or below Park Headquarters each point of interest is located.

_____

_____

_____

_____

d. How many points of interest are less than 1 kilometer above or below Park Headquarters?

_____

---

23. **Use Reasoning** Name a rational number that can replace ■ to make both statements true.

$$■ > {}^-3 \qquad |■| < |{}^-3|$$

_____

24. _THINK SMARTER_ Laila said |4| equals |⁻4|. Is Laila correct? Use the number line and words to support your answer.

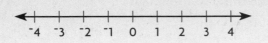

_____

_____

Name

Absolute Value

Find the absolute value.

Common Core **COMMON CORE STANDARDS—6.NS.C.7c**
Apply and extend previous understandings of numbers to the system of rational numbers.

1. $|7|$ Graph 7 on the number line.

7 is ___7___ units from 0.

$|7|$ = ___7___

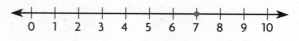

2. $|-8|$ **3.** $|16|$ **4.** $|8.65|$ **5.** $\left|4\frac{3}{20}\right|$ **6.** $|{}^-5{,}000|$

_____   _____   _____   _____   _____

Find all numbers with the given absolute value.

7. 12   **8.** 1.7   **9.** $\frac{3}{5}$ **10.** $3\frac{1}{6}$ **11.** 0

_____   _____   _____   _____   _____

Find the number or numbers that make the statement true.

12. $\left|\;\rule{0.5cm}{0.4cm}\;\right| = 17$ **13.** $\left|\;\rule{0.5cm}{0.4cm}\;\right| = 2.04$ **14.** $\left|\;\rule{0.5cm}{0.4cm}\;\right| = 1\frac{9}{10}$ **15.** $\left|\;\rule{0.5cm}{0.4cm}\;\right| = \frac{19}{24}$

_____   _____   _____   _____

Problem Solving · Real World

16. Which two numbers are 7.5 units away from 0 on a number line?

17. Emilio is playing a game. He just answered a question incorrectly, so his score will change by $^-10$ points. Find the absolute value of $^-10$.

_____   _____

18. **WRITE** ▸ *Math* Write two different real-world examples. One should involve the absolute value of a positive number, and the other should involve the absolute value of a negative number.

_____

_____

_____

Lesson Check (6.NS.C.7c)

1. What is the absolute value of $\frac{8}{9}$?

2. What two numbers have an absolute value of 21.63?

Spiral Review (6.NS.A.1, 6.NS.B.3, 6.NS.B.4, 6.NS.C.7b)

3. Rachel earned $89.70 on Tuesday. She spent $55.89 at the grocery store. How much money does she have left?

4. One carton contains $\frac{17}{20}$ liter of juice. Another carton contains 0.87 liter of juice. Which carton contains the most?

5. Maggie jogged $\frac{7}{8}$ mile on Monday and $\frac{1}{2}$ of that distance on Tuesday. How far did she jog on Tuesday?

6. Trygg has $\frac{3}{4}$ package of marigold seeds. He plants $\frac{1}{6}$ of those seeds in his garden and divides the rest equally into 10 flowerpots. What fraction of a package of seeds is planted in each flowerpot?

FOR MORE PRACTICE GO TO THE
Personal Math Trainer

Name _____

Compare Absolute Values

Essential Question How can you interpret comparisons involving absolute values?

The Number System—
6.NS.C.7d

MATHEMATICAL PRACTICES
MP1, MP2, MP6

 **Unlock the Problem** Real World

🔒 Activity

Carmen is taking a one-day scuba diving class. Completion of the class will allow her to explore the ocean at elevations that are less than ⁻25 feet. Use absolute value to describe the depths to which Carmen will be able to dive after taking the class.

- Graph an elevation of ⁻25 feet on the number line.

- List three elevations less than ⁻25 feet. Then graph these elevations.

  _____

- Elevations less than ⁻25 feet are found _____ ⁻25 feet.

- Because depth represents a distance below sea level, it is never

  negative. In this situation, $|{}^-25|$ ft represents a depth of _____ feet.

- Write each elevation as a depth.

Elevation (ft)	Depth (ft)
⁻30	
⁻35	
⁻40	

- An elevation of less than ⁻25 feet is a depth _____ than 25 feet.

So, Carmen will be able to dive to depths _____ than 25 feet after taking the class.

Elevation (feet)

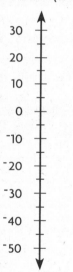

30
20
10
0
⁻10
⁻20
⁻30
⁻40
⁻50

1. Compare a ⁻175-foot elevation and a 175-foot depth. Explain your reasoning.

_____

_____

🔒 Example Cole has an online account for buying video games.

His account balance has always been greater than ⁻$16. Use absolute value to describe Cole's account balance as a debt.

STEP 1 Graph an account balance of ⁻$16 on the number line.

Account balance ($)

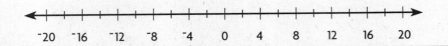

STEP 2 List three account balances greater than ⁻$16. Then graph these account balances on the number line above.

_____

Balances greater than ⁻$16 are found to the _____ of ⁻$16.

_____

STEP 3 Express an account balance of ⁻$16 as a debt.

In this situation |⁻$16| represents a debt of _____.

_____

STEP 4 Complete the table.

Balances Greater Than ⁻$16	Debt
⁻$15	
⁻$14	
	$13

Each debt in the table is _____ than $16.

Cole's account balance is always greater than ⁻$16, so his debt

on the account is always _____ than $16.

Math Talk

MATHEMATICAL PRACTICES ⑥

The temperature at the North Pole was ⁻35°F at noon. **Explain** how you can use absolute value to express a temperature of ⁻35°F.

2. Explain how you can describe a debt as an absolute value.

_____

_____

3. **MATHEMATICAL PRACTICE ①** **Describe** List three numbers that have a magnitude greater than ⁻28. Describe how you determined your answer.

_____

_____

Mifflin Harcourt Publishing Company

Name _____

✓ **1.** On Monday, Allie's bank account balance was ⁻$24. On Tuesday, her account balance was less than it was on Monday. Use absolute value to describe Allie's balance on Tuesday as a debt.

In this situation |⁻$24| represents a debt

of _____.

On Tuesday, Allie had a debt of _____ than $24.

✓ **2.** Matthew scored ⁻36 points in his turn at a video game. In Genevieve's turn, she scored fewer points than Matthew. Use absolute value to describe Genevieve's score as a loss.

Genevieve lost _____ than 36 points.

 Math Talk

MATHEMATICAL PRACTICES ①

Analyze Relationships
Compare a negative bank balance and the amount of the debt owed to the bank. Explain.

On Your Own

3. GO DEEPER One of the cats shown in the table is a tabby. The tabby had a decrease in weight of more than 3.3 ounces. Which cat is the tabby?

_____

Cat	Weight Change (ounces)
Missy	3.8
Angel	⁻3.2
Frankie	⁻2.6
Spot	⁻3.4

Compare. Write <, >, or =.

4. ⁻8 ◯ |⁻8|

5. 13 ◯ |⁻13|

6. |⁻23| ◯ |⁻24|

7. 15 ◯ |⁻14|

8. 34 ◯ |⁻36|

9. ⁻5 ◯ |⁻6|

10. THINK SMARTER Write the values in order from least to greatest.

 |⁻2| |3| |⁻6| |1|

Connect to Reading

Compare and Contrast

When you *compare and contrast*, you look for ways that two or more subjects are alike (compare) and ways they are different (contrast). This helps you to discover information about each subject that you might not have known otherwise. As you read the following passage, think about how the main topics are alike and how they are different.

Trevor mows lawns after school to raise money for a new mountain bike. Last week, it rained every day, and he couldn't work. While waiting for better weather, he spent some of his savings on lawnmower repairs. As a result, his savings balance changed by $^-$$45. This week, the weather was better, and Trevor returned to work. His savings balance changed by $^+$$45 this week.

11. The passage has two main parts. Describe them.

_____

_____

_____

12. Describe the two changes in Trevor's savings balance.

_____

_____

13. (MATHEMATICAL PRACTICE ②) **Reason Quantitatively** Compare the two changes in Trevor's savings balance. How are they alike?

_____

_____

14. (THINK SMARTER) Contrast the two changes in Trevor's savings balance. How are they different?

Math on the Spot

_____

_____

_____

_____

Compare Absolute Values

Common Core

COMMON CORE STANDARD—6.NS.C.7d
Apply and extend previous understandings of
numbers to the system of rational numbers.

Solve.

1. Jamie scored ⁻5 points on her turn at a trivia game. In Veronica's turn, she scored more points than Jamie. Use absolute value to describe Veronica's score as a loss.

   In this situation, |⁻5| represents a loss of

   ____5____ points. Veronica lost ___fewer___ than 5 points.

2. The low temperature on Friday was ⁻10°F. The low temperature on Saturday was colder. Use absolute value to describe the temperature on Saturday as a temperature below zero.

   The temperature on Saturday was _____ than 10 degrees below zero.

3. The table shows changes in the savings accounts of five students. Which student had the greatest increase in money? By how much did the student's account increase?

   _____

   _____

Student	Account Change ($)
Brett	⁻12
Destiny	⁻36
Carissa	15
Rylan	10

Compare. Write <, >, or =.

4. ⁻16 ◯ |⁻16|

5. 20 ◯ |20|

6. 3 ◯ |⁻4|

Problem Solving Real World

7. On Wednesday, Miguel's bank account balance was ⁻$55. On Thursday, his balance was less than that. Use absolute value to describe Miguel's balance on Thursday as a debt.

   In this situation, ⁻$55 represents a debt of

   _____. On Thursday, Miguel had a debt of

   _____ than $55.

8. During a game, Naomi lost points. She lost fewer than 3 points. Use an integer to describe her possible score.

   _____

9. **WRITE** ▸ *Math* Give two numbers that fit this description: a number is less than another number but has a greater absolute value. Describe how you determined the numbers.

   _____

   _____

Lesson Check (6.NS.C.7d)

1. A temperature of ⁻6° is colder than a temperature of 5°F below zero. Is this statement true or false?

2. Long Beach, California has an elevation of ⁻7 feet. New Orleans, Louisiana is 8 feet below sea level. Which city has a lower elevation?

Spiral Review (6.NS.A.1, 6.NS.B.3, 6.NS.B.4)

3. Dawn and Lin took off on skateboards from the same location but traveled in opposite directions. After 20 minutes, Dawn had traveled 6.42 kilometers and Lin had traveled 7.7 kilometers. How far apart were they?

4. Rico and Josh took off on skateboards going in the same direction. After 20 minutes, Rico had traveled 5.98 kilometers and Josh had gone 8.2 kilometers. How far apart were they?

5. Etta bought 11.5 yards of fabric selling for $0.90 per yard. What was the total cost?

6. Yen calculates the product $\frac{5}{8} \times \frac{24}{25}$. Before he multiplies, he simplifies all factors. What does the problem look like after he simplifies the factors?

FOR MORE PRACTICE
GO TO THE
Personal Math Trainer

Rational Numbers and the Coordinate Plane

Essential Question How do you plot ordered pairs of rational numbers on a coordinate plane?

Common Core   The Number System—
6.NS.C.6C

MATHEMATICAL PRACTICES
MP3, MP4, MP7, MP8

A **coordinate plane** is a plane formed by a horizontal number line called the **x-axis** that intersects a vertical number line called the **y-axis**. The axes intersect at 0 on both number lines. The point where the axes intersect is the **origin**.

An **ordered pair** is a pair of numbers, such as (3, 2), that can be used to locate a point on the coordinate plane. The first number is the **x-coordinate**; it tells the distance to move left or right from the origin. The second number is the **y-coordinate**; it tells the distance to move up or down from the origin. The ordered pair for the origin is (0, 0).

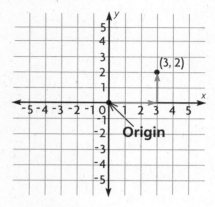

Unlock the Problem   Real World

A screen in a video game shows a coordinate plane. The points *P*, *Q*, *R*, and *S* represent treasure chests. Write the ordered pair for each treasure chest's location.

• If a point is to the left of the *y*-axis, is its *x*-coordinate positive or negative?

_____

 Find the coordinates of each point.

To find the coordinates of point *P*, start at the origin.

To find the *x*-coordinate, move right (positive) or left (negative).   Move 2 units to the _____.

To find the *y*-coordinate, move up (positive) or down (negative).   Move _____ units up.

Point *P* is located at ($^-$2, _____).

Point *Q* is located at (_____, _____).

Point *R* is located at (_____, _____).

Point *S* is located at (_____, _____).

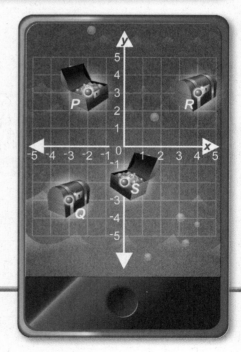

1. **MATHEMATICAL PRACTICE ⑧ Draw Conclusions** Make a conjecture about the *x*-coordinate of any point that lies on the *y*-axis.

_____

2. Explain why (2, 4) represents a different location than (4, 2).

_____

🔑 Example Graph and label the point on the coordinate plane.

A $A(2, \frac{-1}{2})$

Start at the origin.

The x-coordinate is positive.   Move _____ units to the right.

The y-coordinate is negative.   Move $\frac{1}{2}$ unit _____.

Plot the point and label it A.

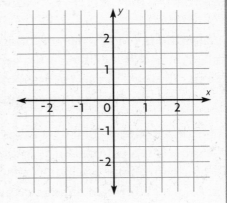

B $B(^-0.5, 0)$

Start at the origin.

The x-coordinate is _____.   Move _____ unit to the _____.

The y-coordinate is 0.   The point lies on the _____-axis.

Plot the point and label it B.

C $C(2\frac{1}{2}, \frac{3}{4})$

Start at the origin.

Move _____ units to the _____.

Move _____ unit _____.

Plot the point and label it C.

D $D(^-1.25, ^-1.75)$

Start at the origin.

Move _____ units to the _____.

Move _____ units _____.

Plot the point and label it D.

MATHEMATICAL PRACTICES ④

Use Symbols Describe the location of a point that has a positive x-coordinate and a negative y-coordinate.

Share and Show

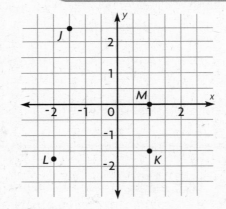

1. Write the ordered pair for point J.

   Start at the origin. Move _____ units to the _____

   and _____ units _____.

   The ordered pair is _____.

Write the ordered pair for the point.

2. K

✓ 3. L

4. M

Name _____

Graph and label the point on the coordinate plane.

5. $P(^-2.5, 2)$

6. $Q(^-2, \frac{1}{4})$

7. $R(0, 1.5)$

8. $S(^-1, \frac{-1}{2})$

✓ **9.** $T(1\frac{1}{2}, ^-2)$

10. $U(0.75, 1.25)$

11. $V(^-0.5, 0)$

12. $W(2, 0)$

13. $X(0, ^-2)$

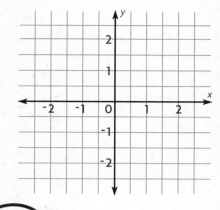

On Your Own

Write the ordered pair for the point. Give approximate coordinates when necessary.

14. A

15. B

16. C

_____ _____ _____

17. D

18. E

19. F

_____ _____ _____

20. G

21. H

22. J

_____ _____ _____

Math Talk

MATHEMATICAL PRACTICES ③

Compare Models Explain how graphing (3, 2) is similar to and different from graphing (3, –2).

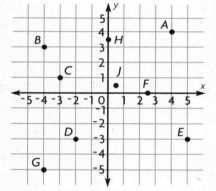

Graph and label the point on the coordinate plane.

23. $M(^-4, 0)$

24. $N(2, 2)$

25. $P(^-3, 3)$

26. $Q(0, ^-2\frac{1}{2})$

27. $R(0.5, 0.5)$

28. $S(^-5, \frac{1}{2})$

29. $T(0, 0)$

30. $U(3\frac{1}{2}, 0)$

31. $V(^-2, ^-4)$

32. **MATHEMATICAL PRACTICE 7** **Look for Structure** A point lies to the left of the y-axis and below the x-axis. What can you conclude about the coordinates of the point?

_____

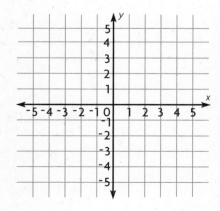

Problem Solving • Applications Real World

Many of the streets in downtown Philadelphia can be modeled by a coordinate plane, as shown on the map. Each unit on the map represents one block. Use the map for 33 and 34.

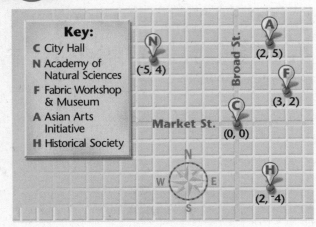

Key:
C City Hall
N Academy of Natural Sciences
F Fabric Workshop & Museum
A Asian Arts Initiative
H Historical Society

33. GO DEEPER Anita works at the Historical Society. She leaves the building and walks 3 blocks north to a restaurant. What ordered pair represents the restaurant?

_____

34. THINK SMARTER **Pose a Problem** Write and solve a new problem that uses a location on the map.

_____

_____

_____

35. THINK SMARTER The points A, B, C, and D on a coordinate plane can be connected to form a rectangle. Point A is located at (2, 0), point B is located at (6, 0), and point C is located at (6, ⁻2.5). Write the ordered pair for point D.

_____

36. MATHEMATICAL PRACTICE ⑦ **Identify Relationships** Explain how you can tell that the line segment connecting two points is vertical without graphing the points.

_____

_____

37. THINK SMARTER For numbers 37a–37d, select True or False for each statement.

37a. Point A (2, ⁻1) is to the right of the y-axis and below the x-axis.   ○ True   ○ False

37b. Point B (⁻5, 2) is to the left of the y-axis and below the x-axis.   ○ True   ○ False

37c. Point C (3, 2) is to the right of the y-axis and above the x-axis.   ○ True   ○ False

37d. Point D (⁻2, ⁻1) is to the left of the y-axis and below the x-axis.   ○ True   ○ False

Rational Numbers and the Coordinate Plane

Common Core **COMMON CORE STANDARD—6.NS.C.6c**
Apply and extend previous understandings of numbers to the system of rational numbers.

Write the ordered pair for the point. Give approximate coordinates when necessary.

1. A

$\left(1, \frac{1}{2}\right)$
_____

2. B

_____

3. C

_____

4. D

_____

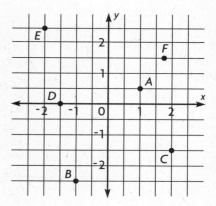

Graph and label the point on the coordinate plane.

5. $G\left(\frac{-1}{2}, 1\frac{1}{2}\right)$

6. $H(0, 2.50)$

7. $J\left(^{-}1\frac{1}{2}, \frac{1}{2}\right)$

8. $K(1, 2)$

9. $L\left(^{-}1\frac{1}{2}, ^{-}2\frac{1}{2}\right)$

10. $M(1, ^{-}0.5)$

11. $N\left(\frac{1}{4}, 1\frac{1}{2}\right)$

12. $P(1.25, 0)$

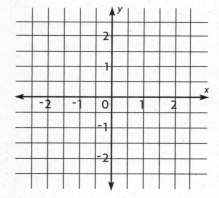

Problem Solving · Real World

Use the map for 13–15.

13. What is the ordered pair for the city hall?

_____

14. The post office is located at $\left(^{-}\frac{1}{2}, 2\right)$. Graph and label a point on the map to represent the post office.

15. **WRITE** ▸*Math* Describe how to graph the ordered pair $(^{-}1, 4.5)$.

_____

_____

Map of Elmwood

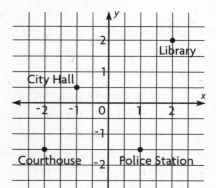

Lesson Check (6.NS.C.6c)

1. An artist uses a coordinate plane to create a design. As part of the design, the artist wants to graph the point ($^-$6.5, 2). How should the artist graph this point?

2. What are the coordinates of the campground?

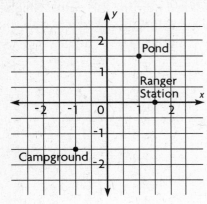

Spiral Review (6.NS.A.1, 6.NS.C.6c)

3. Four students volunteer at the hospital. Casey volunteers 20.7 hours, Danielle, $20\frac{3}{4}$ hours, Javier $18\frac{9}{10}$ hours, and Forrest, $20\frac{18}{25}$ hours. Who volunteered the greatest number of hours?

4. Directions for making a quilt say to cut fifteen squares with sides that are 3.625 inches long. What is the side length written as a fraction?

5. Cam has a piece of plywood that is $6\frac{7}{8}$ feet wide. He is going to cut shelves from the plywood that are each $1\frac{1}{6}$ feet wide. Which is a good estimate for the number of shelves Cam can make?

6. Zach has $\frac{3}{4}$ hour to play video games. It takes him $\frac{1}{12}$ hour to set up the system. Each round of his favorite game takes $\frac{1}{6}$ hour. How many rounds can he play?

FOR MORE PRACTICE
GO TO THE
Personal Math Trainer

Name _____

Ordered Pair Relationships

Essential Question How can you identify the relationship between points on a coordinate plane?

Common Core The Number System—
6.NS.C.6b
MATHEMATICAL PRACTICES
MP1, MP6, MP7

The four regions of the coordinate plane that are separated by the *x*- and *y*-axes are called **quadrants**. Quadrants are numbered with the Roman numerals I, II, III, and IV. If you know the signs of the coordinates of a point, you can determine the quadrant where the point is located.

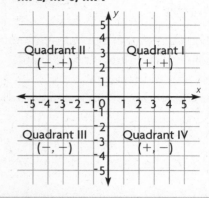

Unlock the Problem

The point (⁻3, 4) represents the location of a bookstore on a map of a shopping mall. Identify the quadrant where the point is located.

• What is the *x*-coordinate of the point? _____

• What is the *y*-coordinate of the point? _____

 Find the quadrant that contains (⁻3, 4).

STEP 1 Examine the *x*-coordinate.

Think: The *x*-coordinate is _____, so the point is _____ units to the _____ of the origin.

Since the point is to the left of the origin, it must be located in either

Quadrant _____ or Quadrant _____.

STEP 2 Examine the *y*-coordinate.

Think: The *y*-coordinate is _____, so the point is _____ units _____ from the origin.

Since the point is above the origin, it must be located in

Quadrant _____.

Check by graphing the point (⁻3, 4) on the coordinate plane.

So, the point representing the bookstore is located in

Quadrant _____.

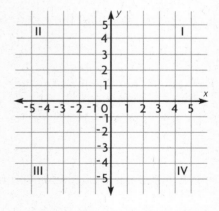

• **MATHEMATICAL PRACTICE 7** **Look for Structure** Look at the signs of the coordinates of points in Quadrants I and II. What do they have in common? How are they different?

_____

_____

A figure has **line symmetry** if it can be folded about a line so that its two parts match exactly. If you cut out the isosceles triangle at the right and fold it along the dashed line, the two parts would match. A line that divides a figure into two halves that are reflections of each other is called a **line of symmetry**.

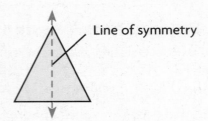
Line of symmetry

You can use the idea of line symmetry to analyze the relationship between points such as (5, ¯1) and (¯5, ¯1) whose coordinates differ only in their signs.

🔑 Activity

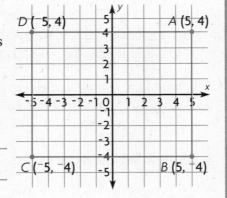

- Identify the lines of symmetry in the rectangle.

   The _____ -axis is a horizontal line of symmetry, and the _____ -axis is a vertical line of symmetry.

- Look at points *A* and *B*. What do you notice about the *x*-coordinates? What do you notice about the *y*-coordinates?

   _____

   _____

- Point *B* is a reflection of point *A* across which axis? How do you know?

   _____

   _____

- Look at points *A* and *D*. What do you notice about the *x*-coordinates? What do you notice about the *y*-coordinates?

   _____

- Point *D* is a reflection of point *A* across which axis? How do you know?

   _____

   _____

- Which point is a reflection of point *B* across the *x*-axis and then the *y*-axis?

   _____

- Compare the coordinates of point *B* with the coordinates of point *D*.

   _____

   _____

Math Talk

MATHEMATICAL PRACTICES ①

Describe Relationships
Describe how the coordinates of a point change if it is reflected across the *x*-axis.

Name _____

Identify the quadrant where the point is located.

1. (2, ⁻5)

To graph the point, first move to the _____ from the origin.

Then move _____.

Quadrant: _____

2. (4, 1)

Quadrant: _____

3. (⁻6, ⁻2)

Quadrant: _____

4. (⁻7, 3)

Quadrant: _____

5. (8, 8)

Quadrant: _____

6. (1, ⁻1)

Quadrant: _____

The two points are reflections of each other across the *x*- or *y*-axis. Identify the axis.

7. (⁻1, 3) and (1, 3)

axis: _____

8. (4, 4) and (4, ⁻4)

axis: _____

9. (2, ⁻9) and (2, 9)

axis: _____

10. (8, 1) and (⁻8, 1)

axis: _____

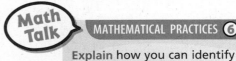

Math Talk MATHEMATICAL PRACTICES ⑥

Explain how you can identify the quadrant where a given point is located.

On Your Own

Identify the quadrant where the point is located.

11. (⁻8, ⁻9)

Quadrant: _____

12. (12, 1)

Quadrant: _____

13. (⁻13, 10)

Quadrant: _____

14. (5, ⁻20)

Quadrant: _____

The two points are reflections of each other across the *x*- or *y*-axis. Identify the axis.

15. (⁻9, ⁻10) and (⁻9, 10)

axis: _____

16. (21, ⁻31) and (21, 31)

axis: _____

17. (15, ⁻20) and (⁻15, ⁻20)

axis: _____

Give the reflection of the point across the given axis.

18. (⁻7, ⁻7), *y*-axis

_____

19. (⁻15, 18), *x*-axis

_____

20. (11, 9), *x*-axis

_____

Problem Solving • Applications

Use the map of Gridville for 21–23.

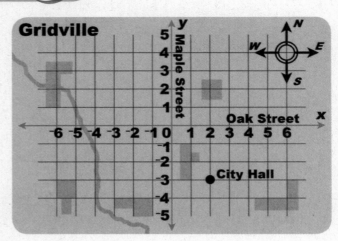

21. GO DEEPER   The library's location has opposite *x*- and *y*-coordinates as City Hall. Across which streets could you reflect City Hall's location to find the library's location?

_____

22. THINK SMARTER   Each unit on the map represents 1 mile. Gregory leaves his house at (⁻5, 4), cycles 4 miles east, 6 miles south, and 1 mile west. In which quadrant of the city is he now?

_____

23. The bus station has the same *x*-coordinate as City Hall but the opposite *y*-coordinate. In which quadrant of the city is the bus station located?

_____

24. MATHEMATICAL PRACTICE ① **Describe Relationships** Describe the relationship between the locations of the points (2, 5) and (2, ⁻5) on the coordinate plane.

_____

_____

25. THINK SMARTER   Identify the quadrant where each point is located. Write each point in the correct box.

(⁻1, 3)   (4, ⁻2)   (⁻3, ⁻2)

(1, ⁻3)   (⁻1, 2)   (3, 4)

Quadrant I	Quadrant II	Quadrant III	Quadrant IV

Name _____

Ordered Pair Relationships

COMMON CORE STANDARD—6.NS.C.6b
Apply and extend previous understandings of numbers to the system of rational numbers.

Identify the quadrant where the point is located.

1. $(10, ^-2)$ Quadrant: ___IV___

2. $(^-5, ^-6)$ Quadrant: _____

3. $(3, 7)$ Quadrant: _____

The two points are reflections of each other across the x- or y-axis. Identify the axis.

4. $(5, 3)$ and $(^-5, 3)$

5. $(^-7, 1)$ and $(^-7, ^-1)$

6. $(^-2, 4)$ and $(^-2, ^-4)$

axis: _____

axis: _____

axis: _____

Give the reflection of the point across the given axis.

7. $(^-6, ^-10)$, y-axis

8. $(^-11, 3)$, x-axis

9. $(8, 2)$, x-axis

_____

_____

_____

Problem Solving · Real World

10. A town's post office is located at the point $(7, 5)$ on a coordinate plane. In which quadrant is the post office located?

11. The grocery store is located at a point on a coordinate plane with the same y-coordinate as the bank but with the opposite x-coordinate. The grocery store and bank are reflections of each other across which axis?

_____

_____

12. **WRITE** *Math* Explain to a new student how a reflection across the y-axis changes the coordinates of the original point.

_____

_____

Lesson Check (6.NS.C.6b)

1. In which quadrant does the point ($^-$4, 15) lie?

2. What are the coordinates of the point (10, $^-$4) if it is reflected across the *y*-axis?

Spiral Review (6.NS.A.1, 6.NS.B.3, 6.NS.B.4)

3. Small juice bottles come in packages of 6. Yogurt treats come in packages of 10. Paula wants to have the exact same number of each item. What is the least number of bottles of juice and individual yogurt treats she will have? How many packages of each will she need?

4. Alison saves $29.26 each month. How many months will it take her to save enough money to buy a stereo for $339.12?

5. The library is 1.75 miles directly north of the school. The park is 0.6 miles directly south of the school. How far is the library from the park?

6. Tours of the art museum are offered every $\frac{1}{3}$ hour starting at 10 A.M. The museum closes at 4:00 P.M. How many tours are offered each day?

FOR MORE PRACTICE
GO TO THE
Personal Math Trainer

Distance on the Coordinate Plane

Essential Question How can you find the distance between two points that lie on a horizontal or vertical line on a coordinate plane?

Common Core The Number System—
6.NS.C.8
MATHEMATICAL PRACTICES
MP1, MP2, MP6, MP7, MP8

 Unlock the Problem

The map of Foggy Mountain Park is marked on a coordinate plane in units of 1 mile. There are two campgrounds in the park. Camp 1 is located at ($^-4$, 3). Camp 2 is located at (5, 3). How far is it from Camp 1 to Camp 2?

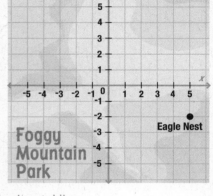

Foggy Mountain Park

Find the distance from Camp 1 to Camp 2.

STEP 1 Graph the points.

Think: The points have the same _____ -coordinate, so they are located on a horizontal line.

STEP 2 Find the horizontal distance from Camp 1 to the *y*-axis.

Find the distance between the *x*-coordinates of the point (_____, 3) and the point (0, 3).

The distance of a number from 0 is the _____ of the number.

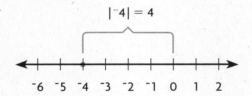

$|{}^-4| = 4$

The distance from ($^-4$, 3) to (0, 3) is $|{}^-4|$ = _____ miles.

STEP 3 Find the horizontal distance from Camp 2 to the *y*-axis.

Find the distance between the *x*-coordinates of (_____ , 3) and (_____ , 3).

The distance from (5, 3) to (0, 3) is |_____| = _____ miles.

STEP 4 Add to find the total distance: _____ + _____ = _____ miles.

So, the distance from Camp 1 to Camp 2 is _____ miles.

ERROR Alert

Remember that distance is never negative. You can find the distance between a negative number and 0 by using absolute value.

 Math Talk

MATHEMATICAL PRACTICES ①

Evaluate Explain how you could check that you found the distance correctly.

---

1. **MATHEMATICAL PRACTICE ⑥** **Explain** how you could use absolute value to find the distance from Camp 2 to the Eagle Nest. What is the distance?

_____

_____

In the problem on the previous page, you used absolute value to find the distance between points in different quadrants. You can also use absolute value to find the distance between points in the same quadrant.

 **Example** Find the distance between the pair of points on the coordinate plane.

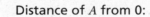

A points *A* and *B*

STEP 1 Look at the coordinates of the points.

The _____ -coordinates of the points are the same, so the points lie on a horizontal line.

Think of the horizontal line passing through *A* and *B* as a number line.

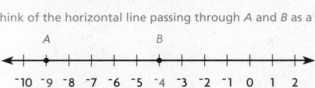

STEP 2 Find the distances of *A* and *B* from 0.

Distance of *A* from 0:

$|^-9| =$ _____ units

Distance of *B* from 0:

$|$ _____ $| =$ _____ units

STEP 3 Subtract to find the distance from *A* to *B*: _____ − _____ = _____ units.

So, the distance from *A* to *B* is _____ units.

B points *C* and *D*

STEP 1 Look at the coordinates of the points.

The _____ -coordinates of the points are the same, so the points lie on a vertical line.

Think of the vertical line passing through *C* and *D* as a number line.

STEP 2 Find the distances of *C* and *D* from 0 on the vertical number line.

Distance of *C* from 0: $|10| =$ _____ units

Distance of *D* from 0: $|$ _____ $| =$ _____ units

STEP 3 Subtract to find the distance from *C* to *D*:

_____ − _____ = _____ units.

So, the distance between *C* and *D* is _____ units.

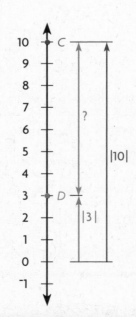

Math Talk

MATHEMATICAL PRACTICES ⑦

Look for Structure Explain how to find the distance from $M(^-5, 1)$ to $N(^-5, 7)$.

Name _____

Find the distance between the pair of points.

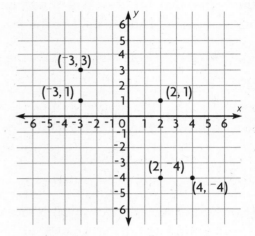

1. (⁻3, 1) and (2, 1)

Horizontal distance from (⁻3, 1) to y-axis:

|_____| = _____

Horizontal distance from (2, 1) to y-axis: |_____| = _____

Distance from (⁻3, 1) to (2, 1): _____

✓ 2. (2, 1) and (2, ⁻4)

_____

✓ 3. (2, ⁻4) and (4, ⁻4)

_____

4. (⁻3, 3) and (⁻3, 1)

_____

Math Talk MATHEMATICAL PRACTICES ⑥

Explain how you can find the distance between two points that have the same y-coordinate.

On Your Own

Practice: Copy and Solve **Graph the pair of points. Then find the distance between them.**

5. (0, 5) and (0, ⁻5)

_____

6. (1, 1) and (1, ⁻3)

_____

7. (⁻2, ⁻5) and (⁻2, ⁻1)

_____

8. (⁻7, 3) and (5, 3)

_____

9. (3, ⁻6) and (3, ⁻10)

_____

10. (8, 0) and (8, ⁻8)

_____

MATHEMATICAL PRACTICE ② **Use Reasoning** **Algebra** **Write the coordinates of a point that is the given distance from the given point.**

11. 4 units from (3, 5)

$\left(3, \right)$

12. 6 units from (2, 1)

$\left(, 1\right)$

13. 7 units from (⁻4, ⁻1)

$\left(⁻4, \right)$

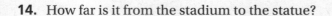
Problem Solving • Applications (Real World)

An archaeologist is digging at an ancient city. The map shows the locations of several important finds. Each unit represents 1 kilometer. Use the map for 14–18.

14. How far is it from the stadium to the statue?

_____

15. 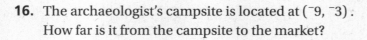 GO DEEPER The archaeologist drives 3 km south from the palace. How far is he from the market?

_____

16. The archaeologist's campsite is located at ($^-$9, $^-$3). How far is it from the campsite to the market?

_____

17. THINK SMARTER The archaeologist rode east on a donkey from the Great Gate, at ($^-$11, 4), to the Royal Road. Then he rode south to the palace. How far did the archaeologist ride?

_____

18. MATHEMATICAL PRACTICE ⑧ Generalize Explain how you could find the distance from the palace to any point on the Imperial Highway.

_____

_____

_____

Archaeological Site

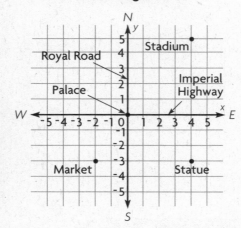

WRITE ▶ Math • Show Your Work

19. 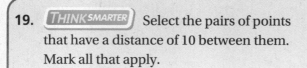 THINK SMARTER Select the pairs of points that have a distance of 10 between them. Mark all that apply.

○ (3, $^-$6) and (3, 4)

○ ($^-$3, 8) and (7, 8)

○ (4, 5) and (6, 5)

○ (4, 1) and (4, 11)

Name _____

Distance on the Coordinate Plane

 COMMON CORE STANDARD—6.NS.C.8
Apply and extend previous understandings of numbers to the system of rational numbers.

Find the distance between the pair of points.

1. (1, 4) and (⁻3, 4)

|1| = 1; |⁻3| = 3;

1 + 3 = 4

_____4_____ units

2. (7, ⁻2) and (11, ⁻2)

_____ units

3. (6, 4) and (6, ⁻8)

_____ units

4. (8, ⁻10) and (5, ⁻10)

_____ units

5. (⁻2, ⁻6) and (⁻2, 5)

_____ units

6. (⁻5, 2) and (⁻5, ⁻4)

_____ units

Write the coordinates of a point that is the given distance from the given point.

7. 5 units from (⁻1, ⁻2)

$\left(\boxed{}, ⁻2 \right)$

8. 8 units from (2, 4)

$\left(2, \boxed{} \right)$

9. 3 units from (⁻7, ⁻5)

$\left(⁻7, \boxed{} \right)$

Problem Solving (Real World)

The map shows the locations of several areas in an amusement park. Each unit represents 1 kilometer.

10. How far is the Ferris wheel from the rollercoaster?

_____

11. How far is the water slide from the restrooms?

_____

Amusement Park

12. **WRITE** ▸*Math* Graph the points (23, 3), (23, 7), and (4, 3) on a coordinate plane. Explain how to find the distance from (23, 3) to (23, 7) and from (23, 3) and (4, 3).

_____

_____

_____

Lesson Check (6.NS.C.8)

1. What is the distance between $(4, \,^-7)$ and $(^-5, \,^-7)$?

2. Point A and point B are 5 units apart. The coordinates of point A are $(3, \,^-9)$. The y–coordinate of point B is $^-9$. What is a possible x–coordinate for point B?

Spiral Review (6.NS.A.1, 6.NS.C.6b, 6.NS.C.6c, 6.NS.C.7b)

3. An apple is cut into 10 pieces. 0.8 of the apple is eaten. Which fraction, in simplest form, represents the amount of apple that is left?

4. A carton contains soup cans weighing a total of 20 pounds. Each can weighs $1\frac{1}{4}$ pounds. How many cans does the carton contain?

5. List $^-1$, $\frac{1}{4}$, and $^-1\frac{2}{3}$ in order from greatest to least.

6. The point located at $(3, \,^-1)$ is reflected across the $y-$axis. What are the coordinates of the reflected point?

FOR MORE PRACTICE
GO TO THE
Personal Math Trainer

Problem Solving • The Coordinate Plane

Essential Question How can you use the strategy *draw a diagram* to help you solve a problem on the coordinate plane?

Common Core
The Number System—6.NS.C.8
MATHEMATICAL PRACTICES
MP1, MP5, MP6

Unlock the Problem

An artist is using an illustration program. The program uses a coordinate plane, with the origin (0, 0) located at the center of the computer screen. The artist draws a dinosaur centered on the point (4, 6). Then she moves it 10 units to the left and 12 units down. What ordered pair represents the dinosaur's new location?

Use the graphic organizer to help you solve the problem.

Read the Problem

What do I need to find?	**What information do I need to use?**	**How will I use the information?**
I need to find the _____ for the dinosaur's new location.	The dinosaur started at the point _____. Then the artist moved it _____ to the left and _____ down.	I can draw a diagram to graph the information on a _____.

Solve the Problem

- Start by graphing and labeling the point _____.

- From this point, count _____ to the left.

- Then count _____ down.

- Graph and label the point at this location, and

  write its coordinates: _____.

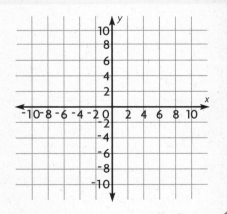

So, the dinosaur's new location is _____.

Analyze Explain how you could check that your answer is correct.

🔑 Try Another Problem

Tyrone and Kyra both walk home from school. Kyra walks 4 blocks east and 3 blocks south to get home. Tyrone lives 3 blocks west and 3 blocks south of the school. How far apart are Tyrone's and Kyra's homes?

Use the graphic organizer to help you solve the problem.

Read the Problem	Solve the Problem
What do I need to find?	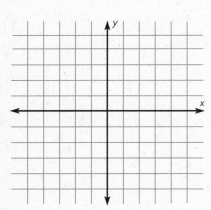
What information do I need to use?	
How will I use the information?	

So, it is _____ blocks from Tyrone's house to Kyra's house.

- **MATHEMATICAL PRACTICE 5** **Use Appropriate Tools** Describe the advantages of using a coordinate plane to solve a problem like the one above.

Math Talk

MATHEMATICAL PRACTICES 6

Explain how you know that your answer is reasonable.

_____

_____

Name _____

Unlock the Problem

✓ Draw a diagram of the situation.
✓ Use absolute value to find distance.

☑ **1.** **GO DEEPER** Busby County is rectangular. A map of the county on a coordinate plane shows the vertices of the county at (⁻5, 8), (8, 8), (8, ⁻10), and (⁻5, ⁻10). Each unit on the map represents 1 mile. What is the county's perimeter?

First, draw a diagram of Busby County.

Busby County

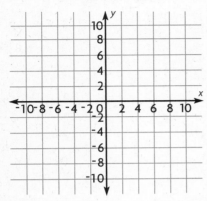

Next, use the diagram to find the length of each side of the rectangle. Then add.

_____

So, the perimeter of Busby County is _____.

2. **THINK SMARTER** What if the vertices of the county were (⁻5, 8), (8, 8), (8, ⁻6), and (⁻5, ⁻6)? What would the perimeter of the county be?

_____

☑ **3.** On a coordinate map of Melville, a restaurant is located at (⁻9, ⁻5). A laundry business is located 3 units to the left of the restaurant on the map. What are the map coordinates of the laundry business?

_____

4. **GO DEEPER** The library is 4 blocks north and 9 blocks east of the school. The museum is 9 blocks east and 11 blocks south of the school. How far is it from the library to the museum?

_____

WRITE ▸ Math • Show Your Work

Problem Solving • Applications (Real World)

5. **MATHEMATICAL PRACTICE ①** **Make Sense of Problems** Diana left her campsite at (2, 6) on a map of Big Trees Park, hiked to Redwood Grove at (⁻5, 6), and continued on to Bass Lake at (⁻5, ⁻3). Each unit on the map represents 1 kilometer. How far did Diana hike?

_____

6. **THINK SMARTER** Hector left his house at (⁻6, 13) on a map of Coleville and walked to the zoo at (⁻6, 2). From there he walked east to his friend's house. He walked a total distance of 25 blocks. If each unit on the map represents one block, what are the coordinates of Hector's friend's house?

_____

7. **GO DEEPER** In November, the price of a cell phone was double the price in March. In December, the price was \$57, which was \$29 less than the price in November. What was the price of the cell phone in March?

_____

Personal Math Trainer

8. **THINK SMARTER +** A map of the city holding the Olympics is placed on a coordinate plane. Olympic Stadium is located at the origin of the map. Each unit on the map represents 2 miles.

Graph the locations of four other Olympic buildings.

Max said the distance between the Aquatics Center and the Olympic Village is greater than the distance between the Media Center and the Basketball Arena. Do you agree with Max? Use words and numbers to support your answer.

Building	Location
Olympic Village	(⁻8, 4)
Aquatics Center	(8, 4)
Media Center	(4, ⁻5)
Basketball Arena	(⁻8, ⁻5)

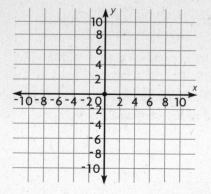

_____

_____

_____

_____

Problem Solving • The Coordinate Plane

Common Core

COMMON CORE STANDARD—6.NS.C.8
Compute fluently with multi-digit numbers
and find common factors and multiples.

Read each problem and solve.

1. On a coordinate map of Clifton, an electronics store is located
   at (6, ⁻7). A convenience store is located 7 units north of the
   electronics store on the map. What are the map coordinates of the
   convenience store?

   (6, 0)

2. Sonya and Lucas walk from the school to the library. They walk 5
   blocks south and 4 blocks west to get to the library. If the school is
   located at a point (9, ⁻1) on a coordinate map, what are the map
   coordinates of the library?

3. On a coordinate map, Sherry's house is at the point
   (10, ⁻2) and the mall is at point (⁻4, ⁻2). If each unit on
   the map represents one block, what is the distance between
   Sherry's house and the mall?

4. Arthur left his job at (5, 4) on a coordinate map and walked to his
   house at (5, ⁻6). Each unit on the map represents 1 block. How far
   did Arthur walk?

5. A fire station is located 2 units east and 6 units north of a hospital.
   If the hospital is located at a point (⁻2, ⁻3) on a coordinate map,
   what are the coordinates of the fire station?

6. Xavier's house is located at the point (4, 6). Michael's house is 10
   blocks west and 2 blocks south of Xavier's house. What are the
   coordinates of Michael's house?

7. **WRITE** ▸*Math* Write a problem that can be solved by
   drawing a diagram on a coordinate plane.

Lesson Check (6.NS.C.8)

1. The points ($^-$4, $^-$4), ($^-$4, 4), (4, 4), and (4, $^-$4) form a square on a coordinate plane. How long is a side length of the square?

2. On a coordinate map, the museum is located at ($^-$5, 7). A park is located 6 units to the right of the museum on the map. What are the coordinates of the park?

Spiral Review (6.NS.A.1, 6.NS.B.3, 6.NS.C.6c, 6.NS.C.7b, 6.NS.C.8)

3. On a grid Joe's house is marked at ($^-$5, $^-$3) and Andy's house is marked at (1, $^-$3). What is the distance, on the grid, between Joe's house and Andy's house?

4. In the last two years, Mari grew $2\frac{1}{4}$ inches, Kim grew 2.4 inches, and Kate grew $2\frac{1}{8}$ inches. Write the amounts they grew in order from least to greatest.

5. A jar of jelly that weighs 4.25 ounces costs $2.89. What is the cost of one ounce of jelly?

6. Jan began with $\frac{5}{6}$ pound of modeling clay. She used $\frac{1}{5}$ of the clay to make decorative magnets. She divided the remaining clay into 8 equal portions. What is the weight of the clay in each portion?

FOR MORE PRACTICE
GO TO THE
Personal Math Trainer

Name _____

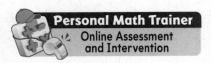

1. For numbers 1a–1d, choose Yes or No to indicate whether the situation can be represented by a negative number.

   1a.   Sherri lost 100 points answering   ○ Yes   ○ No
         a question wrong.

   1b.   The peak of a mountain is   ○ Yes   ○ No
         2,000 feet above sea level.

   1c.   Yong paid $25 for a parking   ○ Yes   ○ No
         ticket.

   1d.   A puppy gained 3 pounds.   ○ Yes   ○ No

2. The low weekday temperatures for a city are shown.

Low Temperatures	
Day	**Low Temperature (°F)**
Monday	$^-5$
Tuesday	$^-3$
Wednesday	2
Thursday	$^-7$
Friday	3

Part A

Using the information in the table, order the temperatures from lowest to highest.

_____

Part B

Explain how to use a vertical number line to determine the order.

3. For numbers 3a–3e, choose Yes or No to indicate whether the number is between ⁻1 and ⁻2.

3a. $-\frac{4}{5}$ ○ Yes ○ No

3b. $1\frac{2}{3}$ ○ Yes ○ No

3c. ⁻1.3 ○ Yes ○ No

3d. $^{-}1\frac{1}{4}$ ○ Yes ○ No

3e. $^{-}2\frac{1}{10}$ ○ Yes ○ No

4. Compare $^{-}\frac{1}{5}$ and ⁻0.9. Use numbers and words to explain your answer.

5. Jeandre said |3| equals |⁻3|. Is Jeandre correct? Use a number line and words to support your answer.

6. Write the values in order from least to greatest.

|⁻4| |2| |⁻12| |8|

_____   _____   _____   _____

7. For numbers 7a–7d, select True or False for each statement.

7a. The *x*-coordinate of any point on the *y*-axis is 0.   ○ True ○ False

7b. Point *D*(⁻2, 1) is to the left of the *y*-axis and below the *x*-axis.   ○ True ○ False

7c. The point where the axes intersect is the origin.   ○ True ○ False

7d. If both the *x*- and *y*- coordinates are positive, the point is to the right of the *y*-axis and below the *x*-axis.   ○ True ○ False

8. Mia's house is located at point (3, 4) on a coordinate plane. The location of Keisha's house is the reflection of the location of Mia's house across the *y*-axis. In what quadrant is Keisha's house in?

_____

9. [THINK SMARTER +] Points *A*(3, 8) and *B*(⁻4, 8) are located on a coordinate plane. Graph the pair of points. Then find the distance between them. Use numbers and words to explain your answer.

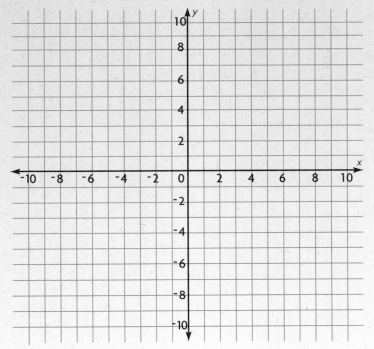

10. **GO DEEPER** The map shows the location *J* of Jose's house and the location *F* of the football field. Jose is going to go to Tyrell's house and then the two of them are going to go to the football field for practice.

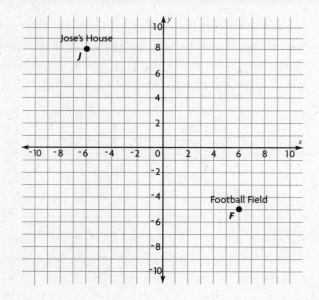

Part A

Tyrell's house is located at point *T*, the reflection of point *J* across the *y*-axis. What are the coordinates of points *T*, *J*, and *F*?

_____

Part B

If each unit on the map represents 1 block, what was the distance Tyrell traveled to the football field and what was the distance Jose traveled to the football field? Use numbers and words to explain your answer.

11. For numbers 11a–11d, choose Yes or No to indicate whether the situation could be represented by the integer $^{+}3$.

11a. A football team gains 3 yards on a play. ○ Yes ○ No

11b. A golfer's score is 3 over par. ○ Yes ○ No

11c. A student answers a 3-point question correctly. ○ Yes ○ No

11d. A cat loses 3 pounds. ○ Yes ○ No

Name _____

12. Jason used a map to record the elevations of five locations.

Elevations	
Location	**Elevation (feet)**
Nob Hill	5
Bear Creek	⁻18
Po Valley	⁻20
Fox Hill	8
Jax River	⁻3

Jason wrote the elevations in order from lowest to highest. Is Jason correct? Use words and numbers to explain why or why not. If Jason is incorrect, what is the correct order?

$$\boxed{^-3, 5, 8, ^-18, ^-20}$$

13. For numbers 13a–13d, select True or False for each statement.

13a. $\frac{1}{5}$ is between 0 and 1. ○ True ○ False

13b. $^-2\frac{2}{3}$ is between $^-1$ and $^-2$. ○ True ○ False

13c. $^-3\frac{5}{8}$ is between $^-3$ and $^-4$. ○ True ○ False

13d. $4\frac{3}{4}$ is between 3 and 4. ○ True ○ False

14. Choose <, >, or =.

14a. 0.25 $\begin{array}{c}<\\>\\=\end{array}$ $\frac{3}{4}$

14b. $\frac{1}{3}$ $\begin{array}{c}<\\>\\=\end{array}$ 0.325

14c. $2\frac{7}{8}$ $\begin{array}{c}<\\>\\=\end{array}$ 2.875

14d. $\frac{-3}{4}$ $\begin{array}{c}<\\>\\=\end{array}$ $\frac{-1}{2}$

15. Graph 4 and ⁻4 on the number line.

Tyler says both 4 and ⁻4 have an absolute value of 4. Is Tyler correct?
Use the number line and words to explain why or why not.

16. Lindsay and Will have online accounts for buying music. Lindsay's
account balance is ⁻$20 and Will's account balance is ⁻$15. Express
each account balance as a debt and explain whose debt is greater.

17. Explain how to graph points $A(⁻3, 0)$, $B(0, 0)$, and $C(0, ⁻3)$ on the
coordinate plane. Then, explain how to graph point D, so that $ABCD$
is a square.

18. Point $A(2, ⁻3)$ is reflected across the x-axis to point B. Point B is reflected
across the y-axis to point C. What are the coordinates of point C? Use
words and numbers to explain your answer.

Critical Area Ratios and Rates

 CRITICAL AREA Connecting ratio and rate to whole number multiplication and division and using concepts of ratio and rate to solve problems

The St. Louis Cardinals, based in St. Louis, Missouri, were founded in 1882.

Meet Me in St. Louis

Baseball teams, like the St. Louis Cardinals, record information about each player on the team. These statistics are used to describe a player's performance.

Get Started 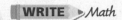 WRITE Math

A batting average is calculated from the ratio of a player's hits to the number of at bats. Batting averages are usually recorded as a decimal to the thousandths place. The table shows the batting results of three baseball players who received the Most Valuable Player award while playing for the St. Louis Cardinals. Write each batting ratio as a fraction. Then write the fraction as a decimal to the thousandths place and as a percent.

Important Facts

Player Name	Batting Results
Albert Pujols (2008)	187 hits in 524 at bats
Stan Musial (1948)	230 hits in 611 at bats
Rogers Hornsby (1925)	203 hits in 504 at bats

The players on a baseball team take their turns batting in the same order or sequence throughout a game. The manager sets the batting order. Suppose you are the manager of a team that includes Pujols, Musial, and Hornsby. What batting order would you use for those three players? Explain your answer.

ALBERT PUJOLS

Completed by _____

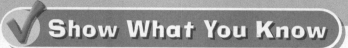 **Show What You Know**

Personal Math Trainer
Online Assessment
and Intervention

Check your understanding of important skills.

Name _____

▶ **Multiply or Divide to Find Equivalent Fractions** **Multiply or divide to find two equivalent fractions for the given fraction.** (4.NF.A.1)

1. $\frac{1}{2}$
_____

2. $\frac{5}{6}$
_____

3. $\frac{12}{18}$
_____

▶ **Extend Patterns** **Write a description of the pattern. Then find the missing numbers.** (4.OA.C.5)

4. 3, _____, 48, 192, 768, _____

_____

5. 625, 575, 525, _____, _____, 375

▶ **Multiply by 2-Digit Numbers** **Find the product.** (5.NBT.B.5)

6.   52
   $\times\ 19$

7.   14
   $\times\ 88$

8.   37
   $\times\ 21$

9.   45
   $\times\ 62$

The student council should have 1 representative for every 25 students. Which of these situations fits the description? Explain your answer.

a. 5 representatives for 100 students
b. 10 representatives for 250 students
c. 15 representatives for 300 students

Vocabulary Builder

▶ **Visualize It** •••••••••••••••••••••••••••••••••••••

Complete the bubble map with review words that are related to fractions.

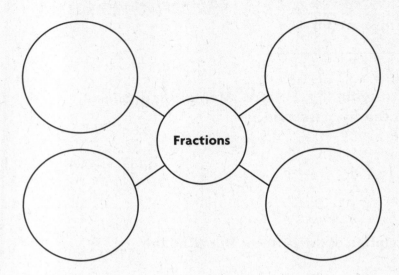

Fractions

Review Words

coordinate plane

denominator

✔ equivalent fractions

numerator

✔ ordered pair

pattern

simplify

x-coordinate

y-coordinate

Preview Words

✔ equivalent ratios

✔ rate

✔ ratio

✔ unit rate

▶ **Understand Vocabulary** •••••••••••••••••••••••••••

Complete the sentences using the checked words.

1. A comparison of one number to another by division is a

    _____.

2. _____ are ratios that name the same comparison.

3. _____ are fractions that name the same amount or part.

4. A ratio that compares quantities with different units is a

    _____.

5. A _____ is a rate that compares a quantity to 1 unit.

6. In an _____ the first number is the *x*-coordinate and the second number is the *y*-coordinate.

GO DIGITAL • Interactive Student Edition
• Multimedia eGlossary

Chapter 4 Vocabulary

denominator

denominador

20

equivalent ratios

razones equivalentes

30

numerator

numerador

66

rate

tasa

86

ratio

razón

87

unit rate

tasa por unidad

103

x-coordinate

coordenada x

109

y-coordinate

coordenada y

111

Ratios that name the same comparison

	Original ratio	2 · 1 ↓	3 · 1 ↓	4 · 1 ↓	5 · 1 ↓
Boxes	1	2	3	4	5
Cards	6	12	18	24	30
		↑ 2 · 6	↑ 3 · 6	↑ 4 · 6	↑ 5 · 6

The number below the bar in a fraction that tells how many equal parts are in the whole or in the group

$\frac{3}{4}$ ← denominator

A ratio that compares two quantities having different units of measure

Example:

An airplane climbs 18,000 feet in 12 minutes. The rate of climb is 18,000 ft to 12 min, $\frac{18{,}000 \text{ ft}}{12 \text{ min}}$, or 18,000 ft : 12 min

---

The number above the bar in a fraction that tells how many equal parts of the whole are being considered

$\frac{3}{4}$ ← numerator

A rate expressed so that the second term in the ratio is one unit

Example: $9 per hour is a *unit rate*.

A comparison of two numbers, *a* and *b*, that can be written as a fraction $\frac{a}{b}$

The ratio of blue squares to red squares is 5 to 1, $\frac{5}{1}$, or 5 : 1.

The second number in an ordered pair; tells the distance to move up or down from (0,0)

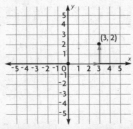

The first number in an ordered pair; tells the distance to move right or left from (0,0)

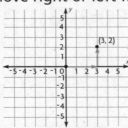

Going to the Baseball Hall of Fame

Word Box

denominator
equivalent ratios
numerator
rate
ratio
unit rate
x-coordinate
y-coordinate

For 2 players

Materials

- 1 each: red and blue playing pieces
- 1 number cube
- Clue Cards

How to Play

1. Choose a playing piece and put it on START.
2. Toss the number cube to take a turn. Move your playing piece that many spaces.
3. If you land on these spaces:

   Blue Space Follow the directions printed in the space.

   Red Space Take a Clue Card from the pile. If you answer the question correctly, keep the card. If you do not, return the card to the bottom of the pile.
4. Collect at least 5 Clue Cards. Move around the track as often as necessary.
5. When you have 5 Clue Cards, you follow the closest center path to reach FINISH.
6. The first player to reach FINISH wins.

TAKE A
CLUE CARD

Win a ticket
to the Hall of
Fame Weekend.
Move ahead 1.

FINISH

TAKE A
CLUE CARD

Get a
behind-the-scene
tour of the museum.
Go back 1.

Have a sleepover in the museum with your family. Lose a turn.

TAKE A CLUE CARD

See your favorite player's baseball cap. Move ahead 1.

FINISH

START ▶

TAKE A CLUE CARD

The Write Way

Reflect

Choose one idea. Write about it.

- Sofia made a beaded necklace with 2 white beads for every 5 purple beads. In all, she used 30 purple beads. Explain how to figure out the total number of white beads she used.
- Write and solve a word problem that includes a rate.
- Tell about a time when you needed to know the unit rate of something.
- Are 3:7 and 6:14 equivalent ratios? Tell how you know.

_____

_____

_____

_____

_____

_____

_____

_____

_____

_____

_____

_____

_____

_____

Model Ratios

Essential Question How can you model ratios?

Common Core Ratios and Proportional Relationships—6.RP.A.1 *Also 6.RP.A.3a*

MATHEMATICAL PRACTICES
MP4, MP5, MP7, MP8

The drawing shows 5 blue squares and 1 red square. You can compare the number of blue squares to the number of red squares by using a ratio. A **ratio** is a comparison of two quantities by division.

The ratio that compares blue squares to red squares is 5 to 1. The ratio 5 to 1 can also be written as 5:1.

Investigate

Materials ■ two-color counters

Julie makes 3 bracelets for every 1 bracelet Beth makes. Use ratios to compare the number of bracelets Julie makes to the number Beth makes.

A. Use red and yellow counters to model the ratio that compares the number of bracelets Julie makes to the number of bracelets Beth makes.

> **Think:** Julie makes _____ bracelets when Beth makes 1 bracelet.

The ratio is _____:1.

B. Model the ratio that shows the number of bracelets Julie makes when Beth makes 2 bracelets. Write the ratio and explain how you modeled it.

_____

_____

C. How could you change the model from Part B to show the number of bracelets Julie makes when Beth makes 3 bracelets? Write the ratio.

_____

_____

Math Talk MATHEMATICAL PRACTICES ⑦

Look for a Pattern For each ratio, divide the number of bracelets Julie makes by the number of bracelets Beth makes. Describe a pattern you notice in the quotients.

Draw Conclusions

1. Explain how you used counters to compare the number of bracelets Julie makes to the number of bracelets Beth makes.

_____

_____

2. **MATHEMATICAL PRACTICE 8** **Generalize** Describe a rule that you can use to find the number of bracelets Julie makes when you know the number of bracelets Beth makes.

_____

3. **THINK SMARTER** How can you use counters to find how many bracelets Beth makes if you know the number Julie makes? Explain and give an example.

_____

_____

_____

Make Connections

You can use a table to compare quantities and write ratios.

A bakery uses 1 packing box for every 4 muffins. Draw a model and make a table to show the ratio of boxes to muffins.

STEP 1 Draw a model to show the ratio that compares boxes to muffins.

> **Think:** There is _____ box for every _____ muffins.
>
> The ratio is _____ : _____.

STEP 2 Complete the table to show the ratio of boxes to muffins.

> **Think:** Each time the number of boxes increases by 1,
>
> the number of muffins increases by _____.

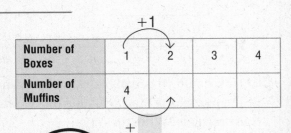

Number of Boxes	1	2	3	4
Number of Muffins	4			

What is the ratio of boxes to muffins when there are 2 boxes? _____

Write another ratio shown by the table. Explain what the ratio represents.

_____

_____

Math Talk

MATHEMATICAL PRACTICES 5

Use Tools Describe the pattern you see in the table comparing the number of boxes to the number of muffins.

Name _____

Write the ratio of yellow counters to red counters.

1.

_____ : _____

2.

_____

Draw a model of the ratio.

 3. 3:2

4. 1:5

Use the ratio to complete the table.

5. Wen is arranging flowers in vases. For every 1 rose she uses, she uses 6 tulips. Complete the table to show the ratio of roses to tulips.

Roses	1	2	3	4
Tulips	6			

 6. On the sixth-grade field trip, there are 8 students for every 1 adult. Complete the table to show the ratio of students to adults.

Students	8		24	
Adults	1	2		4

7. **THINK SMARTER** Zena adds 4 cups of flour for every 3 cups of sugar in her recipe. Draw a model that compares cups of flour to cups of sugar.

Draw Conclusions

The reading skill *draw conclusions* can help you analyze and make sense of information.

Hikers take trail mix as a snack on long hikes because it is tasty, nutritious, and easy to carry. There are many different recipes for trail mix, but it is usually made from different combinations of dried fruit, raisins, seeds, and nuts. Tanner and his dad make trail mix that has 1 cup of raisins for every 3 cups of sunflower seeds.

8. **MATHEMATICAL PRACTICE 4** **Model Mathematics** Explain how you could model the ratio that compares cups of raisins to cups of sunflower seeds when Tanner uses 2 cups of raisins.

_____

_____

_____

_____

The table shows the ratio of cups of raisins to cups of sunflower seeds for different amounts of trail mix. Model each ratio as you complete the table.

Trail Mix					
Raisins (cups)	1	2	3	4	5
Sunflower Seeds (cups)	3				

9. **THINK SMARTER** Describe the pattern you see in the table.

_____

_____

_____

10. **MATHEMATICAL PRACTICE 8** **Draw Conclusions** What conclusion can Tanner draw from this pattern?

_____

_____

11. **GO DEEPER** What is the ratio of cups of sunflower seeds to cups of trail mix when Tanner uses 4 cups of raisins?

_____

Model Ratios

COMMON CORE STANDARD—6.RP.A.1
Understand ratio concepts and use ratio reasoning to solve problems.

Write the ratio of gray counters to white counters.

1.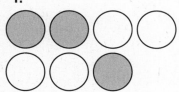

2.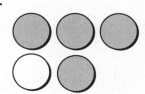

3.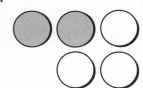

_____ gray:white 3:4 _____   _____   _____

Draw a model of the ratio.

4. 5:1

5. 6:3

Use the ratio to complete the table.

6. Marc is assembling gift bags. For every 2 pencils he places in the bag, he uses 3 stickers. Complete the table to show the ratio of pencils to stickers.

Pencils	2	4	6	8
Stickers	3			

7. Singh is making a bracelet. She uses 5 blue beads for every 1 silver bead. Complete the table to show the ratio of blue beads to silver beads.

Blue	5	10		20
Silver	1		3	

Problem Solving Real World

8. There are 4 quarts in 1 gallon. How many quarts are in 3 gallons?

9. Martin mixes 1 cup lemonade with 4 cups cranberry juice to make his favorite drink. How much cranberry juice does he need if he uses 5 cups of lemonade?

_____   _____

10. **WRITE** ▸ *Math* Suppose there was 1 centerpiece for every 5 tables. Use counters to show the ratio of centerpieces to tables. Then make a table to find the number of tables if there are 3 centerpieces.

_____

_____

Lesson Check (6.RP.A.1)

1. Francine is making a necklace that has 1 blue bead for every 6 white beads. How many white beads will she use if she uses 11 blue beads?

2. A basketball league assigns 8 players to each team. How many players can sign up for the league if there are 24 teams?

_____

Spiral Review (6.NS.B.4, 6.NS.C.6a, 6.NS.C.8)

3. Louis has 45 pencils and 75 pens to divide into gift bags at the fair. He does not want to mix the pens and pencils. He wants to place an equal amount in each bag. What is the greatest number of pens or pencils he can place in each bag?

4. Of the 24 students in Greg's class, $\frac{3}{8}$ ride the bus to school. How many students ride the bus?

5. Elisa made 0.44 of the free throws she attempted. What is that amount written as a fraction in simplest form?

6. On a coordinate plane, the vertices of a rectangle are $(^-1, 1)$, $(3, 1)$, $(^-1, ^-4)$, and $(3, ^-4)$. What is the perimeter of the rectangle?

FOR MORE PRACTICE
GO TO THE
Personal Math Trainer

Ratios and Rates

Essential Question How do you write ratios and rates?

Ratios and Proportional Relationships—6.RP.A.1 *Also 6.RP.A.2*

MATHEMATICAL PRACTICES
MP2, MP5, MP6

Unlock the Problem *Real World*

A bird rescue group is caring for 3 eagles, 2 hawks, and 5 owls in their rescue center.

You can compare the numbers of different types of birds using ratios. There are three ways to write the ratio of owls to eagles in the rescue center.

Using words	As a fraction	With a colon
5 to 3	$\frac{5}{3}$	5:3

Ratios can be written to compare a part to a part, a part to a whole, or a whole to a part.

🔑 **Write each ratio using words, as a fraction, and with a colon.**

Ⓐ Owls to hawks

_____ to _____ | ─── | _____ : _____

Part to part

Ⓑ Eagles to total birds in the rescue center

_____ to _____ | ─── | _____ : _____

Part to whole

Ⓒ Total birds in the rescue center to hawks

_____ to _____ | ─── | _____ : _____

Whole to part

1. The ratio of owls to total number of birds is 5:10. Explain what this ratio means.

_____

🔑 Example

A restaurant sells veggie burgers at the rate of $4 for 1 burger. What rate gives the cost of 5 veggie burgers? Write the rate for 5 burgers using words, as a fraction, and with a colon.

A **rate** is a ratio that compares two quantities that have different units of measure.

A **unit rate** is a rate that makes a comparison to 1 unit. The unit rate for cost per veggie burger is $4 to 1 burger or $\frac{\$4}{1 \text{ burger}}$.

Complete the table to find the rate that gives the cost of 5 veggie burgers.

Think: 1 veggie burger costs $4, so 2 veggie burgers cost $4 + _____ , or 2 × _____ .

	Unit Rate	2 • $4 ↓	3 • $4 ↓	☐ • $4 ↓	☐ • $4 ↓
Cost	$4	$8			
Veggie Burgers	1	2	3	4	

                                ↑   ↑   ↑   ↑

                      2 • 1   ☐ • 1   4 • 1   ☐ • 1

The table shows that 5 veggie burgers cost _____ .

So, the rate that gives the cost for 5 veggie burgers is

$_____ to _____ burgers, $\dfrac{\$ \boxed{}}{\boxed{} \text{ burgers}}$, or $_____ : _____ burgers.

Try This! Write the rate in three different ways.

A The rate that gives the cost of 3 veggie burgers

_____

B The rate that gives the cost of 4 veggie burgers

_____

2. Explain why the ratio $\frac{\$4}{1 \text{ burger}}$ is a unit rate.

_____

3. **MATHEMATICAL PRACTICE ⑤** **Use Patterns** Explain the pattern you see in the table in the Example.

_____

_____

Share and Show

1. Write the ratio of the number of red bars to blue stars.

_____
_____

Write the ratio in two different ways.

2. 8 to 16

_____

3. $\frac{4}{24}$

_____

4. 1:3

_____

✓ 5. 7 to 9

_____

✓ 6. Marilyn saves $15 per week. Complete the table to find the rate that gives the amount saved in 4 weeks. Write the rate in three different ways.

_____

Savings		$30	$45		$75
Weeks	1	2	3	4	5

Math Talk

MATHEMATICAL PRACTICES ⑥

Explain Are the ratios 5:2 and 2:5 the same or different? How do you know?

On Your Own

Write the ratio in two different ways.

7. $\frac{16}{40}$

_____

8. 8:12

_____

9. 4 to 11

_____

10. 2:13

_____

11. There are 24 baseball cards in 4 packs. Complete the table to find the rate that gives the number of cards in 2 packs. Write this rate in three different ways.

_____

Cards			18	24
Packs	1	2	3	4

12. **MATHEMATICAL PRACTICE ⑥** Make Connections Explain how the statement "There is $\frac{3}{4}$ cup per serving" represents a rate.

_____
_____
_____

Problem Solving • Applications

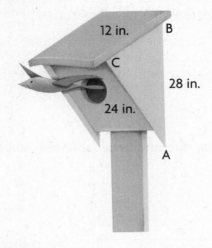

Use the diagram of a birdhouse for 13–15.

13. Write the ratio of *AB* to *BC* in three different ways.

_____

14. GO DEEPER   Write the ratio of the shortest side length of triangle *ABC* to the perimeter of the triangle in three different ways.

_____

15. MATHEMATICAL PRACTICE ②   **Represent a Problem**   Write the ratio of the perimeter of triangle *ABC* to the longest side length of the triangle in three different ways.

_____

WRITE ▸ Math • **Show Your Work**

16. Leandra places 6 photos on each page in a photo album. Find the rate that gives the number of photos on 2 pages. Write the rate in three different ways.

_____

17. THINK SMARTER   **What's the Question?**   The ratio of total students in Ms. Murray's class to students in the class who have an older brother is 3 to 1. The answer is 1:2. What is the question?

_____

_____

18. WRITE ▸ Math   What do all unit rates have in common?

_____

_____

19. THINK SMARTER   Julia has 2 green reusable shopping bags and 5 purple reusable shopping bags. Select the ratios that compare the number of purple reusable shopping bags to the total number of reusable shopping bags. Mark all that apply.

○ 5 to 7   ○ 5 : 2   ○ 2 to 7

○ 5 : 7   ○ $\frac{2}{5}$ ○ $\frac{5}{7}$

Ratios and Rates

Common Core

COMMON CORE STANDARD—6.RP.A.1
Understand ratio concepts and use ratio reasoning to solve problems.

Write the ratio in two different ways.

1. $\frac{4}{5}$ 2. 16 to 3   3. 9:13   4. $\frac{15}{8}$

    4 to 5

    4:5
_____   _____   _____   _____

5. There are 20 light bulbs in 5 packages. Complete the table to find the rate that gives the number of light bulbs in 3 packages. Write this rate in three different ways.

Light Bulbs		8		16	20
Packages	1	2	3	4	5

_____

_____

![Problem Solving Real World]

6. Gemma spends 4 hours each week playing soccer and 3 hours each week practicing her clarinet. Write the ratio of hours spent practicing clarinet to hours spent playing soccer three different ways.

7. Randall bought 2 game controllers at Electronics Plus for $36. What is the unit rate for a game controller at Electronics Plus?

_____   _____

8. **WRITE** ▸*Math* Explain how to determine if a given rate is also a unit rate.

_____

_____

Lesson Check (6.RP.A.1)

1. At the grocery store, Luis bought 10 bananas and 4 apples. What are three different ways to write the ratio of apples to bananas?

2. Rita checked out 7 books from the library. She had 2 non-fiction books. The rest were fiction. What are three different ways to write the ratio of non-fiction to fiction?

Spiral Review (6.RP.A.1, 6.NS.B.4, 6.NS.C.6c)

3. McKenzie bought 1.2 pounds of coffee for $11.82. What was the cost per pound?

4. Pedro has a bag of flour that weighs $\frac{9}{10}$ pound. He uses $\frac{2}{3}$ of the bag to make gravy. How many pounds of flour does Pedro use to make gravy?

5. Gina draws a map of her town on a coordinate plane. The point that represents the town's civic center is 1 unit to the right of the origin and 4 units above it. What are the coordinates of the point representing the civic center?

6. Stefan draws these shapes. What is the ratio of triangles to stars?

**FOR MORE PRACTICE
GO TO THE
Personal Math Trainer**

Equivalent Ratios and Multiplication Tables

Essential Question How can you use a multiplication table to find equivalent ratios?

Common Core   Ratios and Proportional Relationships—6.RP.A.3a
MATHEMATICAL PRACTICES
MP1, MP5, MP6

The table below shows two rows from the multiplication table: the row for 1 and the row for 6. The ratios shown in each column of the table are equivalent to the original ratio. Ratios that name the same comparison are **equivalent ratios**.

	Original ratio	2 • 1 ↓	3 • 1 ↓	4 • 1 ↓	5 • 1 ↓
Bags	1	2	3	4	5
Apples	6	12	18	24	30
		↑ 2 • 6	↑ 3 • 6	↑ 4 • 6	↑ 5 • 6

×	1	2	3	4	5
1	1	2	3	4	5
2	2	4	6	8	10
3	3	6	9	12	15
4	4	8	12	16	20
5	5	10	15	20	25
6	6	12	18	24	30

You can use a multiplication table to find equivalent ratios.

Unlock the Problem   Real World

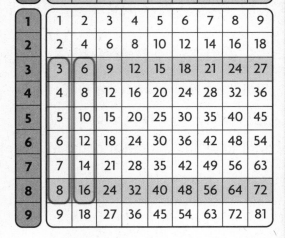

×	1	2	3	4	5	6	7	8	9
1	1	2	3	4	5	6	7	8	9
2	2	4	6	8	10	12	14	16	18
3	3	6	9	12	15	18	21	24	27
4	4	8	12	16	20	24	28	32	36
5	5	10	15	20	25	30	35	40	45
6	6	12	18	24	30	36	42	48	54
7	7	14	21	28	35	42	49	56	63
8	8	16	24	32	40	48	56	64	72
9	9	18	27	36	45	54	63	72	81

The ratio of adults to students on a field trip is $\frac{3}{8}$.

Write two ratios that are equivalent to $\frac{3}{8}$.

Use the multiplication table.

STEP 1 Shade the rows that show the original ratio.

Think: The original ratio is . Shade the row for _____ and

the row for _____ on the multiplication table.

STEP 2 Circle the column that shows the original ratio.

Think: There is one group of 3 adults for every group of 8 students.

STEP 3 Circle two columns that show equivalent ratios.

The column for 2 shows there are 2 • 3 , or _____ adults when

there are 2 • 8, or _____ students.

The column for 3 shows there are 3 • 3, or _____ adults when

there are 3 • 8, or _____ students.

So, _____ and _____ are equivalent to $\frac{3}{8}$.

Math Talk   MATHEMATICAL PRACTICES ⑥

Explain whether the multiplication table shown represents all of the ratios that are equivalent to 3:8.

CONNECT You can find equivalent ratios by using a table or by multiplying or dividing by a form of one.

🔑 One Way Use a table.

Jessa made fruit punch by mixing 2 pints of orange juice with 5 pints of pineapple juice. To make more punch, she needs to mix orange juice and pineapple juice in the same ratio. Write three equivalent ratios for $\frac{2}{5}$.

Think: Use rows from the multiplication table to help you complete a table of equivalent ratios.

×	1	2	3	4	5
1	1	2	3	4	5
2	2	4	6	8	10
3	3	6	9	12	15
4	4	8	12	16	20
5	5	10	15	20	25

$\longrightarrow$

	Original ratio	2 • 2 ↓	3 • 2 ↓	⬚ • 2 ↓
Orange juice (pints)	2			8
Pineapple juice (pints)	5		15	

2 • 5   ⬚ • 5   4 • 5

So, $\frac{2}{5}$, _____, _____, and _____ are equivalent ratios.

🔑 Another Way Multiply or divide by a form of one.

Write two equivalent ratios for $\frac{6}{8}$.

Ⓐ Multiply by a form of one.

Multiply the numerator and denominator by the same number.

$$\frac{6 \cdot \square}{8 \cdot \square} = \frac{\square}{\square}$$

> ⚠ **ERROR Alert**
>
> Be sure to multiply or divide the numerator and the denominator by the same number.

Ⓑ Divide by a form of one.

Divide the numerator and denominator by the same number.

$$\frac{6 \div \square}{8 \div \square} = \frac{\square}{\square}$$

So, $\frac{6}{8}$, _____, and _____ are equivalent ratios.

- **MATHEMATICAL PRACTICE ⑥** **Compare** Explain how ratios are similar to fractions. Explain how they are different.

_____

_____

Name _____

Write two equivalent ratios.

1. Use a multiplication table to write two ratios that are equivalent to $\frac{4}{7}$.

   Find the rows that show $\frac{4}{7}$.

   Find columns that show equivalent ratios. $\frac{4}{7} =$ _____ $=$ _____

 2.

3		
7		

3.

5		
2		

4.

	2	
	10	

5. $\frac{4}{5}$

_____

 6. $\frac{12}{30}$

_____

7. $\frac{2}{9}$

_____

 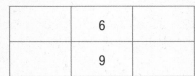

MATHEMATICAL PRACTICES ⑤

Use Tools Explain how the multiplication table helps you find equivalent ratios.

On Your Own

Write two equivalent ratios.

8.

9		
8		

9.

5		
4		

10.

	6	
	9	

11. $\frac{8}{7}$

_____

12. $\frac{2}{6}$

_____

13. $\frac{4}{11}$

_____

Determine whether the ratios are equivalent.

14. $\frac{2}{3}$ and $\frac{8}{12}$

_____

15. $\frac{8}{10}$ and $\frac{6}{10}$

_____

16. $\frac{16}{60}$ and $\frac{4}{15}$

_____

17. $\frac{3}{14}$ and $\frac{8}{28}$

_____

Problem Solving • Applications

×	1	2	3	4	5	6	7	8	9
1	1	2	3	4	5	6	7	8	9
2	2	4	6	8	10	12	14	16	18
3	3	6	9	12	15	18	21	24	27
4	4	8	12	16	20	24	28	32	36
5	5	10	15	20	25	30	35	40	45
6	6	12	18	24	30	36	42	48	54
7	7	14	21	28	35	42	49	56	63
8	8	16	24	32	40	48	56	64	72
9	9	18	27	36	45	54	63	72	81

Use the multiplication table for 18 and 19.

18. In Keith's baseball games this year, the ratio of times he has gotten on base to the times he has been at bat is $\frac{4}{14}$. Write two ratios that are equivalent to $\frac{4}{14}$.

_____

19. **THINK SMARTER** **Pose a Problem** Use the multiplication table to write a new problem involving equivalent ratios. Then solve the problem.

_____

_____

_____

20. **MATHEMATICAL PRACTICE 1** **Describe** how to write an equivalent ratio for $\frac{9}{27}$ without using a multiplication table.

_____

_____

_____

21. **GO DEEPER** Write a ratio that is equivalent to $\frac{6}{9}$ and $\frac{16}{24}$.

_____

22. **THINK SMARTER** Determine whether each ratio is equivalent to $\frac{1}{3}$, $\frac{5}{10}$, or $\frac{3}{5}$. Write the ratio in the correct box.

| $\frac{2}{4}$ | $\frac{3}{9}$ | $\frac{7}{21}$ | $\frac{18}{30}$ | $\frac{10}{30}$ | $\frac{6}{10}$ | $\frac{1}{2}$ | $\frac{8}{16}$ |

$\frac{1}{3}$	$\frac{5}{10}$	$\frac{3}{5}$

Equivalent Ratios and Multiplication Tables

Common Core COMMON CORE STANDARD—6.RP.A.3a
Understand ratio concepts and use ratio reasoning to solve problems.

Write two equivalent ratios.

1. Use a multiplication table to write two ratios that are equivalent to $\frac{5}{3}$.

$$\frac{5}{3} = \frac{10}{6}, \frac{15}{9}$$

2.

6		
7		

3.

3		
2		

4. $\frac{6}{8}$

_____

5. $\frac{11}{1}$

_____

Determine whether the ratios are equivalent.

6. $\frac{2}{3}$ and $\frac{5}{6}$

7. $\frac{5}{10}$ and $\frac{1}{6}$

8. $\frac{8}{3}$ and $\frac{32}{12}$

9. $\frac{9}{12}$ and $\frac{3}{4}$

_____ _____ _____ _____

Problem Solving Real World

10. Tristan uses 7 stars and 9 diamonds to make a design. Write two ratios that are equivalent to $\frac{7}{9}$.

11. There are 12 girls and 16 boys in Javier's math class. There are 26 girls and 14 boys in Javier's choir class. Are the ratios of girls to boys in the two classes equivalent? Explain.

_____ _____

12. **WRITE** ▸ *Math* Explain how to determine whether two ratios are equivalent.

_____

_____

_____

Lesson Check (6.RP.A.3a)

1. A pancake recipe calls for 4 cups of flour and 3 cups milk. Does a recipe calling for 2 cups flour and 1.5 cups milk use the same ratio of flour to milk?

2. A bracelet is made of 14 red beads and 19 gold beads. A necklace is made of 84 red beads and 133 gold beads. Do the two pieces of jewelry have the same ratio of red beads to gold beads?

Spiral Review (6.NS.A.1, 6.NS.B.4, 6.NS.C.6c)

3. Scissors come in packages of 3. Glue sticks come in packages of 10. Martha wants to buy the same number of each. What is the fewest glue sticks Martha can buy?

4. Cole had $\frac{3}{4}$ hour of free time before dinner. He spent $\frac{2}{3}$ of the time playing the guitar. How long did he play the guitar?

5. Delia has $3\frac{5}{8}$ yards of ribbon. About how many $\frac{1}{4}$-yard-long pieces can she cut?

6. Which point is located at ⁻1.1?

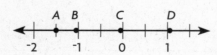

FOR MORE PRACTICE GO TO THE Personal Math Trainer

Name _____

Problem Solving •
Use Tables to Compare Ratios

Essential Question How can you use the strategy *find a pattern* to help you compare ratios?

 Common Core Ratios and Proportional Relationships—6.RP.A.3a

MATHEMATICAL PRACTICES
MP1, MP5, MP7

Unlock the Problem

A paint store makes rose-pink paint by mixing 3 parts red paint to 8 parts white paint. A clerk mixes 4 parts red paint to 7 parts white paint. Did the clerk mix the paint correctly to make rose-pink paint? Use tables of equivalent ratios to support your answer.

Use the graphic organizer to help you solve the problem.

Read the Problem

What do I need to find?	**What information do I need to use?**	**How will I use the information?**
I need to find whether the ratio used by the clerk is _____ to the ratio for rose-pink paint.	I need to use the rose-pink paint ratio and the ratio used by the clerk.	I will make tables of equivalent ratios to compare the ratios _____ to _____ and _____ to _____.

Solve the Problem

Rose-Pink Paint				
Parts Red	3	6	9	12
Parts White	8			

Clerk's Paint Mixture				
Parts Red	4			
Parts White	7	14	21	28

Look for a pattern to determine whether the ratios in the first table are equivalent to the ratios in the second table.

Think: The number 12 appears in the first row of both tables.

$\dfrac{12}{}$ is/is not equivalent to $\dfrac{12}{}$.

The ratios have the same numerator and _____ denominators.

So, the clerk _____ mix the paint correctly.

Math Talk

MATHEMATICAL PRACTICES ①

Evaluate How can you check that your answer is correct?

Chapter 4   229

🔒 Try Another Problem

In Amy's art class, the ratio of brushes to students is 6 to 4. In Traci's art class, the ratio of brushes to students is 9 to 6. Is the ratio of brushes to students in Amy's class equivalent to the ratio of brushes to students in Traci's class? Use tables of equivalent ratios to support your answer.

Read the Problem

What do I need to find?	What information do I need to use?	How will I use the information?

Solve the Problem

So, the ratio of brushes to students in Amy's class is/is not equivalent to the ratio of brushes to students in Traci's class.

1. **MATHEMATICAL PRACTICE ⑤ Use Patterns** Explain how you used a pattern to determine whether the ratios in the two tables are equivalent.

_____

_____

_____

2. Tell how writing the ratios in simplest form can help you justify your answer.

_____

Share and Show MATH BOARD

1. In Jawan's school, 4 out of 10 students chose basketball as a sport they like to watch, and 3 out of 5 students chose football. Is the ratio of students who chose basketball (4 to 10) equivalent to the ratio of students who chose football (3 to 5)?

First, make tables to show the ratios.

Basketball				

Football				

Next, compare the ratios in the tables. Find a ratio in the first table that has the same numerator as a ratio in the second table.

$\dfrac{12}{}$ _____ equivalent to $\dfrac{12}{}$.

So, the ratios _____ equivalent.

2. **THINK SMARTER** What if 20 out of 50 students chose baseball as a sport they like to watch? Is this ratio equivalent to the ratio for either basketball or football? Explain.

_____

_____

_____

3. **MATHEMATICAL PRACTICE 7 Look for Structure** The table shows the results of the quizzes Hannah took in one week. Did Hannah get the same score on her math and science quizzes? Explain.

_____

_____

Hannah's Quiz Results	
Subject	**Questions Correct**
Social Studies	4 out of 5
Math	8 out of 10
Science	3 out of 4
English	10 out of 12

4. Did Hannah get the same score on the quizzes in any of her classes? Explain.

_____

_____

On Your Own

5. **GO DEEPER** For every $10 that Julie makes, she saves $3. For every $15 Liam makes, he saves $6. Is Julie's ratio of money saved to money earned equivalent to Liam's ratio of money saved to money earned?

_____

_____

6. **THINK SMARTER** A florist offers three different bouquets of tulips and irises. The list shows the ratios of tulips to irises in each bouquet. Determine the bouquets that have equivalent ratios.

_____

_____

Bouquet Ratios

Spring Mix

4 tulips to 6 irises

Morning Melody

9 tulips to 12 irises

Splash of Sun

10 tulips to 15 irises

7. The ratio of boys to girls in a school's soccer club is 3 to 5. The ratio of boys to girls in the school's chess club is 13 to 15. Is the ratio of boys to girls in the soccer club equivalent to the ratio of boys to girls in the chess club? Explain.

_____

_____

 **WRITE** ▸ *Math*
Show Your Work

8. **MATHEMATICAL PRACTICE ①** **Analyze** Thad, Joey, and Mia ran in a race. The finishing times were 4.56 minutes, 3.33 minutes, and 4.75 minutes. Thad did not finish last. Mia had the fastest time. What was each runner's time?

_____

_____

9. **THINK SMARTER** Fernando donates $2 to a local charity organization for every $15 he earns. Cleo donates $4 for every $17 she earns. Is Fernando's ratio of money donated to money earned equivalent to Cleo's ratio of money donated to money earned? Explain.

_____

_____

Problem Solving • Use Tables to Compare Ratios

COMMON CORE STANDARD—6.RP.A.3a
Understand ratio concepts and use ratio reasoning to solve problems.

Read each problem and solve.

1. Sarah asked some friends about their favorite colors. She found that 4 out of 6 people prefer blue, and 8 out of 12 people prefer green. Is the ratio of friends who chose blue to the total asked equivalent to the ratio of friends who chose green to the total asked?

Blue				
Friends who chose blue	4	8	12	16
Total asked	6	12	18	24

Green				
Friends who chose green	8	16	24	32
Total asked	12	24	36	48

Yes, $\frac{4}{6}$ is equivalent to $\frac{8}{12}$.

2. Lisa and Tim make necklaces. Lisa uses 5 red beads for every 3 yellow beads. Tim uses 9 red beads for every 6 yellow beads. Is the ratio of red beads to yellow beads in Lisa's necklace equivalent to the ratio in Tim's necklace?

_____

3. Mitch scored 4 out of 5 on a quiz. Demetri scored 8 out of 10 on a quiz. Did Mitch and Demetri get equivalent scores?

_____

4. **WRITE** ▸*Math* Use tables to show which of these ratios are equivalent: $\frac{4}{6}$, $\frac{10}{25}$, and $\frac{6}{15}$.

_____

_____

_____

Lesson Check (6.RP.A.3a)

1. Mrs. Sahd distributes pencils and paper to students in the ratio of 2 pencils to 10 sheets of paper. Three of these ratios are equivalent to $\frac{2}{10}$. Which one is NOT equivalent?

$\frac{1}{5}$ $\frac{7}{15}$ $\frac{4}{20}$ $\frac{8}{40}$

2. Keith uses 18 cherries and 3 peaches to make a pie filling. Lena uses an equivalent ratio of cherries to peaches when she makes pie filling. Can Lena use a ratio of 21 cherries to 6 peaches? Explain.

Spiral Review (6.RP.A.1, 6.NS.A.1, 6.NS.C.7a, 6.NS.C.8)

3. What is the quotient $\frac{3}{20} \div \frac{7}{10}$?

4. Which of these numbers is greater than ⁻2.25 but less than ⁻1?

1   ⁻1.5   0   ⁻2.5

5. Alicia plots a point at (0, 5) and (0, ⁻2). What is the distance between the points?

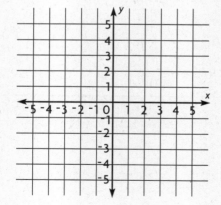

6. Morton sees these stickers at a craft store. What is the ratio of clouds to suns?

FOR MORE PRACTICE
GO TO THE
Personal Math Trainer

Use Equivalent Ratios

Essential Question How can you use tables to solve problems involving equivalent ratios?

Common Core **Ratios and Proportional Relationships—6.RP.A.3a**
MATHEMATICAL PRACTICES
MP2, MP3, MP8

🔑 Unlock the Problem (Real World)

In warm weather, the Anderson family likes to spend time on the family's boat. The boat uses 2 gallons of gas to travel 12 miles on the lake. How much gas would the boat use to travel 48 miles?

What are you asked to find?

_____

_____

🔒 **Solve by finding equivalent ratios.**

Let ▪ represent the unknown number of gallons.

$$\dfrac{\text{gallons}}{\text{miles}} \rightarrow \dfrac{2}{12} = \dfrac{\blacksquare}{48} \leftarrow \dfrac{\text{gallons}}{\text{miles}}$$

Make a table of equivalent ratios.

	Original ratio	2 · 2 ↓	▪ · 2 ↓	▪ · 2 ↓
Gas used (gallons)	2		6	
Distance (miles)	12	24		48

▪ · 12   3 · 12   ▪ · 12

The ratios $\frac{2}{12}$ and _____ are equivalent ratios,

so $\dfrac{2}{12} = \dfrac{\blacksquare}{48}$.

So, the boat will use _____ gallons of gas to travel 48 miles.

• What if the boat uses 14 gallons of gas? Explain how you can use equivalent ratios to find the number of miles the boat travels when it uses 14 gallons of gas.

_____

_____

_____

🔑 Example Use equivalent ratios to find the unknown value.

Ⓐ $\frac{3}{4} = \frac{\blacksquare}{20}$

Use common denominators to write equivalent ratios.

_____ is a multiple of 4, so _____ is a common denominator.

Multiply the _____ and denominator by _____ to write the ratios using a common denominator.

The _____ are the same, so the _____ are equal to each other.

$$\frac{3}{4} = \frac{\blacksquare}{20}$$

$$\frac{3 \times \blacksquare}{4 \times \blacksquare} = \frac{\blacksquare}{20}$$

$$\frac{\blacksquare}{20} = \frac{\blacksquare}{20}$$

So, the unknown value is _____ and $\frac{3}{4} = \frac{\square}{20}$.

Check your answer by making a table of equivalent ratios.

Original ratio $\blacksquare$ •3 $\blacksquare$ •3 $\blacksquare$ •3 $\blacksquare$ •3

3	6			
4	8			

$\blacksquare$ •4 $\blacksquare$ •4 $\blacksquare$ •4 $\blacksquare$ •4

Ⓑ $\frac{56}{42} = \frac{8}{\blacksquare}$

Write an equivalent ratio with 8 in the numerator.

Think: Divide 56 by _____ to get 8.

So, divide the denominator by _____ as well.

The _____ are the same, so the _____ are equal to each other.

$$\frac{56}{42} = \frac{8}{\blacksquare}$$

$$\frac{56 \div \blacksquare}{42 \div \blacksquare} = \frac{8}{\blacksquare}$$

$$\frac{8}{\blacksquare} = \frac{8}{\blacksquare}$$

So, the unknown value is _____ and $\frac{56}{42} = \frac{8}{\square}$.

Check your answer by making a table of equivalent ratios.

Original ratio $\blacksquare$ •8 $\blacksquare$ •8 $\blacksquare$ •8 $\blacksquare$ •8 $\blacksquare$ •8 $\blacksquare$ •8

8	16				
6	12				

$\blacksquare$ •6 $\blacksquare$ •6 $\blacksquare$ •6 $\blacksquare$ •6 $\blacksquare$ •6 $\blacksquare$ •6

Math Talk

MATHEMATICAL PRACTICES 8

Use Repeated Reasoning
Give an example of two equivalent ratios. Explain how you know that they are equivalent.

Name _____

Use equivalent ratios to find the unknown value.

1. $\dfrac{\blacksquare}{10} = \dfrac{4}{5}$

   $\dfrac{\blacksquare}{10} = \dfrac{4 \cdot}{5 \cdot }$

   $\dfrac{\blacksquare}{10} = \dfrac{\blacksquare}{10}$

   So, the unknown value is _____.

2. $\dfrac{18}{24} = \dfrac{6}{\blacksquare}$

   $\dfrac{18 \div }{24 \div } = \dfrac{6}{\blacksquare}$

   $\dfrac{6}{\blacksquare} = \dfrac{6}{\blacksquare}$

   So, the unknown value is _____.

3. $\dfrac{3}{6} = \dfrac{15}{\blacksquare}$

4. $\dfrac{\blacksquare}{5} = \dfrac{8}{10}$

5. $\dfrac{7}{4} = \dfrac{\blacksquare}{12}$

6. $\dfrac{10}{\blacksquare} = \dfrac{40}{12}$

_____ | _____ | _____ | _____

Math Talk

MATHEMATICAL PRACTICES ❸

Apply Explain whether you can always find an equivalent ratio by subtracting the same number from the numerator and denominator. Give an example to support your answer.

On Your Own

Use equivalent ratios to find the unknown value.

7. $\dfrac{2}{6} = \dfrac{\blacksquare}{30}$

8. $\dfrac{5}{\blacksquare} = \dfrac{55}{110}$

9. $\dfrac{3}{9} = \dfrac{9}{\blacksquare}$

10. $\dfrac{\blacksquare}{6} = \dfrac{16}{24}$

_____ | _____ | _____ | _____

11. Mavis walks 3 miles in 45 minutes. How many minutes will it take Mavis to walk 9 miles?

12. **GO DEEPER** The ratio of boys to girls in a choir is 3 to 8. There are 32 girls in the choir. How many members are in the choir?

_____

13. **MATHEMATICAL PRACTICE ❷** **Use Reasoning** Is the unknown value in $\dfrac{2}{3} = \dfrac{\blacksquare}{18}$ the same as the unknown value in $\dfrac{3}{2} = \dfrac{18}{\blacksquare}$? Explain.

_____

Problem Solving • Applications

Solve by finding an equivalent ratio.

14. It takes 8 minutes for Sue to make 2 laps around the go-kart track. How many laps can Sue complete in 24 minutes?

_____

15. GO DEEPER The width of Jay's original photo is 8 inches. The length of the original photo is 10 inches. He prints a smaller version that has an equivalent ratio of width to length. The width of the smaller version is 4 inches less than the width of the original. What is the length of the smaller version?

_____

16. Ariel bought 3 raffle tickets for $5. How many tickets could Ariel buy for $15?

_____

17. THINK SMARTER **What's the Error?** Greg used the steps shown to find the unknown value. Describe his error and give the correct solution.

$$\frac{2}{6} = \frac{\blacksquare}{12}$$

$$\frac{2+6}{6+6} = \frac{\blacksquare}{12}$$

$$\frac{8}{12} = \frac{\blacksquare}{12}$$

The unknown value is 8.

_____

_____

_____

18. THINK SMARTER Courtney bought 3 maps for $10. Use the table of equivalent ratios to find how many maps she can buy for $30.

3	6	
10	20	30

Use Equivalent Ratios

Common Core

COMMON CORE STANDARD—6.RP.A.3a
Understand ratio concepts and use ratio reasoning to solve problems.

Use equivalent ratios to find the unknown value.

1. $\dfrac{4}{10} = \dfrac{\blacksquare}{40}$

$\dfrac{4 \times 4}{10 \times 4} = \dfrac{\blacksquare}{40}$

$\dfrac{16}{40} = \dfrac{\blacksquare}{40}$

$\blacksquare = 16$

2. $\dfrac{3}{24} = \dfrac{33}{\blacksquare}$

3. $\dfrac{7}{\blacksquare} = \dfrac{21}{27}$

4. $\dfrac{\blacksquare}{9} = \dfrac{12}{54}$

5. $\dfrac{3}{2} = \dfrac{12}{\blacksquare}$

6. $\dfrac{4}{5} = \dfrac{\blacksquare}{40}$

7. $\dfrac{\blacksquare}{2} = \dfrac{45}{30}$

8. $\dfrac{45}{\blacksquare} = \dfrac{5}{6}$

Problem Solving · Real World

9. Honeybees produce 7 pounds of honey for every 1 pound of beeswax they produce. Use equivalent ratios to find how many pounds of honey are produced when 25 pounds of beeswax are produced.

10. A 3-ounce serving of tuna provides 21 grams of protein. Use equivalent ratios to find how many grams of protein are in 9 ounces of tuna.

11. **WRITE** ▸*Math* Explain how using equivalent ratios is like adding fractions with unlike denominators.

_____

_____

_____

_____

Lesson Check (6.RP.A.3a)

1. Jaron paid $2.70 for 6 juice boxes. How much should Jaron expect to pay for 18 juice boxes?

2. A certain shade of orange paint is made by mixing 3 quarts of red paint with 2 quarts of yellow paint. To make more paint of the same shade, how many quarts of yellow paint should be mixed with 6 quarts of red paint?

Spiral Review (6.RP.A.3a, 6.NS.A.1, 6.NS.C.7c, 6.NS.C.8)

3. What is the quotient $2\frac{4}{5} \div 1\frac{1}{3}$?

4. What is the absolute value of $^-2\frac{2}{3}$?

5. On a map, a clothing store is located at $(^-2, ^-3)$. A seafood restaurant is located 6 units to the right of the clothing store. What are the coordinates of the restaurant?

6. Marisol plans to make 9 mini-sandwiches for every 2 people attending her party. Write a ratio that is equivalent to Marisol's ratio.

FOR MORE PRACTICE
GO TO THE
Personal Math Trainer

✓ Mid-Chapter Checkpoint

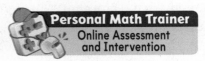

Personal Math Trainer
Online Assessment
and Intervention

Vocabulary

Choose the best term from the box to complete the sentence.

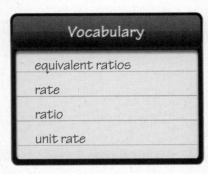

Vocabulary
equivalent ratios
rate
ratio
unit rate

1. A _____ is a rate that makes a comparison to 1 unit. (p. 218)

2. Two ratios that name the same comparison are

   _____. (p. 223)

Concepts and Skills

3. Write the ratio of red circles to blue squares. (6.RP.A.1)

   _____

Write the ratio in two different ways. (6.RP.A.1)

4. 8 to 12

   _____

5. 7:2

   _____

6. $\frac{5}{9}$

   _____

7. 11 to 3

   _____

Write two equivalent ratios. (6.RP.A.3a)

8. $\frac{2}{7}$

   _____

9. $\frac{6}{5}$

   _____

10. $\frac{9}{12}$

   _____

11. $\frac{18}{6}$

   _____

Find the unknown value. (6.RP.A.3a)

12. $\frac{15}{\blacksquare} = \frac{5}{10}$

13. $\frac{\blacksquare}{9} = \frac{12}{3}$

14. $\frac{48}{16} = \frac{\blacksquare}{8}$

15. $\frac{9}{36} = \frac{3}{\blacksquare}$

16. There are 36 students in the chess club, 40 students in the drama club, and 24 students in the film club. What is the ratio of students in the drama club to students in the film club? (6.RP.A.3a)

_____

17. A trail mix has 4 cups of raisins, 3 cups of dates, 6 cups of peanuts, and 2 cups of cashews. Which ingredients are in the same ratio as cashews to raisins? (6.RP.A.3a)

_____

18. There are 32 adults and 20 children at a school play. What is the ratio of children to people at the school play? (6.RP.A.3a)

_____

19. GO DEEPER Sonya got 8 out of 10 questions right on a quiz. She got the same score on a quiz that had 20 questions. How many questions did Sonya get right on the second quiz? How many questions did she get wrong on the second quiz? (6.RP.A.3a)

_____

242

Name _____

Find Unit Rates

Essential Question How can you use unit rates to make comparisons?

Common Core
Ratios and Proportional Relationships—6.RP.A.2 *Also 6.RP.A.3b*
MATHEMATICAL PRACTICES
MP2, MP3, MP6, MP8

Unlock the Problem

The star fruit, or carambola, is the fruit of a tree that is native to Indonesia, India, and Sri Lanka. Slices of the fruit are in the shape of a five-pointed star. Lara paid $9.60 for 16 ounces of star fruit. Find the price of 1 ounce of star fruit.

Recall that a unit rate makes a comparison to 1 unit. You can find a unit rate by dividing the numerator and denominator by the number in the denominator.

- Underline the sentence that tells you what you are trying to find.
- Circle the numbers you need to use to solve the problem.

 Write the unit rate for the price of star fruit.

Write a ratio that compares _____

to _____.

Divide the numerator and denominator by

the number in the _____.

$$\frac{price}{weight} \to \frac{\$ \rule{1cm}{0.15mm}}{\rule{1cm}{0.15mm} \text{ oz}}$$

$$\frac{\$9.60 \div \rule{0.8cm}{0.15mm}}{16 \text{ oz} \div \rule{0.8cm}{0.15mm}}$$

$$\frac{\$ \rule{1cm}{0.15mm}}{1 \text{ oz}}$$

So, the unit rate is _____. The price is _____ per ounce.

 Math Talk

MATHEMATICAL PRACTICES ⑥

Explain What is the difference between a ratio and a rate?

1. **MATHEMATICAL PRACTICE ⑥** **Explain** why the unit rate is equivalent to the original rate.

_____

_____

2. **MATHEMATICAL PRACTICE ③** **Make Arguments** Explain a way to convince others that you found the unit rate correctly.

_____

_____

🔐 Example

A During migration, a hummingbird can fly 210 miles in 7 hours, and a goose can fly 165 miles in 3 hours. Which bird flies at a faster rate?

Write the rate for each bird.

Hummingbird: $\dfrac{\boxed{}\text{ miles}}{7\text{ hours}}$　　　Goose: $\dfrac{165\text{ miles}}{\boxed{}\text{ hours}}$

Write the unit rates.

$\dfrac{210\text{ mi} \div \boxed{}}{7\text{ hr} \div \boxed{}}$　　　$\dfrac{165\text{ mi} \div \boxed{}}{3\text{ hr} \div \boxed{}}$

$\dfrac{\boxed{}\text{ mi}}{1\text{ hr}}$　　　$\dfrac{\boxed{}\text{ mi}}{1\text{ hr}}$

Compare the unit rates.　　_____ miles per hour is faster than _____ miles per hour.

So, the _____ flies at a faster rate.

B A 64-ounce bottle of apple juice costs $5.76. A 15-ounce bottle of apple juice costs $1.80. Which item costs less per ounce?

Write the rate for each bottle.

64-ounce bottle: $\dfrac{\boxed{}}{64\text{ ounces}}$　　　15-ounce bottle: $\dfrac{\boxed{}}{\boxed{}\text{ ounces}}$

Write the unit rates.

$\dfrac{\boxed{} \div \boxed{}}{64\text{ oz} \div \boxed{}}$　　　$\dfrac{\$1.80 \div \boxed{}}{\boxed{}\text{ oz} \div \boxed{}}$

$\dfrac{\boxed{}}{1\text{ oz}}$　　　$\dfrac{\boxed{}}{1\text{ oz}}$

Compare the unit rates.　　_____ per ounce is less expensive than _____ per ounce.

So, the _____ -ounce bottle costs less per ounce.

Try This! At one grocery store, a dozen eggs cost $1.20. At another store, $1\frac{1}{2}$ dozen eggs cost $2.16. Which is the better buy?

Store 1:　　　　　　　　　　　　　　Store 2:

The unit price is lower at Store _____ , so a dozen eggs for _____ is the better buy.

Name _____

 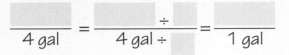
Write the rate as a fraction. Then find the unit rate.

1. Sara drove 72 miles on 4 gallons of gas.

$$\frac{}{4\ gal} = \frac{\div}{4\ gal \div } = \frac{}{1\ gal}$$

2. Dean paid $27.00 for 4 movie tickets.

_____

3. Amy and Mai have to read *Bud, Not Buddy* for a class. Amy reads 20 pages in 2 days. Mai reads 35 pages in 3 days. Who reads at a faster rate?

_____

4. An online music store offers 5 downloads for $6.25. Another online music store offers 12 downloads for $17.40. Which store offers the better deal?

_____

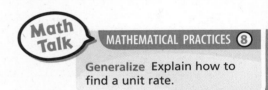

Math Talk MATHEMATICAL PRACTICES ⑧

Generalize Explain how to find a unit rate.

On Your Own

Write the rate as a fraction. Then find the unit rate.

5. A company packed 108 items in 12 boxes.

_____

6. There are 112 students for 14 teachers.

_____

7. **GO DEEPER** Geoff charges $27 for 3 hours of swimming lessons. Anne charges $31 for 4 hours. How much more does Geoff charge per hour than Anne?

_____

8. **MATHEMATICAL PRACTICE ⑥ Compare** One florist made 16 bouquets in 5 hours. A second florist made 40 bouquets in 12 hours. Which florist makes bouquets at a faster rate?

_____

Tell which rate is faster by comparing unit rates.

9. $\frac{160\ mi}{2\ hr}$ and $\frac{210\ mi}{3\ hr}$

10. $\frac{270\ ft}{9\ min}$ and $\frac{180\ ft}{9\ min}$

11. $\frac{250\ m}{10\ s}$ and $\frac{120\ m}{4\ s}$

_____

Unlock the Problem Real World

12. **THINK SMARTER** Ryan wants to buy treats for his puppy. If Ryan wants to buy the treats that cost the least per pack, which treat should he buy? Explain.

a. What do you need to find?

_____

_____

Cost of Dog Treats		
Name	**Cost**	**Number of Packs**
Pup Bites	$5.76	4
Doggie Treats	$7.38	6
Pupster Snacks	$7.86	6
Nutri-Biscuits	$9.44	8

b. Find the price per pack for each treat.

_____

_____

_____

_____

_____

_____

c. Complete the sentences.
The treat with the highest price per pack is

_____.

The treat with the lowest price per pack is

_____.

Ryan should buy _____

because _____

_____

_____.

13. **MATHEMATICAL PRACTICE ② Reason Abstractly** What information do you need to consider in order to decide whether one product is a better deal than another? When might the lower unit rate not be the best choice? Explain.

_____

_____

_____

_____

_____

14. **THINK SMARTER** Select the cars that get a higher mileage per gallon of gas than a car that gets 25 miles per gallon. Mark all that apply.

○ Car A: 22 miles per 1 gallon

○ Car B: 56 miles per 2 gallons

○ Car C: 81 miles per 3 gallons

○ Car D: 51 miles per 3 gallons

Find Unit Rates

Common Core

COMMON CORE STANDARD—6.RP.A.2
Understand ratio concepts and use ratio reasoning to solve problems.

Write the rate as a fraction. Then find the unit rate.

1. A wheel rotates through 1,800° in 5 revolutions.

$$\frac{1{,}800°}{5 \text{ revolutions}}$$

$$\frac{1{,}800° \div 5}{5 \text{ revolutions} \div 5} = \frac{360°}{1 \text{ revolution}}$$

2. There are 312 cards in 6 decks of playing cards.

_____

3. Bana ran 18.6 miles of a marathon in 3 hours.

_____

4. Cameron paid $30.16 for 8 pounds of almonds.

_____

Compare unit rates.

5. An online game company offers a package that includes 2 games for $11.98. They also offer a package that includes 5 games for $24.95. Which package is a better deal?

_____

6. At a track meet, Samma finished the 200-meter race in 25.98 seconds. Tom finished the 100-meter race in 12.54 seconds. Which runner ran at a faster average rate?

_____

Problem Solving (Real World)

7. Sylvio's flight is scheduled to travel 1,792 miles in 3.5 hours. At what average rate will the plane have to travel to complete the trip on time?

_____

8. Rachel bought 2 pounds of apples and 3 pounds of peaches for a total of $10.45. The apples and peaches cost the same amount per pound. What was the unit rate?

_____

9. **WRITE** ▸*Math* Write a word problem that involves comparing unit rates.

_____

_____

Lesson Check (6.RP.A.2, 6.RP.A.3b)

1. Cran–Soy trail mix costs $2.99 for 5 ounces, Raisin–Nuts mix costs $3.41 for 7 ounces, Lots of Cashews mix costs $7.04 for 8 ounces, and Nuts for You mix costs $2.40 for 6 ounces. List the trail mix brands in order from the least expensive to the most expensive.

2. Aaron's heart beats 166 times in 120 seconds. Callie's heart beats 88 times in 60 seconds. Emma's heart beats 48 times in 30 seconds. Galen's heart beats 22 times in 15 seconds. Which two students' heart rates are equivalent?

Spiral Review (6.RP.A.1, 6.RP.A.3a, 6.NS.A.1, 6.NS.7d)

3. Courtlynn combines $\frac{7}{8}$ cup sour cream with $\frac{1}{2}$ cup cream cheese. She then divides the mixture between 2 bowls. How much mixture does Courtlynn put in each bowl?

4. Write a comparison using $<$ or $>$ to show the relationship between $\left| \frac{-2}{3} \right|$ and $\frac{-5}{6}$.

5. There are 18 tires on one truck. How many tires are on 3 trucks of the same type?

6. Write two ratios that are equivalent to $\frac{5}{6}$.

FOR MORE PRACTICE
GO TO THE
Personal Math Trainer

Name _____

Use Unit Rates

Essential Question How can you solve problems using unit rates?

 Ratios and Proportional Relationships—6.RP.A.3b
MATHEMATICAL PRACTICES
MP1, MP3, MP5

Unlock the Problem

The Champie family is traveling from Arizona to Texas. On the first part of the trip, they drove 500 miles in 10 hours. If they continue driving at the same rate, how many hours will it take them to drive 750 miles?

You can use equivalent ratios to find the number of hours it will take the Champie family to drive 750 miles. You may need to find a unit rate before you can write equivalent ratios.

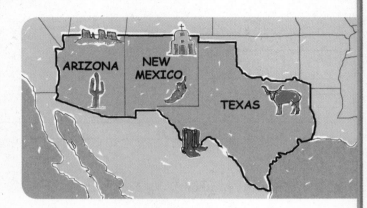

Find equivalent ratios by using a unit rate.

Write ratios that compare miles to hours.

750 is not a multiple of 500.

Write the known ratio as a unit rate.

Write an equivalent rate by multiplying the

_____ and _____ by the same value.

Think: Multiply 50 by _____ to get 750.

So, multiply the denominator by _____ also.

The _____ are the same, so the

_____ are equal to each other.

The unknown value is _____.

So, it will take the family _____ hours to drive 750 miles.

$$\dfrac{\text{miles}}{\text{hours}} \rightarrow \dfrac{500}{10} = \dfrac{750}{\blacksquare} \leftarrow \dfrac{\text{miles}}{\text{hours}}$$

$$\dfrac{500 \div \boxed{}}{10 \div 10} = \dfrac{750}{\blacksquare}$$

$$\dfrac{\boxed{}}{1} = \dfrac{750}{\blacksquare}$$

$$\dfrac{50 \cdot \boxed{}}{1 \cdot \boxed{}} = \dfrac{750}{\blacksquare}$$

$$\dfrac{\boxed{}}{15} = \dfrac{750}{\blacksquare}$$

 Math Talk MATHEMATICAL PRACTICES ①

Analyze Why did you need to find a unit rate first?

🔑 Example

Kenyon earns $105 for mowing 3 lawns. How much would Kenyon earn for mowing 10 lawns?

STEP 1 Draw a bar model to represent the situation:

$105

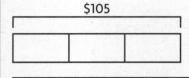

$?

STEP 2 Solve the problem.

The model shows that 3 units represent $105.

You need to find the value represented by _____ units.

Write a unit rate:

1 unit represents $_____.

$$\frac{\$105}{3} = \frac{\$105 \div \boxed{}}{3 \div \boxed{}} = \frac{\$\boxed{}}{1}$$

10 units are equal to 10 times 1 unit,

so 10 units = 10 × $_____.   10 × $_____ = $_____

So, Kenyon will earn $_____ for mowing 10 lawns.

Try This!

Last summer, Kenyon earned $210 for mowing 7 lawns. How much did he earn for mowing 5 lawns last summer?

STEP 1 Draw a bar model to represent the situation.

STEP 2 Solve the problem.

Name _____

Use a unit rate to find the unknown value.

1. $\dfrac{10}{\blacksquare} = \dfrac{6}{3}$

$\dfrac{10}{\blacksquare} = \dfrac{6 \div \blacksquare}{3 \div 3}$

$\dfrac{10}{\blacksquare} = \dfrac{\blacksquare}{1}$

$\dfrac{10}{\blacksquare} = \dfrac{2 \cdot \blacksquare}{1 \cdot \blacksquare}$

$\dfrac{10}{\blacksquare} = \dfrac{10}{\blacksquare}$

$\blacksquare = \underline{\hspace{1cm}}$

2. $\dfrac{6}{8} = \dfrac{\blacksquare}{20}$

$\dfrac{6 \div \blacksquare}{8 \div 8} = \dfrac{\blacksquare}{20}$

$\dfrac{\blacksquare}{1} = \dfrac{\blacksquare}{20}$

$\dfrac{0.75 \cdot 20}{1 \cdot \blacksquare} = \dfrac{\blacksquare}{20}$

$\dfrac{\blacksquare}{20} = \dfrac{\blacksquare}{20}$

$\blacksquare = \underline{\hspace{1cm}}$

On Your Own

Use a unit rate to find the unknown value.

3. $\dfrac{40}{8} = \dfrac{45}{\blacksquare}$

4. $\dfrac{42}{14} = \dfrac{\blacksquare}{5}$

5. $\dfrac{\blacksquare}{2} = \dfrac{56}{8}$

6. $\dfrac{\blacksquare}{4} = \dfrac{26}{13}$

_____ _____ _____ _____

Practice: Copy and Solve Draw a bar model to find the unknown value.

7. $\dfrac{4}{32} = \dfrac{9}{\blacksquare}$

8. $\dfrac{9}{3} = \dfrac{\blacksquare}{4}$

9. $\dfrac{\blacksquare}{14} = \dfrac{9}{7}$

10. $\dfrac{3}{\blacksquare} = \dfrac{2}{1.25}$

11. **MATHEMATICAL PRACTICE ⑤ Communicate** Explain how to find an unknown value in a ratio by using a unit rate.

_____

_____

_____

12. **GO DEEPER** Savannah is tiling her kitchen floor. She bought 8 cases of tile for $192. She realizes she bought too much tile and returns 2 unopened cases to the store. What was her final cost for tile?

_____

Problem Solving • Applications 〔Real World〕

Pose a Problem

13. ｛THINK SMARTER｝ Josie runs a T-shirt printing company. The table shows the length and width of four sizes of T-shirts. The measurements of each size T-shirt form equivalent ratios.

Adult T-Shirt Sizes		
Size	Length (inches)	Width (inches)
Small	27	18
Medium	30	20
Large	?	22
X-large	?	24

What is the length of an extra-large T-shirt?

Write two equivalent ratios and find the unknown value:

$$\frac{\text{Length of medium}}{\text{Width of medium}} \rightarrow \frac{30}{20} = \frac{\blacksquare}{24} \begin{array}{l} \leftarrow \text{Length of X-large} \\ \leftarrow \text{Width of X-large} \end{array}$$

$$\frac{30 \div 20}{20 \div 20} = \frac{\blacksquare}{24} \rightarrow \frac{1.5}{1} = \frac{\blacksquare}{24} \rightarrow \frac{1.5 \cdot 24}{1 \cdot 24} = \frac{\blacksquare}{24} \rightarrow \frac{36}{24} = \frac{\blacksquare}{24}$$

The length of an extra-large T-shirt is 36 inches.

Write a problem that can be solved by using the information in the table and could be solved by using equivalent ratios.

Pose a Problem	Solve Your Problem

14. ｛THINK SMARTER ＋｝ Peri earned $27 for walking her neighbor's dog 3 times. If Peri earned $36, how many times did she walk her neighbor's dog? Use a unit rate to find the unknown value.

Personal Math Trainer

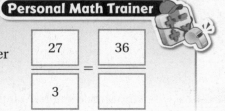

$$\frac{27}{3} = \frac{36}{}$$

Use Unit Rates

Common Core

COMMON CORE STANDARD—6.RP.A.3b
Understand ratio concepts and use ratio reasoning to solve problems.

Use a unit rate to find the unknown value.

1. $\dfrac{34}{17} = \dfrac{\blacksquare}{7}$

$\dfrac{34 \div 17}{17 \div 17} = \dfrac{\blacksquare}{7}$

$\dfrac{2}{1} = \dfrac{\blacksquare}{7}$

$\dfrac{2 \times 7}{1 \times 7} = \dfrac{\blacksquare}{7}$

$\dfrac{14}{7} = \dfrac{\blacksquare}{7}$

$\blacksquare = 14$

2. $\dfrac{16}{32} = \dfrac{\blacksquare}{14}$

3. $\dfrac{18}{\blacksquare} = \dfrac{21}{7}$

4. $\dfrac{\blacksquare}{16} = \dfrac{3}{12}$

_____   _____   _____

Draw a bar model to find the unknown value.

5. $\dfrac{15}{45} = \dfrac{6}{\blacksquare}$

6. $\dfrac{3}{6} = \dfrac{\blacksquare}{7}$

_____   _____

Problem Solving Real World

7. To stay properly hydrated, a person should drink 32 fluid ounces of water for every 60 minutes of exercise. How much water should Damon drink if he rides his bike for 135 minutes?

8. Lillianne made 6 out of every 10 baskets she attempted during basketball practice. If she attempted to make 25 baskets, how many did she make?

_____   _____

9. **WRITE** *Math* Give some examples of real-life situations in which you could use unit rates to solve an equivalent ratio problem.

_____

_____

Lesson Check (6.RP.A.3b)

1. Randi's school requires that there are 2 adult chaperones for every 18 students when the students go on a field trip to the museum. If there are 99 students going to the museum, how many adult chaperones are needed?

2. Landry's neighbor pledged $5.00 for every 2 miles he swims in a charity swim-a-thon. If Landry swims 3 miles, how much money will his neighbor donate?

Spiral Review (6.RP.A.2, 6.RP.A.3a, 6.NS.C.6a, 6.NS.C.6c)

3. Describe a situation that could be represented by ⁻8.

4. What are the coordinates of point *G*?

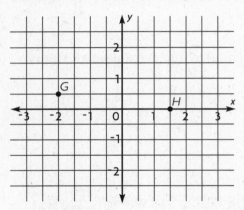

5. Gina bought 6 containers of yogurt for $4. How many containers of yogurt could Gina buy for $12?

6. A bottle containing 64 fluid ounces of juice costs $3.84. What is the unit rate?

FOR MORE PRACTICE
GO TO THE
Personal Math Trainer

Equivalent Ratios and Graphs

Essential Question How can you use a graph to represent equivalent ratios?

 Common Core Ratios and Proportional Relationships—6.RP.A.3a

MATHEMATICAL PRACTICES
MP4, MP5, MP7

 Unlock the Problem

A car travels at a rate of 50 miles per hour. Use equivalent ratios to graph the distance the car travels over time. Graph time on the *x*-axis and distance on the *y*-axis.

● **What words in the problem tell the unit rate?**

_____

🔑 **Write and graph equivalent ratios.**

STEP 1 Use the unit rate to write equivalent ratios.

Write the unit rate. $\dfrac{\boxed{}\ \text{miles}}{1\ \text{hour}}$

Write an equivalent ratio. $\dfrac{\boxed{}\ \text{mi} \times 2}{1\ \text{hr} \times 2}$

$= \dfrac{\boxed{}\ \text{mi}}{\boxed{}\ \text{hr}}$

Complete the table of equivalent ratios.

Distance (mi)			150	200	
Time (hr)	1	2			5

STEP 2 Use an ordered pair to represent each ratio in the table.

Let the *x*-coordinate represent time in hours and the *y*-coordinate represent distance in miles.

$$\dfrac{50\ \text{mi}}{1\ \text{hr}} \rightarrow (1, 50)$$

(1, _____)

(2, _____)

(_____, 150)

(_____, 200)

(5, _____)

Remember

The first number in an ordered pair is the *x*-coordinate, and the second number is the *y*-coordinate.

STEP 3 Use the ordered pairs to graph the car's distance over time.

Think: The graph represents the same relationship as the unit rate.

For every 1 hour the car travels, the distance increases by

_____ miles.

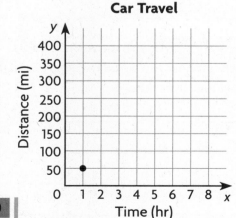

Car Travel

 Math Talk

MATHEMATICAL PRACTICES ⑦

Look for a Pattern Identify a pattern in the graph.

© Houghton Mifflin Harcourt Publishing Company

🔑 Example During a heavy rainstorm, the waters of the
Blue River rose at a steady rate for 8 hours. The graph shows the river's
increase in height over time. Use the graph to complete the table of
equivalent ratios. How many inches did the river rise in 8 hours?

Think: On the graph, x-coordinates represent

time in _____, and y-coordinates represent

the river's increase in height in _____.

The ordered pair (1, _____) means that after _____

hour, the river rose _____ inches.

Increase in Blue River Height

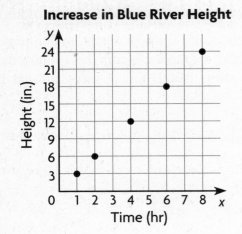

Increase in height (in.)	3				
Time (hr)	1	2	4	6	8

So, the river rose _____ inches in 8 hours.

---

1. **MATHEMATICAL PRACTICE ⑦ Look for a Pattern** Describe the pattern you see in the
graph and the table.

_____

_____

2. Explain how you know that the ratios in the table are equivalent.

_____

_____

3. **MATHEMATICAL PRACTICE ⑤ Use Appropriate Tools** Matt earns $12 per hour.
Explain how you could use equivalent ratios to draw a graph of his
earnings over time.

_____

_____

_____

_____

Name _____

A redwood tree grew at a rate of 4 feet per year. Use this information for 1–3.

1. Complete the table of equivalent ratios for the first 5 years.

Height (ft)					
Time (yr)	1	2			

2. Write ordered pairs, letting the x-coordinate represent time in years and the y-coordinate represent height in feet.

(1, _____), (2, _____), (_____, _____)

(_____, _____), (_____, _____)

On Your Own

The graph shows the rate at which Luis's car uses gas, in miles per gallon. Use the graph for 4–8.

4. Complete the table of equivalent ratios.

Distance (mi)	30				
Gas (gal)	1	2	3	4	5

5. Find the car's unit rate of gas usage. $\dfrac{\text{miles}}{\text{gallon}}$

6. How far can the car go on 5 gallons of gas? _____

7. Estimate the amount of gas needed to travel 50 miles.

_____

8. GODEEPER Ellen's car averages 35 miles per gallon of gas. If you used equivalent ratios to graph her car's gas usage, how would the graph differ from the graph of Luis's car's gas usage?

_____

_____

3. Use the ordered pairs to graph the tree's growth over time.

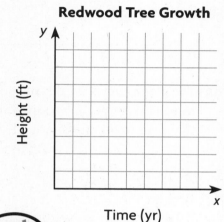

Redwood Tree Growth

Math Talk MATHEMATICAL PRACTICES ④

Use Graphs Explain what the point (1, 4) represents on the graph of the redwood tree's growth.

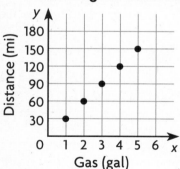

Gas Usage in Luis's Car

Problem Solving · Applications

9. **MATHEMATICAL PRACTICE 7** **Look for Structure** The graph shows the depth of a submarine over time. Use equivalent ratios to find the number of minutes it will take the submarine to descend 1,600 feet.

_____

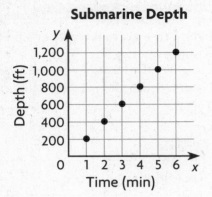

Submarine Depth

10. The graph shows the distance that a plane flying at a steady rate travels over time. Use equivalent ratios to find how far the plane travels in 13 minutes.

_____

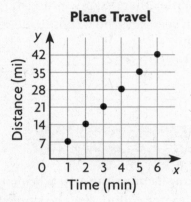

Plane Travel

11. **THINK SMARTER** **Sense or Nonsense?**
Emilio types at a rate of 84 words per minute. He claims that he can type a 500-word essay in 5 minutes. Is Emilio's claim sense or nonsense? Use a graph to help explain your answer.

_____

_____

_____

_____

Emilio's Typing Rate

12. **THINK SMARTER +** The Tuckers drive at a rate of 20 miles per hour through the mountains. Use the ordered pairs to graph the distance traveled over time.

Distance (miles)	20	40	60	80	100
Time (hours)	1	2	3	4	5

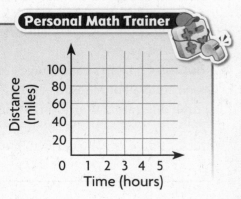

Personal Math Trainer

Equivalent Ratios and Graphs

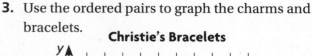

COMMON CORE STANDARD—6.RP.A.3a
*Understand ratio concepts and use ratio
reasoning to solve problems.*

**Christie makes bracelets. She uses 8 charms for each bracelet. Use
this information for 1–3.**

1. Complete the table of equivalent ratios for the
   first 5 bracelets.

Charms	8	16	24	32	40
Bracelets	1	2	3	4	5

2. Write ordered pairs, letting the *x*-coordinate
   represent the number of bracelets and the
   y-coordinate represent the number of charms.

   (1, __8__), (2, __16__), (_____ , _____),

   (_____ , _____), (_____ , _____)

3. Use the ordered pairs to graph the charms and
   bracelets.

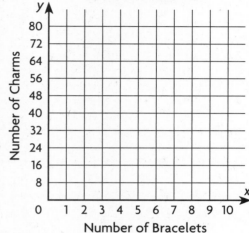

Christie's Bracelets

**The graph shows the number of granola
bars that are in various numbers of boxes
of Crunch N Go. Use the graph for 4–5.**

4. Complete the table of equivalent ratios.

Bars				
Boxes	1	2	3	4

5. Find the unit rate of granola bars per box.

   _____

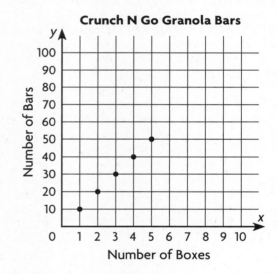

Crunch N Go Granola Bars

Problem Solving · Real World

6. Look at the graph for Christie's Bracelets. How
   many charms are needed for 7 bracelets?

   _____

7. Look at the graph for Crunch N Go Granola Bars.
   Stefan needs to buy 90 granola bars. How many
   boxes must he buy?

   _____

8. **WRITE** ▸ *Math* Choose a real-life example of a unit rate.
   Draw a graph of the unit rate. Then explain how another
   person could use the graph to find the unit rate.

   _____

Lesson Check (6.RP.A.3a)

1. A graph shows the distance a car traveled over time. The x-axis represents time in hours, and the y-axis represents distance in miles. The graph contains the point (3, 165). What does this point represent?

2. Maura charges $11 per hour to babysit. She makes a graph comparing the amount she charges (the y-coordinate) to the time she babysits (the x-coordinate). Which ordered pair shown is NOT on the graph?

(4, 44)   (11, 1)   (1, 11)   (11, 121)

Spiral Review (6.RP.A.3b, 6.NS.C.6b, 6.NS.C.7a, 6.NS.C.7c)

3. List 0, ⁻4, and 3 from least to greatest.

4. What two numbers can be used in place of the ■ to make the statement true?

$$|■| = \frac{8}{9}$$

5. Morgan plots the point (4, ⁻7) on a coordinate plane. If she reflects the point across the y-axis, what are the coordinates of the reflected point?

6. Jonathan drove 220 miles in 4 hours. Assuming he drives at the same rate, how far will he travel in 7 hours?

FOR MORE PRACTICE
GO TO THE
Personal Math Trainer

Name _____

1. Kendra has 4 necklaces, 7 bracelets, and 5 rings. Draw a model to show the ratio that compares rings to bracelets.

2. There are 3 girls and 2 boys taking swimming lessons. Write the ratio that compares the girls taking swimming lessons to the total number of students taking swimming lessons.

   _____

3. Luis adds 3 strawberries for every 2 blueberries in his fruit smoothie. Draw a model to show the ratio that compares strawberries to blueberries.

4. Write the ratio 3 to 10 in two different ways.

   _____

5. Alex takes 3 steps every 5 feet he walks. As Alex continues walking, he takes more steps and walks a longer distance. Complete the table by writing two equivalent ratios.

Steps	3		
Distance (feet)	5		

6. Sam has 3 green apples and 4 red apples. Select the ratios that compare the number of red apples to the total number of apples. Mark all that apply.

○ 4 to 7

○ 3 to 7

○ 4 : 7

○ 4 : 3

○ $\frac{3}{7}$

○ $\frac{4}{7}$

7. Jeff ran 2 miles in 12 minutes. Ju Chan ran 3 miles in 18 minutes. Did Jeff and Ju Chan run the same number of miles per minute? Complete the tables of equivalent ratios to support your answer.

Jeff				
Distance (miles)	2			
Time (minutes)	12			

Ju Chan				
Distance (miles)	3			
Time (minutes)	18			

8. Jen bought 2 notebooks for $10. Write the rate as a fraction. Then find the unit rate.

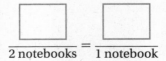

$$\frac{\boxed{}}{2 \text{ notebooks}} = \frac{\boxed{}}{1 \text{ notebook}}$$

9. Determine whether each ratio is equivalent to $\frac{1}{2}$, $\frac{2}{3}$, or $\frac{4}{7}$. Write the ratio in the correct box.

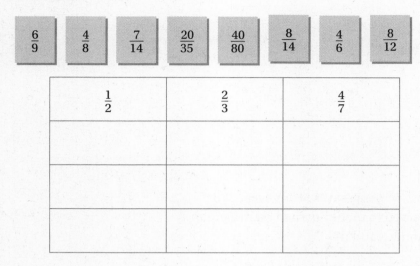

$\frac{1}{2}$	$\frac{2}{3}$	$\frac{4}{7}$

10. Amos bought 5 cantaloupes for $8. How many cantaloupes can he buy for $24? Show your work.

11. Camille said $\frac{4}{5}$ is equivalent to $\frac{24}{30}$. Check her work by making a table of equivalent ratios.

4					
5					

12. **GO DEEPER** A box of oat cereal costs $3.90 for 15 ounces. A box of rice cereal costs $3.30 for 11 ounces. Which box of cereal costs less per ounce? Use numbers and words to explain your answer.

13. Scotty earns $35 for babysitting for 5 hours. If Scotty charges the same rate, how many hours will it take him to earn $42?

_____ hours

14. Use a unit rate to find the unknown value.

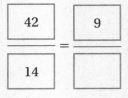

$$\frac{42}{14} = \frac{9}{\boxed{}}$$

15. Jenna saves $3 for every $13 she earns. Vanessa saves $6 for every $16 she earns. Is Jenna's ratio of money saved to money earned equivalent to Vanessa's ratio of money saved to money earned?

_____

16. The Hendersons are on their way to a national park. They are traveling at a rate of 40 miles per hour. Use the ordered pairs to graph the distance traveled over time.

Distance (miles)	40	80	120	160	200
Time (minutes)	1	2	3	4	5

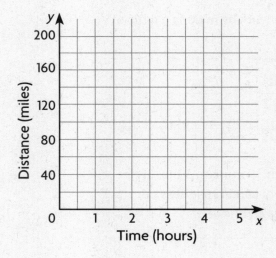

Name _____

17. THINK SMARTER + Abby goes to the pool to swim laps. The graph shows how far Abby swam over time. Use equivalent ratios to find how far Abby swam in 7 minutes.

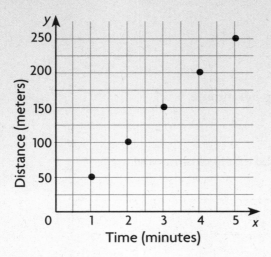

_____ meters

18. Caleb bought 6 packs of pencils for $12.

Part A

How much will he pay for 9 packs of pencils? Use numbers and words to explain your answer.

Part B

Describe how to use a bar model to solve the problem.

19. A rabbit runs 35 miles per hour. Select the animals who run at a faster unit rate per hour than the rabbit. Mark all that apply.

○ Reindeer: 100 miles in 2 hours

○ Ostrich: 80 miles in 2 hours

○ Zebra: 90 miles in 3 hours

○ Squirrel: 36 miles in 3 hours

20. Water is filling a bathtub at a rate of 3 gallons per minute.

Part A

Complete the table of equivalent ratios for the first five minutes of the bathtub filling up.

Amount of Water (gallons)	3				
Time (minutes)	1				

Part B

Emily said there will be 36 gallons of water in the bathtub after 12 minutes. Explain how Emily could have found her answer.

Percents

✓ Show What You Know

Personal Math Trainer
Online Assessment
and Intervention

Check your understanding of important skills.

Name _____

▶ **Decimal Models** **Shade the model to show the decimal.** (4.NF.C.6)

1. 0.31   **2.** 0.7   **3.** 1.7

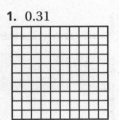   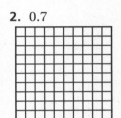   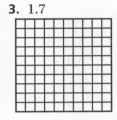 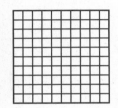

▶ **Division** **Find the quotient.** (5.NBT.B.6)

4. 2,002 ÷ 91   **5.** 98)3,038   **6.** 24,487 ÷ 47   **7.** 22)2,332

_____   _____   _____   _____

▶ **Multiply Whole Numbers by Decimals** **Find the product.** (5.NBT.B.7)

8.   2.38
      × 4
   _____

9.   32.06
      × 7
   _____

10.   4.60
       × 18
    _____

11.   7.04
       × 32
    _____

Esmeralda likes to listen to music while she works out. She had
a playlist on her MP3 player that lasted 40 minutes, but she
accidentally deleted 25% of the music. Does Esmeralda have
enough music left on her playlist for a 30-minute workout?
Explain your answer.

© Houghton Mifflin Harcourt Publishing Company • Image Credits: (b) ©Cathy Maler Callanan/Getty Images

Vocabulary Builder

▶ **Visualize It** •

Complete the bubble map with review and preview words that are related to ratios.

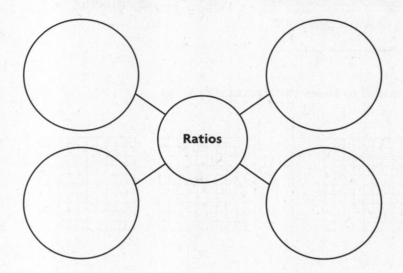

Review Words
decimal
equivalent ratios
factor
quotient
rate
ratio
simplify

Preview Word
percent

▶ **Understand Vocabulary** •

Complete the sentences using review and preview words.

1. A comparison of one number to another by division is a

   _____.

2. _____ name the same comparison.

3. A ratio that compares quantities with different units is a

   _____.

4. A _____ is a ratio, or rate, that compares a number to 100.

5. _____ a fraction or a ratio by dividing the numerator and denominator by a common factor.

GO DIGITAL • **Interactive Student Edition** • **Multimedia eGlossary**

Chapter 5 Vocabulary

decimal

decimal

19

equivalent ratios

razones equivalentes

30

factor

factor

33

percent

porcentaje

74

quotient

cociente

84

rate

tasa

86

ratio

razón

87

simplest form

mínima expresión

92

Ratios that name the same comparison

	Original ratio	2 • 1 ↓	3 • 1 ↓	4 • 1 ↓	5 • 1 ↓
Boxes	1	2	3	4	5
Cards	6	12	18	24	30
		↑ 2 • 6	↑ 3 • 6	↑ 4 • 6	↑ 5 • 6

A number with one or more digits to the right of the decimal point

Examples: 2.6 and 7.053

A comparison of a number to 100; percent means "per hundred"

Example:

$\frac{45}{100} = 45\%$

A number multiplied by another number to find a product

$2 \times 3 \times 7 = 42$

↑ ↑ ↑
factors

A ratio that compares two quantities having different units of measure

Example:

An airplane climbs 18,000 feet in 12 minutes. The rate of climb is 18,000 ft to 12 min, $\frac{18,000 \text{ ft}}{12 \text{ min}}$, or 18,000 ft : 12 min

---

The number that results from dividing

$80 \div 4 = 20$ 　　$4\overline{)80}$ ← quotient
　　　　　　　　　　　　20

↑
quotient

A fraction is in simplest form when the numerator and denominator have only 1 as a common factor

Example: $\frac{6 \div 2}{8 \div 2} = \frac{3}{4}$

A comparison of two numbers, a and b, that can be written as a fraction $\frac{a}{b}$

The ratio of blue squares to red squares is 5 to 1, $\frac{5}{1}$, or 5 : 1.

Game

Matchup

For 2–3 players

Materials

• 1 set of word cards

How to Play

1. Place the cards face-down in even rows. Take turns to play.

2. Choose two cards and turn them face-up.

   • If the cards show a word and its meaning, it's a match. Keep the pair and take another turn.

   • If the cards do not match, turn them over again.

3. The game is over when all cards have been matched. The players count their pairs. The player with the most pairs wins.

Word Box

decimal

equivalent ratios

factor

percent

quotient

rate

ratio

simplest form

Image Credits: (bg) ©Morgan Lane Photography/Shutterstock; (b) ©Mark Andersen/Rubberball/Corbis

© Houghton Mifflin Harcourt Publishing Company

The Write Way

Reflect

Choose one idea. Write about it.

- Which is greatest: $\frac{3}{5}$, .70, or 65%? Tell how you know.
- Explain how to write $\frac{4}{80}$ as a decimal and as a percent.
- A soccer team needs to sell 200 T-shirts to raise enough money for a trip. So far they have sold 55% percent of the shirts. Explain how to figure out how many more shirts they need to sell.
- Tell how to solve this problem: 15 is 20% of _____.

Name _____

Model Percents

Essential Question How can you use a model to show a percent?

Common Core · Ratios and Proportional Relationships—6.RP.A.3c
MATHEMATICAL PRACTICES
MP2, MP5, MP6

Investigate

Materials ■ 10-by-10 grids

Not many people drive electric cars today. But one expert estimates that by 2025, 35 percent of all cars will be powered by electricity.

A **percent** is a ratio, or rate, that compares a number to 100. Percent means "per hundred." The symbol for percent is %.

A. Model 35% on the 10-by-10 grid. Then tell what the percent represents.

The large square represents the whole, or 100%. Each small square represents 1%.

- Shade the grid to show 35%.

   Think: 35% is _____ out of 100.

- Write 35% as a ratio comparing 35 to 100.

   Think: 35 out of 100 squares is 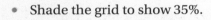.

- 35% =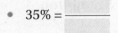

So, by 2025, _____ out of _____ cars may be powered by electricity.

B. Model 52% on a 10-by-10 grid.

- _____ out of _____ squares is .

- 52% = $\frac{}{100}$

C. Model 18% on a 10-by-10 grid.

- _____ out of _____ squares is $\frac{}{100}$.

- 18% = $\frac{}{100}$

Draw Conclusions

1. Explain how you would use a 10-by-10 grid to model 7%.

_____

2. Model $\frac{1}{4}$ on a 10-by-10 grid. What percent is shaded? Explain.

_____

3. MATHEMATICAL PRACTICE ⑤ **Use a Concrete Model** Explain how you could model 0.5% on a 10-by-10 grid.

_____

_____

4. THINK SMARTER How would you model 181% using 10-by-10 grids?

_____

Make Connections

The table shows the types of meteorites in Meg's collection. Shade a grid to show the ratio comparing the number of each type to the total number. Then write the ratio as a percent.

Meg's Meteorite Collection	
Type	**Number**
Iron	21
Stone	76
Stony-iron	3

Think: A percent is a ratio that compares a number to _____.

Iron

_____ out of _____ meteorites are iron.

$$\frac{}{100} = \underline{\quad}\%$$

Stone

_____ out of _____ meteorites are stone.

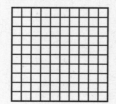

$$\frac{}{} = \underline{\quad}\%$$

Stony-iron

_____ out of _____ meteorites are stony-iron.

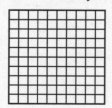

$$\frac{}{} = \underline{\quad}\%$$

Math Talk MATHEMATICAL PRACTICES ②

Connect Symbols and Words Explain what this statement means: 13% of the students at Harding Middle School are left-handed.

Name _____

Write a ratio and a percent to represent the shaded part.

1.

ratio: _____ percent: _____

2.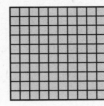

ratio: _____ percent: _____

3.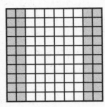

ratio: _____ percent: _____

Model the percent and write it as a ratio.

4. 30%

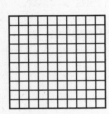

ratio: _____

5. 5%

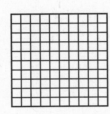

ratio: _____

6. 75%

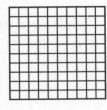

ratio: _____

Problem Solving • Applications

7. **MATHEMATICAL PRACTICE ⑤ Use a Concrete Model** Explain how to model 32% on a 10-by-10 grid. How does the model represent the ratio of 32 to 100?

_____

_____

_____

8. **GO DEEPER** A floor has 100 tiles. There are 24 black tiles and 35 brown tiles. The rest of the tiles are white. What percent of the tiles are white?

_____

Pose a Problem

9. THINK SMARTER Javier designed a mosaic wall mural using 100 tiles in 3 different colors: yellow, blue, and red. If 64 of the tiles are yellow, what percent of the tiles are either red or blue?

To find the number of tiles that are either red or blue, count the red and blue squares. Or subtract the number of yellow squares, 64, from the total number of squares, 100.

36 out of 100 tiles are red or blue.

The ratio of red or blue tiles to all tiles is $\frac{36}{100}$.

So, the percent of the tiles that are either red or blue is 36%.

Write another problem involving a percent that can be solved by using the mosaic wall mural.

Pose a Problem

_____

_____

_____

_____

_____

Solve Your Problem

_____

_____

_____

_____

_____

10. THINK SMARTER Select the 10-by-10 grids that model 45%. Mark all that apply.

○    ○ 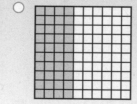   ○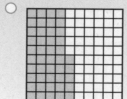

○ 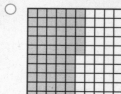   ○

Model Percents

COMMON CORE STANDARD—
6.RP.A.3c *Understand ratio concepts and use ratio reasoning to solve problems.*

Write a ratio and a percent to represent the shaded part.

1.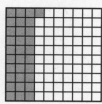

2.

3.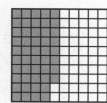

ratio: $\frac{31}{100}$ percent: __31%__

ratio: _____ percent: _____

ratio: _____ percent: _____

Model the percent and write it as a ratio.

4. 97%

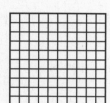

ratio: _____

5. 24%

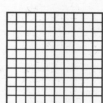

ratio: _____

6. 50%

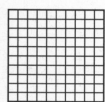

ratio: _____

Problem Solving

The table shows the pen colors sold at the school supply store one week. Write the ratio comparing the number of the given color sold to the total number of pens sold. Then shade the grid.

Pens Sold	
Color	**Number**
Blue	36
Black	49
Red	15

7. Black

_____

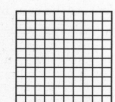

8. Not blue

_____

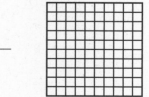

9. **WRITE** ▸*Math* Is every percent a ratio? Is every ratio a percent? Explain.

_____

_____

Lesson Check (6.RP.A.3c)

1. What percent of the large square is shaded?

_____

2. What is the ratio of shaded squares to unshaded squares?

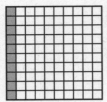

_____

Spiral Review (6.RP.A.1, 6.NS.C.6a, 6.NS.C.6c, 6.NS.C.8)

3. Write a number that is less than $^-2\frac{4}{5}$ and greater than $^-3\frac{1}{5}$.

4. On a coordinate grid, what is the distance between (2, 4) and (2, $^-$3)?

5. Each week, Diana spends 4 hours playing soccer and 6 hours babysitting. Write a ratio to compare the time Diana spends playing soccer to the time she spends babysitting.

6. Antwone earns money at a steady rate mowing lawns. The points (1, 25) and (5, 125) appear on a graph of the amount earned versus number of lawns mowed. What are the coordinates of the point on the graph with an x-value of 3?

© Houghton Mifflin Harcourt Publishing Company

**FOR MORE PRACTICE
GO TO THE
Personal Math Trainer**

Write Percents as Fractions and Decimals

Essential Question How can you write percents as fractions and decimals?

To write a percent as a fraction or a decimal, first write the percent as a ratio that compares a number to 100. For example, $37\% = \frac{37}{100}$.

 Unlock the Problem Real World

Carlos eats a banana, an orange, and a blueberry muffin for breakfast. What fraction of the daily value of vitamin C does each item contain?

Vitamin C Content	
Item	**Percent of Daily Value**
Banana	15%
Orange	113%
Blueberry Muffin	0.5%

 Write each percent as a fraction.

A Write 15% as a fraction.

$$15\% = \frac{\boxed{}}{100} = \frac{}{}$$

15% is 15 out of 100.

Write the fraction in simplest form.

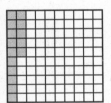

So, 15% = _____.

B Write 113% as a fraction.

$$113\% = \frac{\boxed{}}{100} + \frac{13}{100}$$

$$= \underline{} + \frac{13}{100}$$

113% is 100 out of 100 plus 13 out of 100.

$\frac{100}{100} = 1$

Write the sum as a mixed number.

 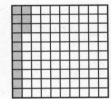

So, 113% = _____.

C Write 0.5% as a fraction.

$$0.5\% = \frac{\boxed{}}{100}$$

$$= \frac{0.5 \cdot 10}{100 \cdot 10} = \frac{\boxed{}}{1,000}$$

$$= \frac{1}{\boxed{}}$$

0.5% is 0.5 out of 100.

Multiply the numerator and denominator by 10 to get a whole number in the numerator.

Write the fraction in simplest form.

So, 0.5% = _____.

- **MATHEMATICAL PRACTICE ②** **Reason Quantitatively** Explain why two 10-by-10 grids were used to show 113%.

_____

_____

🔑 Example

A Write 72% as a decimal.

$$72\% = \frac{\boxed{}}{100}$$

= _____

So, 72% = _____ .

72% is 72 out of 100.

Use place value to write 72 hundredths as a decimal.

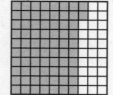

B Write 4% as a decimal.

$$4\% = \frac{\boxed{}}{100}$$

$$100\overline{)4.00}$$
$$\underline{-0}\downarrow$$
$$40\downarrow$$
$$\underline{-0}\downarrow$$
$$400$$
$$\underline{-400}$$
$$0$$

4% is 4 out of 100.

Use division to write 4% as a decimal.

Divide the ones. Since 4 ones cannot be shared among 100 groups, write a zero in the quotient.

Place a decimal point after the ones place in the quotient.

So, 4% = _____ .

> **Remember**
> When you divide decimal numbers by powers of 10, you move the decimal point one place to the left for each factor of 10.

C Write 25.81% as a decimal.

$$25.81\% = \frac{\boxed{}}{100}$$

= _____

So, 25.81% = _____ .

25.81% is 25.81 out of 100.

To divide by 100, move the decimal point 2 places to the left: 0.2581

Share and Show MATH BOARD

Write the percent as a fraction.

1. 80%

$$80\% = \frac{\boxed{}}{100} = \frac{\boxed{}}{\boxed{}}$$

2. 150%

_____

✓ **3.** 0.2%

_____

Write the percent as a decimal.

✓ **4.** 58%

_____

5. 9%

_____

Math Talk

MATHEMATICAL PRACTICES ⑥

Explain How would you use estimation to check that your answer is reasonable when you write a percent as a fraction or decimal?

Name _____

On Your Own

Write the percent as a fraction or mixed number.

6. 17%

7. 20%

8. 125%

9. 355%

10. 0.1%

11. 2.5%

Write the percent as a decimal.

12. 89%

13. 30%

14. 2%

15. 122%

16. 3.5%

17. 6.33%

18. **MATHEMATICAL PRACTICE ②** **Use Reasoning** Write $<$, $>$, or $=$.

$21.6\% \bigcirc \frac{1}{5}$

19. _GO DEEPER_ Georgianne completed 60% of her homework assignment. Write the portion of her homework that she still needs to complete as a fraction.

Problem Solving • Applications

Use the table for 20 and 21.

20. What fraction of computer and video game players are 50 years old or more?

   _____

21. What fraction of computer and video game players are 18 years old or more?

   _____

22. **THINK SMARTER** Box A and Box B each contain black tiles and white tiles. They have the same total number of tiles. In Box A, 45% of the tiles are black. In Box B, $\frac{11}{20}$ of the tiles are white. Compare the number of black tiles in the boxes. Explain your reasoning.

   _____

   _____

   _____

   _____

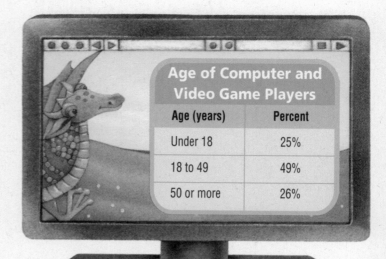

Age of Computer and Video Game Players	
Age (years)	**Percent**
Under 18	25%
18 to 49	49%
50 or more	26%

23. **THINK SMARTER** Mr. Truong is organizing a summer program for 6th grade students. He surveyed students to find the percent of students interested in each activity. Complete the table by writing each percent as a fraction or decimal.

Activity	Percent	Fraction	Decimal
Sports	48%	$\frac{12}{25}$	
Cooking	23%		0.23
Music	20%		0.2
Art	9%	$\frac{9}{100}$	

COMMON CORE STANDARD—6.RP.A.3c
Understand ratio concepts and use ratio reasoning to solve problems.

Write the percent as a fraction or mixed number.

1. 44%

$$44\% = \frac{44}{100}$$
$$= \frac{11}{25}$$

2. 32%

3. 116%

4. 250%

5. 0.3%

6. 0.4%

7. 1.5%

8. 12.5%

Write the percent as a decimal.

9. 63%

10. 110%

11. 42.15%

12. 0.1%

Problem Solving · Real World

13. An online bookstore sells 0.8% of its books to foreign customers. What fraction of the books are sold to foreign customers?

14. In Mr. Klein's class, 40% of the students are boys. What decimal represents the portion of the students that are girls?

15. **WRITE** ▸Math Explain how percents, fractions, and decimals are related. Use a 10-by-10 grid to make a model that supports your explanation.

Lesson Check (6.RP.A.3c)

1. The enrollment at Sonya's school this year is 109% of last year's enrollment. What decimal represents this year's enrollment compared to last year's?

2. An artist's paint set contains 30% watercolors and 25% acrylics. What fraction represents the portion of the paints that are watercolors or acrylics? Write the fraction in simplest form.

Spiral Review (6.RP.A.3a, 6.RP.A.3c, 6.NS.C.7a, 6.NS.C.7b, 6.NS.C.8)

3. Write the numbers in order from least to greatest.

$$^-5.25 \qquad 1.002 \qquad ^-5.09$$

4. On a coordinate plane, the vertices of a rectangle are (2, 4), (2, $^-$1), ($^-$5, $^-$1), and ($^-$5, 4). What is the perimeter of the rectangle?

5. The table below shows the widths and lengths, in feet, for different playgrounds. Which playgrounds have equivalent ratios of width to length?

	A	B	C	D
Width	12	15	20	16.5
Length	20	22.5	25	27.5

6. What percent represents the shaded part?

FOR MORE PRACTICE
GO TO THE
Personal Math Trainer

Write Fractions and Decimals as Percents

Essential Question How can you write fractions and decimals as percents?

Common Core Ratios and Proportional Relationships—6.RP.A.3c
MATHEMATICAL PRACTICES
MP2, MP6, MP7

 Unlock the Problem Real World

During the 2008–2009 season of the National Basketball Association (NBA), the Phoenix Suns won about $\frac{11}{20}$ of their games. The Miami Heat won about 0.524 of their games. Which team was more successful during the season?

To compare the season performances of the Suns and the Heat, it is helpful to write the fraction and the decimal as a percent.

- Underline the sentence that tells you what you are trying to find.
- Circle the numbers you need to use.

 Write the fraction or decimal as a percent.

 A $\frac{11}{20}$

Multiply the _____ and $\frac{11}{20} = \frac{11 \times \boxed{}}{20 \times \boxed{}}$

_____ by the same value to write an equivalent fraction with a denominator of 100.

$= \dfrac{\boxed{}}{100}$

A percent is a ratio comparing a number

to _____. Write the ratio $=$ _____

as a _____.

So, the percent of games won by the Phoenix Suns is _____.

B 0.524

To write a percent as a decimal, divide by _____.
To write a decimal as a percent,

_____ by 100. $0.524 \times 100 = 52.4$

To multiply by 100, move the decimal

point 2 places to the _____. $0.524 =$ _____ %

So, the percent of games won by the Miami Heat is _____.

Because they won a greater percentage of their games, the _____ were more successful during the 2008–2009 season.

CONNECT You can use what you know about fractions, decimals, and percents to write numbers in different forms.

🔑 Example

Ⓐ Write 0.7 as a fraction and as a percent.

0.7 means 7 _____. Write 0.7 as a fraction.

To write as a percent, first write an equivalent fraction with a denominator

of _____.

Write the ratio of _____ to

_____ as a percent.

$$0.7 = \frac{7}{\boxed{}}$$

$$= \frac{7 \times \boxed{}}{10 \times \boxed{}}$$

$$= \frac{\boxed{}}{100}$$

$$= \_\_\_\_$$

So, 0.7 written as a fraction is _____, and

0.7 written as a percent is _____.

Ⓑ Write $\frac{3}{40}$ as a decimal and as a percent.

Since 40 is not a factor of 100, it is more difficult to find an equivalent fraction with a denominator of 100.

Use division to write $\frac{3}{40}$ as a decimal.

Divide 3 by 40.

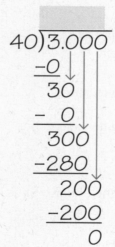

To write a decimal as a percent,

_____ by 100.

Move the decimal point 2 places to the

_____.

$$\frac{3}{40} = 0.075$$

$$0.075 = _____$$

So, $\frac{3}{40}$ written as a decimal is _____, and

$\frac{3}{40}$ written as a percent is _____.

MATHEMATICAL PRACTICES ⑥

Explain Why does it make sense that $\frac{3}{40}$ is less than 10%?

Name _____

Write the fraction or decimal as a percent.

1. $\frac{3}{25}$

$$\frac{3 \times \boxed{}}{25 \times \boxed{}} = \frac{\boxed{}}{100}$$

_____

 2. $\frac{3}{10}$

_____

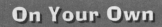 3. 0.717

_____

4. 0.02

_____

On Your Own

**Write the number in two other forms (fraction, decimal, or percent).
Write the fraction in simplest form.**

5. 0.01

_____

6. $\frac{13}{40}$

_____

7. $\frac{6}{5}$

_____

8. 0.008

_____

The table shows the portion of Kim's class that participates
in each sport. Use the table for 9–10.

Participation in Sports	
Sport	**Part of Class**
Baseball	23%
Soccer	$\frac{1}{5}$
Swimming	0.09

9. **GO DEEPER** Do more students take part in soccer or in
swimming? Explain your reasoning.

_____

10. **MATHEMATICAL PRACTICE ⑥ Explain** What percent of Kim's class participates
in one of the sports listed? Explain how you found your answer.

_____

_____

11. **THINK SMARTER** For their reading project, students chose to either complete a character study,
or write a book review. $\frac{1}{5}$ of the students completed a character study, and 0.8 of the students
wrote a book review. Joia said that more students wrote a book review than completed a
character study. Do you agree with Joia? Use numbers and words to support your answer.

_____

_____

Connect to Art

Sand Sculptures

Every year, dozens of teams compete in the U.S. Open Sandcastle Competition. Recent winners have included complex sculptures in the shape of flowers, elephants, and racing cars.

Teams that participate in the contest build their sculptures using a mixture of sand and water. Finding the correct ratios of these ingredients is essential for creating a stable sculpture.

The table shows the recipes that three teams used. Which team used the greatest percent of sand in their recipe?

Convert to percents. Then order from least to greatest.

Team A	$\dfrac{30}{30 + 10} = \dfrac{30}{40} = 0.75 = \underline{}\%$
Team B	$\dfrac{19}{20} = \dfrac{19 \times \square}{20 \times \square} = \dfrac{\square}{100} = \underline{}\%$
Team C	$0.84 = \underline{}\%$

Sand Sculpture Recipes

Team	Sand	Water
A	30 cups	10 cups
B	$\frac{19}{20}$ cup	$\frac{1}{20}$ cup
C	0.84 cup	0.16 cup

From least to greatest, the percents are _____.

So, Team _____ used the greatest percent of sand.

Solve.

12. Which team used the greatest percent of water in their recipe?

_____

13. Some people say that the ideal recipe for sand sculptures contains 88.9% sand. Which team's recipe is closest to the ideal recipe?

_____

14. THINK SMARTER   Team D used a recipe that consists of 20 cups of sand, 2 cups of flour, and 3 cups of water. How does the percent of sand in Team D's recipe compare to that of the other teams?

_____

_____

Math on the Spot

Write Fractions and Decimals as Percents

COMMON CORE STANDARD—
6.RP.A.3c *Understand ratio concepts and use ratio reasoning to solve problems.*

Write the fraction or decimal as a percent.

1. $\frac{7}{20}$

2. $\frac{3}{50}$

3. $\frac{1}{25}$

4. $\frac{5}{5}$

$$\frac{7}{20} = \frac{7 \times 5}{20 \times 5}$$

$$= \frac{35}{100} = 35\%$$

5. 0.622

6. 0.303

7. 0.06

8. 2.45

Write the number in two other forms (fraction, decimal, or percent).
Write the fraction in simplest form.

9. $\frac{19}{20}$

10. $\frac{9}{16}$

11. 0.4

12. 0.22

Problem Solving (Real World)

13. According to the U.S. Census Bureau, $\frac{3}{25}$ of all adults in the United States visited a zoo in 2007. What percent of all adults in the United States visited a zoo in 2007?

14. A bag contains red and blue marbles. Given that $\frac{17}{20}$ of the marbles are red, what percent of the marbles are blue?

15. **WRITE** ⟶ *Math* Explain two ways to write $\frac{4}{5}$ as a percent.

_____

_____

Lesson Check (6.RP.A.3c)

1. The portion of shoppers at a supermarket who pay by credit card is 0.36. What percent of shoppers at the supermarket do NOT pay by credit card?

_____

2. About $\frac{23}{40}$ of a lawn is planted with Kentucky bluegrass. What percent of the lawn is planted with Kentucky bluegrass?

_____

Spiral Review (6.RP.A.1, 6.RP.A.2, 6.RP.A.3a, 6.RP.A.3c)

3. A basket contains 6 peaches and 8 plums. What is the ratio of peaches to total pieces of fruit?

_____

4. It takes 8 minutes for 3 cars to move through a car wash. At the same rate, how many cars can move through the car wash in 24 minutes?

_____

5. A 14-ounce box of cereal sells for $2.10. What is the unit rate?

_____

6. A model railroad kit contains curved tracks and straight tracks. Given that 35% of the tracks are curved, what fraction of the tracks are straight? Write the fraction in simplest form.

_____

FOR MORE PRACTICE GO TO THE
Personal Math Trainer

✓ Mid-Chapter Checkpoint

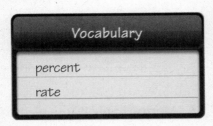

Personal Math Trainer
Online Assessment
and Intervention

Vocabulary

Vocabulary
percent
rate

Choose the best term from the box to complete the sentence.

1. A _____ is a ratio that compares a quantity to 100. (p. 269)

Concepts and Skills

Write a ratio and a percent to represent the shaded part. (6.RP.A.3c)

2.

_____

3.

_____

4.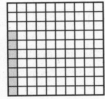

_____

5.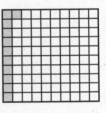

_____

6.

_____

7.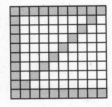

_____

Write the number in two other forms (fraction, decimal, or percent). (6.RP.A.3c)
Write the fraction in simplest form.

8. 0.04

9. $\frac{3}{10}$

10. 1%

11. $1\frac{1}{5}$

_____ _____ _____ _____

12. 0.9

13. 0.5%

14. $\frac{7}{8}$

15. 355%

_____ _____ _____ _____

16. About $\frac{9}{10}$ of the avocados grown in the United States are grown in California. About what percent of the avocados grown in the United States are grown in California? (6.RP.A.3c)

_____

17. Morton made 36 out of 48 free throws last season. What percent of his free throws did Morton make? (6.RP.A.3c)

_____

18. Sarah answered 85% of the trivia questions correctly. What fraction describes this percent? (6.RP.A. 3c)

_____

19. About $\frac{4}{5}$ of all the orange juice in the world is produced in Brazil. About what percent of all the orange juice in the world is produced in Brazil? (6.RP.A.3c)

_____

20. GO DEEPER If you eat 4 medium strawberries, you get 48% of your daily recommended amount of vitamin C. What fraction of your daily amount of vitamin C do you still need? (6.RP.A.3c)

_____

Name _____

Percent of a Quantity

Essential Question How do you find a percent of a quantity?

Common Core

Ratios and Proportional Relationships—6.RP.A.3c

MATHEMATICAL PRACTICES
MP1, MP2, MP3, MP5

 Unlock the Problem Real World

A typical family of four uses about 400 gallons of water each day, and 30% of this water is for outdoor activities, such as gardening. How many gallons of water does a typical family of four use each day for outdoor activities?

• Will the number of gallons of water for outdoor activities be greater than or less than 200 gallons? Explain.

_____

_____

One Way Use ratio reasoning.

Draw a bar model.

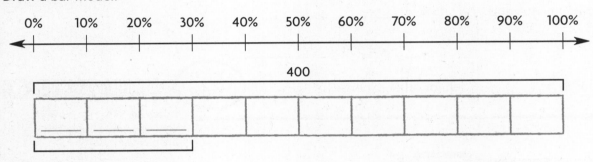

The model shows that 100% represents 400 gallons.

Think: 30% is 3 groups of 10%, so divide the model into 10 equal groups.

Find the value of 10% of 400.

$$10\% \text{ of } 400 = \frac{1}{10} \times 400 = \frac{400}{\ \ \ } = \underline{\ \ \ \ }$$

Find the value of 30% of 400.

$$30\% \text{ of } 400 = 3 \times \underline{\ \ \ \ } = \underline{\ \ \ \ }$$

Another Way Multiply.

You can find 30% of 400 by multiplying.

Write the percent as a rate per 100.

$$30\% = \frac{30}{100}$$

Multiply to find $\frac{30}{100}$ of 400.

$$\frac{30}{100} \times 400 = \underline{\ \ \ \ }$$

So, 30% of 400 gallons is _____ gallons.

 Math Talk

MATHEMATICAL PRACTICES ②

Reason Quantitatively How can you find the number of gallons of water used for indoor activities?

Try This! Find 65% of 300.

$$65\% = \underline{\ \ \ \ }$$

$$\underline{\ \ \ \ } \times 300 = \underline{\ \ \ \ }$$

Chapter 5 289

Example

Charla earns $4,000 per month. She spends 40% of her salary on rent and 15% of her salary on groceries. How much money does Charla have left for other expenses?

STEP 1 Add to find the total percent of Charla's salary that is used for rent and groceries.

40% + _____ % = _____ %

STEP 2 Subtract the total percent from 100% to find the percent that is left for other expenses.

100% − _____ % = 45%

STEP 3 Write the percent from Step 2 as a rate per 100 and multiply.

45% = _____

_____ × 4,000 = _____

So, Charla has $ _____ left for other expenses.

Math Talk

MATHEMATICAL PRACTICES ①

Describe What is another way you could solve the problem?

Share and Show | MATH BOARD

Find the percent of the quantity.

0%   25%   50%   75%   100%

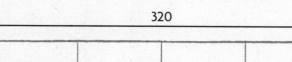

1. 25% of 320

$25\% = \frac{1}{4}$, so use _____ equal groups.

$\frac{1}{4} \times 320 = \dfrac{320}{} = $ _____

320

2. 80% of 50

_____

3. 175% of 24

_____

4. 60% of 210

_____

5. A jar contains 125 marbles. Given that 4% of the marbles are green, 60% of the marbles are blue, and the rest are red, how many red marbles are in the jar?

_____

6. There are 32 students in Mr. Moreno's class and 62.5% of the students are girls. How many boys are in the class?

_____

Math Talk

MATHEMATICAL PRACTICES ⑤

Use Tools What strategy could you use to estimate 49.3% of 3,000?

Name _____

Find the percent of the quantity.

7. 60% of 90

8. 25% of 32.4

9. 110% of 300

10. 0.2% of 6,500

_____

_____

_____

_____

11. A baker made 60 muffins for a cafe. By noon, 45% of the muffins were sold. How many muffins were sold by noon?

_____

12. There are 30 treasures hidden in a castle in a video game. LaToya found 80% of them. How many of the treasures did LaToya find?

_____

13. A school library has 260 DVDs in its collection. Given that 45% of the DVDs are about science and 40% are about history, how many of the DVDs are about other subjects?

_____

14. **GO DEEPER** Mitch planted cabbage, squash, and carrots on his 150-acre farm. He planted half the farm with squash and 22% with carrots. How many acres did he plant with cabbage?

_____

Compare. Write <, >, or =.

15. 45% of 60 ◯ 60% of 45

16. 10% of 90 ◯ 90% of 100

17. 75% of 8 ◯ 8% of 7.5

18. **THINK SMARTER** Sarah had 12 free throw attempts during a game and made at least 75% of the free throws. What is the greatest number of free throws Sarah could have missed during the game?

_____

19. **MATHEMATICAL PRACTICE ❸** Chrissie likes to tip a server in a restaurant a minimum of 20%. She and her friend have a lunch bill that is $18.34. Chrissie says the tip will be $3.30. Her friend says that is not a minimum of 20%. Who is correct? Explain.

_____

_____

Unlock the Problem

20. One-third of the juniors in the Linwood High School Marching Band play the trumpet. The band has 50 members and the table shows what percent of the band members are freshmen, sophomores, juniors, and seniors. How many juniors play the trumpet?

a. What do you need to find?

_____

_____

b. How can you use the table to help you solve the problem?

_____

_____

_____

Linwood High School Marching Band

Freshmen	26%
Sophomores	30%
Juniors	24%
Seniors	20%

c. What operation can you use to find the number of juniors in the band?

_____

d. Show the steps you use to solve the problem.

e. Complete the sentences.

The band has _____ members. There

are _____ juniors in the band. The number of juniors who play the

trumpet is _____ .

---

21. THINK SMARTER   Compare. Circle <, >, or =.

21a.   25% of 44 $\begin{matrix}<\\>\\=\end{matrix}$ 20% of 50   21b.   10% of 30 $\begin{matrix}<\\>\\=\end{matrix}$ 30% of 100

21c.   35% of 60 $\begin{matrix}<\\>\\=\end{matrix}$ 60% of 35

Percent of a Quantity

Common Core **COMMON CORE STANDARD—6.RP.A.3c**
Understand ratio concepts and use ratio reasoning to solve problems.

Find the percent of the quantity.

1. 60% of 140

$$60\% = \frac{60}{100}$$

$$\frac{60}{100} \times 140$$

$$= 84$$

2. 55% of 600

_____

3. 4% of 50

_____

4. 10% of 2,350

_____

5. 160% of 30

_____

6. 105% of 260

_____

7. 0.5% of 12

_____

8. 40% of 16.5

_____

Problem Solving Real World

9. The recommended daily amount of vitamin C for children 9 to 13 years old is 45 mg. A serving of a juice drink contains 60% of the recommended amount. How much vitamin C does the juice drink contain?

_____

10. During a 60-minute television program, 25% of the time is used for commercials and 5% of the time is used for the opening and closing credits. How many minutes remain for the program itself?

_____

11. **WRITE** ▸*Math* Explain two ways you can find 35% of 700.

_____

_____

_____

_____

Lesson Check (6.RP.A.3c)

1. A store has a display case with cherry, peach, and grape fruit chews. There are 160 fruit chews in the display case. Given that 25% of the fruit chews are cherry and 40% are peach, how many grape fruit chews are in the display case?

2. Kelly has a ribbon that is 60 inches long. She cuts 40% off the ribbon for an art project. While working on the project, she decides she only needs 75% of the piece she cut off. How many inches of ribbon does Kelly end up using for her project?

Spiral Review (6.NS.C.7d, 6.RP.A.3b, 6.RP.A.3c)

3. Three of the following statements are true. Which one is NOT true?

$|^-12| > 1$ $|0| > ^-4$

$|20| > |^-10|$ $6 < |^-3|$

4. Miyuki can type 135 words in 3 minutes. How many words can she expect to type in 8 minutes?

5. Which percent represents the model?

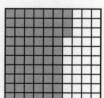

6. About $\frac{3}{5}$ of the students at Roosevelt Elementary School live within one mile of the school. What percent of students live within one mile of the school?

FOR MORE PRACTICE
GO TO THE
Personal Math Trainer

Problem Solving • Percents

Essential Question How can you use the strategy *use a model* to help you solve a percent problem?

 Ratios and Proportional Relationships—6.RP.A.3c
MATHEMATICAL PRACTICES
MP1, MP2, MP6

 Unlock the Problem (Real World)

The recommended daily amount of protein is about 50 grams. One Super Protein Cereal Bar contains 16% of that amount of protein. If Stefon eats one Super Protein Cereal Bar per day, how much protein will he need to get from other sources to meet the recommended daily amount?

Use the graphic organizer to help you solve the problem.

Read the Problem

What do I need to find?	**What information do I need to use?**	**How will I use the information?**
Write what you need to find.	Write the important information.	What strategy can you use?
_____		_____
_____	_____	_____
_____	_____	_____
_____	_____	_____
		_____

Solve the Problem

Draw a bar model.

100%

Recommended Daily Amount | 50 g

Cereal Bar

16%

The model shows that 100% = 50 grams,

so 1% of 50 = $\frac{50}{100}$ = _____.

16% of 50 = 16 × _____ = _____

So, the cereal bar contains _____ of protein.

50 − _____ = _____

So, _____ of protein should come from other sources.

Math Talk

MATHEMATICAL PRACTICES ①

Describe How can you use estimation to show that your answer is reasonable?

🔐 Try Another Problem

Lee has saved 65% of the money she needs to buy a pair of jeans that cost $24. How much money does Lee have, and how much more money does she need to buy the jeans?

Read the Problem

What do I need to find?	What information do I need to use?	How will I use the information?

Solve the Problem

1. Does your answer make sense? Explain how you know.

_____

_____

2. **MATHEMATICAL PRACTICE ⑥** **Explain** how you could solve this problem in a different way.

_____

_____

MATHEMATICAL PRACTICES ⑥

Compare How is the model you used to solve this problem similar to and/or different from the model on page 295?

Name _____

Share and Show MATH BOARD

1. A geologist visits 40 volcanoes in Alaska and California. 15% of the volcanoes are in California. How many volcanoes does the geologist visit in California and how many in Alaska?

First, draw a bar model.

100%

Total Volcanoes	40

California

15%

Next, find 1%.

$100\% = 40$, so 1% of $40 = \frac{40}{100} =$ _____

Then, find 15%, the number of volcanoes in California.

15% of $40 = 15 \times$ _____ $=$ _____

Finally, subtract to find the number of volcanoes in Alaska.

So, the geologist visited _____ volcanoes in California

and _____ volcanoes in Alaska.

2. **THINK SMARTER** **What if** 30% of the volcanoes were in California? How many volcanoes would the geologist have visited in California and how many in Alaska?

_____

3. Ricardo has $25 to spend on school supplies. He spends 72% of the money on a backpack and the rest on a large binder. How much does he spend on the backpack? How much does he spend on the binder?

_____

4. Kevin is hiking on a trail that is 4.2 miles long. So far, he has hiked 80% of the total distance. How many more miles does Kevin have to hike in order to complete the trail?

_____

© Houghton Mifflin Harcourt Publishing Company

WRITE ▸ Math
Show Your Work

On Your Own

5. **GO DEEPER** Jordan takes 50% of the cherries from a bowl. Then Mei takes 50% of the remaining cherries. Finally, Greg takes 50% of the remaining cherries. There are 3 cherries left. How many cherries were in the bowl before Jordan arrived?

_____

6. **THINK SMARTER** Each week, Tasha saves 65% of the money she earns babysitting and spends the rest. This week she earned $40. How much more money did she save than spend this week?

_____

7. **THINK SMARTER** An employee at a state park has 53 photos of animals found at the park. She wants to arrange the photos in rows so that every row except the bottom row has the same number of photos. She also wants there to be at least 5 rows. Describe two different ways she can arrange the photos.

_____

_____

8. **MATHEMATICAL PRACTICE** ⑥ **Explain a Method** Maya wants to mark a length of 7 inches on a sheet of paper, but she does not have a ruler. She has pieces of wood that are 4 inches, 5 inches, and 6 inches long. Explain how she can use these pieces to mark a length of 7 inches.

_____

_____

_____

Personal Math Trainer

9. **THINK SMARTER +** Pierre's family is driving 380 miles from San Francisco to Los Angeles. On the first day, they drive 30% of the distance. On the second day, they drive 50% of the distance. On the third day, they drive the remaining distance and arrive in Los Angeles. How many miles did Pierre's family drive each day? Write the number of miles in the correct box.

| 76 miles | 190 miles | 114 miles |

First Day	Second Day	Third Day

Problem Solving • Percents

Common Core   **COMMON CORE STANDARD—6.RP.A.3c**
*Understand ratio concepts and use ratio
reasoning to solve problems.*

Read each problem and solve.

1. On Saturday, a souvenir shop had
   125 customers. Sixty-four percent of
   the customers paid with a credit card.
   The other customers paid with cash.
   How many customers paid with cash?

   1% of 125 = $\frac{125}{100}$ = 1.25

   64% of 125 = 64 × 1.25 = 80

   125 − 80 = 45 customers

2. A carpenter has a wooden stick that is
   84 centimeters long. She cuts off 25% from the end
   of the stick. Then she cuts the remaining stick into 6
   equal pieces. What is the length of each piece?

   _____

3. A car dealership has 240 cars in the parking lot and
   17.5% of them are red. Of the other 6 colors in the lot,
   each color has the same number of cars. If one of the
   colors is black, how many black cars are in the lot?

   _____

4. The utilities bill for the Millers' home in April was
   $132. Forty-two percent of the bill was for gas, and the
   rest was for electricity. How much did the Millers pay
   for gas, and how much did they pay for electricity?

   _____

5. Andy's total bill for lunch is $20. The cost of the drink
   is 15% of the total bill and the rest is the cost of the
   food. What percent of the total bill did Andy's food
   cost? What was the cost of his food?

   _____

6. **WRITE** *Math* Write a word problem that involves
   finding the additional amount of money needed to
   purchase an item, given the cost and the percent of
   the cost already saved.

   _____

   _____

   _____

Lesson Check (6.RP.A.3c)

1. Milo has a collection of DVDs. Out of 45 DVDs, 40% are comedies and the remaining are action-adventures. How many action-adventure DVDs does Milo own?

2. Andrea and her partner are writing a 12-page science report. They completed 25% of the report in class and 50% of the remaining pages after school. How many pages do Andrea and her partner still have to write?

Spiral Review (6.RP.A.3a, 6.RP.A.3c, 6.NS.C.6c, 6.NS.C.7c)

3. What is the absolute value of $\frac{-4}{25}$?

4. Ricardo graphed a point by starting at the origin and moving 5 units to the left. Then he moved up 2 units. What is the ordered pair for the point he graphed?

5. The population of birds in a sanctuary increases at a steady rate. The graph of the population over time has the points (1, 105) and (3, 315). Name another point on the graph.

6. Alicia's MP3 player contains 1,260 songs. Given that 35% of the songs are rock songs and 20% of the songs are rap songs, how many of the songs are other types of songs?

FOR MORE PRACTICE
GO TO THE
Personal Math Trainer

Find the Whole From a Percent

Essential Question How can you find the whole given a part and the percent?

 Ratios and Proportional Relationships—6.RP.A.3c
MATHEMATICAL PRACTICES
MP1, MP2, MP8

A percent is equivalent to the ratio of a part to a whole. Suppose there are 20 marbles in a bag and 5 of them are blue. The *whole* is the total number of marbles, 20. The *part* is the number of blue marbles, 5. The ratio of the part to the whole, $\frac{5}{20}$, is equal to the *percent* of marbles that are blue, 25%.

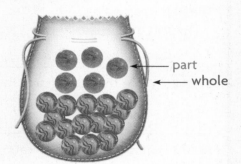

$$\frac{\text{part} \rightarrow}{\text{whole} \rightarrow} \frac{5}{20} = \frac{5 \times 5}{20 \times 5} = \frac{25}{100} = 25\% \leftarrow \text{percent}$$

You can use the relationship among the part, the whole, and the percent to solve problems.

🔑 Unlock the Problem Real World

Emily has sent 28 text messages so far this week. That is 20% of the total number of text messages she is allowed in one week. What is the total number of text messages Emily can send in one week?

🔓 One Way Use a double number line.

Think: The *whole* is the total number of messages Emily can send. The *part* is the number of messages Emily has sent so far.

The double number line shows that 20% represents 28 messages.

Find the number of messages represented by 100%.

Think: I want to find 100%. What can I multiply 20 by to get 100?

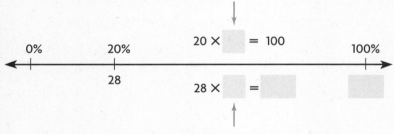

$20 \times \boxed{} = 100$

$28 \times \boxed{} = \boxed{}$ \qquad $\boxed{}$

Multiply 28 by the same factor.

So, 28 is 20% of _____. Emily can send _____ messages in one week.

 Math Talk

MATHEMATICAL PRACTICES ①

Analyze Relationships Explain the relationship among the part, the whole, and the percent using the information in this problem.

🔓 Another Way Use equivalent ratios.

STEP 1 Write the relationship among the percent, part, and whole.

$$percent = \frac{part}{whole}$$

Think: The percent is _____%. The part is _____ messages. The _____ is unknown.

$$20\% = \frac{\boxed{}}{\boxed{}}$$

STEP 2 Write the percent as a ratio.

$$\frac{20}{\boxed{}} = \frac{28}{\boxed{}}$$

STEP 3 Simplify the known ratio.

$$\frac{20 \div 20}{100 \div \boxed{}} = \frac{1}{\boxed{}} = \frac{28}{\boxed{}}$$

STEP 4 Write an equivalent ratio.

Think: The numerator should be _____.

$$\frac{1 \times 28}{5 \times \boxed{}} = \frac{28}{\boxed{}}$$

$$\frac{28}{\boxed{}} = \frac{28}{\boxed{}}$$

So, 28 is 20% of _____. Emily can send _____ messages in one week.

> ### Math Idea
> The denominator of the percent ratio will always be 100 because 100% represents the whole.

🔓 Example 24 is 5% of what number?

STEP 1 Write the relationship among the percent, part, and whole.

$$percent = \frac{part}{whole}$$

Think: The percent is _____%. The part is _____. The _____ is unknown.

$$5\% = \frac{\boxed{}}{\boxed{}}$$

STEP 2 Write the percent as a ratio.

$$\frac{5}{\boxed{}} = \frac{24}{\boxed{}}$$

STEP 3 Simplify the known ratio.

$$\frac{5 \div \boxed{}}{100 \div \boxed{}} = \frac{1}{\boxed{}} = \frac{24}{\boxed{}}$$

STEP 4 Write an equivalent ratio.

Think: The numerator should be _____.

$$\frac{1 \times \boxed{}}{20 \times \boxed{}} = \frac{24}{\boxed{}}$$

$$\frac{24}{\boxed{}} = \frac{24}{\boxed{}}$$

So, 24 is 5% of _____.

Math Talk

MATHEMATICAL PRACTICES ❶

Evaluate What method could you use to check your answer to the Example?

Name _____

Share and Show [MATH BOARD]

Find the unknown value.

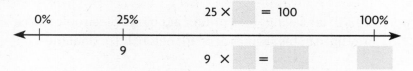

✓ **1.** 9 is 25% of _____

2. 14 is 10% of _____   ✓ **3.** 3 is 5% of _____   **4.** 12 is 60% of _____

Math Talk

MATHEMATICAL PRACTICES ⑧

Use Repeated Reasoning
Explain how to solve a problem involving a part, a whole, and a percent.

On Your Own

Find the unknown value.

5. 16 is 20% of _____

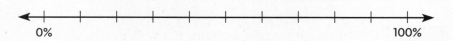

6. 42 is 50% of _____   **7.** 28 is 40% of _____   **8.** 60 is 75% of _____

9. 27 is 30% of _____   **10.** 21 is 60% of _____   **11.** 12 is 15% of _____

Solve.

12. 40% of the students in the sixth grade at Andrew's school participate in sports. If 52 students participate in sports, how many sixth graders are there at Andrew's school?

13. [GO DEEPER] There were 136 students and 34 adults at the concert. If 85% of the seats were filled, how many seats are in the auditorium?

MATHEMATICAL PRACTICE ② Use Reasoning **Algebra** Find the unknown value.

14. $40\% = \dfrac{32}{}$ **15.** $65\% = \dfrac{91}{}$ **16.** $45\% = \dfrac{54}{}$

Problem Solving • Applications

Use the advertisement for 17 and 18.

17. Corey spent 20% of his savings on a printer at Louie's Electronics. How much did Corey have in his savings account before he bought the printer?

_____

18. **THINK SMARTER** Kai spent 90% of his money on a laptop that cost $423. Does he have enough money left to buy a scanner? Explain.

_____

19. Maurice has completed 17 pages of the research paper he is writing. That is 85% of the required length of the paper. What is the required length of the paper?

_____

20. **GO DEEPER** Of 250 seventh-grade students, 175 walk to school. What percent of seventh-graders do not walk to school?

_____

21. **What's the Error?** Kate has made 20 free throws in basketball games this year. That is 80% of the free throws she has attempted. To find the total number of free throws she attempted, Kate wrote the equation $\frac{80}{100} = \frac{}{20}$. What error did Kate make?

_____

_____

Personal Math Trainer

22. **THINK SMARTER +** Maria spent 36% of her savings to buy a smart phone. The phone cost $90. How much money was in Maria's savings account before she purchased the phone? Find the unknown value.

$36\% = \dfrac{90}{\boxed{}}$

Find the Whole from a Percent

Common Core

COMMON CORE STANDARD—6.RP.A.3C
Understand ratio concepts and use ratio reasoning
to solve problems.

Find the unknown value.

1. 9 is 15% of ___60___

$$\frac{15}{100} = \frac{9}{\boxed{}}$$

$$\frac{15 \div 5}{100 \div 5} = \frac{3 \times 3}{20 \times 3} = \frac{9}{60}$$

2. 54 is 75% of _____

3. 12 is 2% of _____

4. 18 is 50% of _____

5. 16 is 40% of _____

6. 56 is 28% of _____

7. 5 is 10% of _____

8. 24 is 16% of _____

9. 15 is 25% of _____

Problem Solving · Real World

10. Michaela is hiking on a weekend camping trip. She has walked 6 miles so far. This is 30% of the total distance. What is the total number of miles she will walk?

    _____

11. A customer placed an order with a bakery for muffins. The baker has completed 37.5% of the order after baking 81 muffins. How many muffins did the customer order?

    _____

12. **WRITE** ▸Math Write a question that involves finding what number is 25% of another number. Solve using a double number line and check using equivalent ratios. Compare the methods.

    _____

    _____

Lesson Check (6.RP.3c)

1. Kareem saves his coins in a jar. 30% of the coins are pennies. If there are 24 pennies in the jar, how many coins does Kareem have?

2. A guitar shop has 19 acoustic guitars on display. This is 19% of the total number of guitars. What is the total number of guitars the shop has?

Spiral Review (6.RP.A.3a, 6.RP.A.3c, 6.NS.C.6b)

3. On a coordinate grid, in which quadrant is the point ($^-$5, 4) located?

4. A box contains 16 cherry fruit chews, 15 peach fruit chews, and 12 plum fruit chews. Which two flavors are in the ratio 5 to 4?

5. During basketball season, Marisol made $\frac{19}{25}$ of her free throws. What percent of her free throws did Marisol make?

6. Landon is entering the science fair. He has a budget of $115. He has spent 20% of the money on new materials. How much does Landon have left to spend?

Houghton Mifflin Harcourt Publishing Company

FOR MORE PRACTICE
GO TO THE
Personal Math Trainer

✓ Chapter 5 Review/Test

Personal Math Trainer
Online Assessment and Intervention

1. What percent is represented by the shaded part?

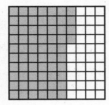

   A 46%

   B 60%

   C 64%

   D 640%

2. Write a percent to represent the shaded part.

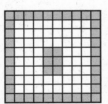

_____

3. Rosa made a mosaic wall mural using 42 black tiles, 35 blue tiles and 23 red tiles. Write a percent to represent the number of red tiles in the mural.

_____

4. Model 39%.

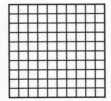

5. For 5a–5d, choose Yes or No to indicate whether the percent and the fraction represent the same amount.

5a. 50% and $\frac{1}{2}$ ○ Yes   ○ No

5b. 45% and $\frac{4}{5}$ ○ Yes   ○ No

5c. $\frac{3}{8}$ and 37.5%   ○ Yes   ○ No

5d. $\frac{2}{10}$ and 210%   ○ Yes   ○ No

6. The school orchestra has 25 woodwind instruments, 15 percussion instruments, 30 string instruments, and 30 brass instruments. Select the portion of the instruments that are percussion. Mark all that apply.

○ 15%

○ 1.5

○ $\frac{3}{20}$

○ 0.15

7. For a science project, $\frac{3}{4}$ of the students chose to make a poster and 0.25 of the students wrote a report. Rosa said that more students made a poster than wrote a report. Do you agree with Rosa? Use numbers and words to support your answer.

8. Select other ways to write 0.875. Mark all that apply.

○ 875%

○ 87.5%

○ $\frac{7}{8}$

○ $\frac{875}{100}$

Name _____

9. There are 88 marbles in a bin and 25% of the marbles are red.

There are | 22 25 62 66 | red marbles in the bin.

10. Harrison has 30 CDs in his music collection. If 40% of the CDs are country music and 30% are pop music, how many CDs are other types of music?

_____ CDs

11. For numbers 11a–11b, choose <, >, or =.

11a. 30% of 90 | < > = | 35% of 80

11b. 25% of 16 | < > = | 20% of 25

12. GO DEEPER There were 200 people who voted at the town council meeting. Of these people, 40% voted for building a new basketball court in the park. How many people voted against building the new basketball court? Use numbers and words to explain your answer.

13. James and Sarah went out to lunch. The price of lunch for both of them was $20. They tipped their server 20% of that amount. How much did each person pay if they shared the price of lunch and the tip equally?

_____

14. A sandwich shop has 30 stores and 60% of the stores are in California. The rest of the stores are in Nevada.

Part A

How many stores are in California and how many are in Nevada?

_____

Part B

The shop opens 10 new stores. Some are in California, and some are in Nevada. Complete the table.

Locations of Sandwich Shops		
	Percent of Stores	**Number of Stores**
California		
Nevada	45%	

Personal Math Trainer

15. THINK SMARTER ✚ Juanita has saved 35% of the money that she needs to buy a new bicycle. If she has saved $63, how much money does the bicycle cost? Use numbers and words to explain your answer.

16. For 16a–16d, choose Yes or No to indicate whether the statement
is correct.

16a.   12 is 20% of 60.   ○ Yes   ○ No

16b.   24 is 50% of 48.   ○ Yes   ○ No

16c.   14 is 75% of 20.   ○ Yes   ○ No

16d.   9 is 30% of 30.   ○ Yes   ○ No

17. Heather and her family are going to the grand opening of a new
amusement park. There is a special price on tickets this weekend.
Tickets cost $56 each. This is 70% of the cost of a regular price ticket.

Part A

What is the cost of a regular price ticket? Show your work.

Part B

Heather's mom says that they would save more than $100 if they buy
4 tickets for their family on opening weekend. Do you agree or disagree
with Heather's mom? Use numbers and words to support your answer.
If her statement is incorrect, explain the correct way to solve it.

18. Elise said that 0.2 equals 2%. Use words and numbers to explain
her mistake.

19. Write 18% as a fraction.

_____

20. Noah wants to put a variety of fish in his new fish tank. His tank is large enough to hold a maximum of 70 fish.

Part A

Complete the table.

Type of Fish	Percent of Maximum Number	Number of Fish in Tank
Rainbow fish	20%	
Swordtail	40%	
Molly	30%	

Part B

Has Noah put the maximum number of fish in his tank? Use number and words to explain how you know. If he has not put the maximum number of fish in the tank, how many more fish could he put in the tank?

6 Units of Measure

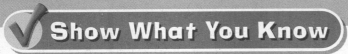

Show What You Know

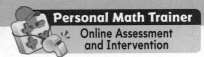

Personal Math Trainer
Online Assessment
and Intervention

Check your understanding of important skills.

Name _____

▶ **Choose the Appropriate Unit** **Circle the more reasonable unit to measure the object.** (4.MD.A.1)

1. the length of a car
inches or feet

2. the length of a soccer field
meters or kilometers

▶ **Multiply and Divide by 10, 100, and 1,000** **Use mental math.** (5.NBT.A.2)

3. 2.51×10

_____

4. 5.3×100

_____

5. $0.71 \times 1{,}000$

_____

6. $3.25 \div 10$

_____

7. $8.65 \div 100$

_____

8. $56.2 \div 1{,}000$

_____

▶ **Convert Units** **Complete.** (5.MD.A.1)

9. $12 \text{ lb} = \blacksquare \text{ oz}$
Think: 1 lb = 16 oz

_____

10. $8 \text{ c} = \blacksquare \text{ pt}$
Think: 2 c = 1 pt

_____

11. $84 \text{ in.} = \blacksquare \text{ ft}$
Think: 12 in. = 1 ft

_____

A cheetah can run at a rate of 105,600 yards per hour. Find the number of miles the cheetah could run at this rate in 5 minutes.

Vocabulary Builder

▶ **Visualize It** ••••••••••••••••••••••••••••••••••

Sort the review words into the Venn diagram.

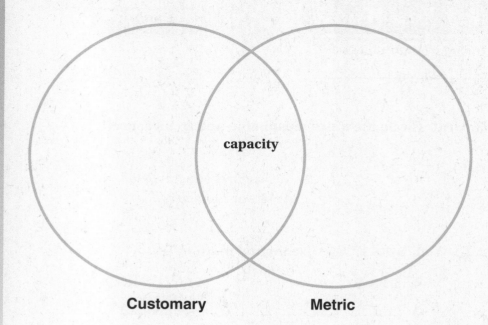

Customary   Metric

▶ **Understand Vocabulary** ••••••••••••••••••••••••

Complete the sentences by using the checked words.

1. A rate in which the two quantities are equal but use different

   units is called a _____.

2. _____ is the the amount of matter in an object.

3. _____ is the amount a container can hold.

4. The _____ of an object tells how heavy the
   object is.

5. Inches, feet, and yards are all customary units used to measure

   _____.

6. A _____ is a larger unit of capacity than a quart.

GO DIGITAL
• Interactive Student Edition
• Multimedia eGlossary

Chapter 6 Vocabulary

capacity

capacidad

9

common factor

factor común

12

conversion factor

factor de conversión

16

denominator

denominador

20

formula

fórmula

34

numerator

numerador

66

square unit

unidad cuadrada

96

weight

peso

107

A number that is a factor of two or more numbers

Example:

Factors of 16: 1, 2, 4, 8, 16

Factors of 20: 1, 2, 4, 5, 10, 20

The amount a container can hold

Examples: $\frac{1}{2}$ gallon, 2 quarts

The number below the bar in a fraction that tells how many equal parts are in the whole or in the group

$\frac{3}{4}$ ⟵ denominator

A rate in which two quantities are equal, but use different units

Example: 1 yard = 3 feet, so use the rate $\frac{1 \text{ yd}}{3 \text{ ft}}$ to convert yards from feet

The number above the bar in a fraction that tells how many equal parts of the whole are being considered

$\frac{3}{4}$ ⟵ numerator

A set of symbols that expresses a mathematical rule

Example: Use $d = r \times t$ to find distance.

How heavy an object is

Example:

soccer ball
14–16 ounces

A unit used to measure area such as square foot (ft²), square meter (m²), and so on

Bingo

For 3–6 players

Word Box

capacity

common factor

conversion factor

denominator

formula

numerator

square unit

weight

Materials

- 1 set of word cards
- 1 Bingo board for each player
- game markers

How to Play

1. The caller chooses a card and reads the definition. Then the caller puts the card in a second pile.
2. Players put a marker on the word that matches the definition each time they find it on their Bingo boards.
3. Repeat Steps 1 and 2 until a player marks 5 boxes in a line going down, across, or on a slant and calls "Bingo."
4. To check the answers, the player who said "Bingo" reads the words aloud while the caller checks the definitions.

The Write Way

Reflect

Choose one idea. Write about it.

- Describe a situation in which you might use a conversion factor.
- Sumeer has a jar that holds 4 cups of water. Eliza has a bottle that holds 3 pints of water. Explain whose container has the greater capacity.
- If the area of a room is 20 feet by 6 yards, tell how to figure out the room's area in square feet.
- Write and solve a word problem that uses the formula $d = r \times t$.

Name _____

Convert Units of Length

Essential Question How can you use ratio reasoning to convert from one unit of length to another?

Common Core Ratios and Proportional Relationships—6.RP.A.3d
MATHEMATICAL PRACTICES
MP2, MP6, MP8

In the customary measurement system, some of the common units of length are inches, feet, yards, and miles. You can multiply by an appropriate conversion factor to convert between units. A **conversion factor** is a rate in which the two quantities are equal, but use different units.

> **Customary Units of Length**
>
> 1 foot (ft) = 12 inches (in.)
> 1 yard (yd) = 36 inches
> 1 yard = 3 feet
> 1 mile (mi) = 5,280 feet
> 1 mile = 1,760 yards

Unlock the Problem

In a soccer game, Kyle scored a goal. Kyle was 33 feet from the goal. How many yards from the goal was he?

> **Math Idea**
> When the same unit appears in a numerator and a denominator, you can divide by the common unit before multiplying as you would with a common factor.

🔑 **Convert 33 feet to yards.**

Choose a conversion factor. **Think:** I'm converting *to* yards *from* feet.

1 yard = 3 feet, so use the rate $\frac{1 \text{ yd}}{3 \text{ ft}}$.

Multiply 33 feet by the conversion factor. Units of *feet* appear in a numerator and a denominator, so you can divide the units before multiplying.

$$33 \text{ ft} \times \frac{1 \text{ yd}}{3 \text{ ft}} = \frac{33 \cancel{\text{ft}}}{1} \times \frac{1 \text{ yd}}{3 \cancel{\text{ft}}} = \underline{\hspace{1.5cm}} \text{ yd}$$

So, Kyle was _____ yards from the goal.

🔑 **How many inches from the goal was Kyle?**

Choose a conversion factor. **Think:** I'm converting *to* inches *from* feet.

12 inches = 1 foot, so use the rate $\frac{12 \text{ in.}}{1 \text{ ft}}$.

Multiply 33 ft by the conversion factor.

$$33 \text{ ft} \times \frac{12 \text{ in.}}{1 \text{ ft}} = \frac{33 \cancel{\text{ft}}}{1} \times \frac{12 \text{ in.}}{1 \cancel{\text{ft}}} = \underline{\hspace{2.5cm}} \text{ in.}$$

So, Kyle was _____ inches from the goal.

 Math Talk

MATHEMATICAL PRACTICES ⑥

Explain How do you know which unit to use in the numerator and which unit to use in the denominator of a conversion factor?

Metric Units You can use a similar process to convert metric units. Metric units are used throughout most of the world. One advantage of using the metric system is that the units are related by powers of 10.

Metric Units of Length

1,000 millimeters (mm) = 1 meter (m)
100 centimeters (cm) = 1 meter
10 decimeters (dm) = 1 meter
1 dekameter (dam) = 10 meters
1 hectometer (hm) = 100 meters
1 kilometer (km) = 1,000 meters

🔑 **Example** A passenger airplane is 73.9 meters long. What is the length of the airplane in centimeters? What is the length in kilometers?

⚠️ **ERROR Alert**

Be sure to use the correct conversion factor. The units you are converting from should simplify to 1, leaving only the units you are converting to.

🔑 **One Way** Use a conversion factor.

$$73.9 \text{ meters} = \blacksquare \text{ centimeters}$$

Choose a conversion factor.

100 cm = 1 m, so use the rate $\dfrac{\boxed{} \text{ cm}}{\boxed{} \text{ m}}$.

Multiply 73.9 meters by the conversion factor. Simplify the common units before multiplying.

$$\dfrac{73.9 \, \cancel{m}}{1} \times \dfrac{\boxed{} \, cm}{\boxed{} \, \cancel{m}} = \underline{\hspace{2cm}} cm$$

So, 73.9 meters is equal to _____ centimeters.

🔑 **Another Way** Use powers of 10.

Metric units are related to each other by factors of 10.

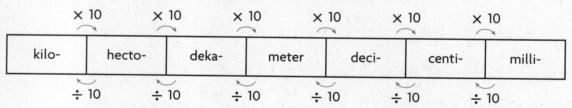

| kilo- | hecto- | deka- | meter | deci- | centi- | milli- |

73.9 meters = ⬛ kilometers

Use the chart.

Kilometers are 3 places to the left of meters in the chart. Move the decimal point 3 places to the left. This is the same as dividing by 1,000.

73.9   0.0739

So, 73.9 meters is equal to _____ kilometer.

Math Talk

MATHEMATICAL PRACTICES ②

Reasoning If you convert 285 centimeters to decimeters, will the number of decimeters be greater or less than the number of centimeters? Explain.

316

Name _____

Convert to the given unit.

1. 3 miles = ▇ yards

   conversion factor: $\dfrac{\boxed{}\ \text{yd}}{\boxed{}\ \text{mi}}$

   3 miles = $\dfrac{3\ \text{mi}}{1} \times \dfrac{1{,}760\ \text{yd}}{1\ \text{mi}} =$ _____ yd

2. 43 dm = _____ hm

3. 9 yd = _____ in.

4. 72 ft = _____ yd

5. 7,500 mm = _____ dm

MATHEMATICAL PRACTICES ⑧

Generalize How do you convert from inches to yards and yards to inches?

On Your Own

6. Rohan used 9 yards of ribbon to wrap gifts. How many inches of ribbon did he use?

7. One species of frog can grow to a maximum length of 12.4 millimeters. What is the maximum length of this frog species in centimeters?

8. The height of the Empire State Building measured to the top of the lightning rod is approximately 443.1 meters. What is this height in hectometers?

9. **GO DEEPER** A snail moves at a speed of 2.5 feet per minute. How many yards will the snail have moved in half of an hour?

Practice: Copy and Solve Compare. Write <, >, or =.

10. 32 feet ◯ 11 yards

11. 537 cm ◯ 5.37 m

12. 75 inches ◯ 6 feet

Problem Solving • Applications (Real World)

What's the Error?

13. **THINK SMARTER** The Redwood National Park is home to some of the largest trees in the world. Hyperion is the tallest tree in the park, with a height of approximately 379 feet. Tom wants to find the height of the tree in yards.

Tom converted the height this way:

3 feet = 1 yard

conversion factor: $\dfrac{3 \text{ ft}}{1 \text{ yd}}$

$$\dfrac{379 \text{ ft}}{1} \times \dfrac{3 \text{ ft}}{1 \text{ yd}} = 1{,}137 \text{ yd}$$

Find and describe Tom's error.	**Show how to correctly convert from 379 feet to yards.**

So, 379 feet = _____ yards.

• **MATHEMATICAL PRACTICE ⑥ Explain** how you knew Tom's answer was incorrect.

_____

_____

---

14. **THINK SMARTER** Choose <, >, or =.

14a. 12 yards [< / > / =] 432 inches   14b. 321 cm [< / > / =] 32.1 m

Common Core   COMMON CORE STANDARD—6.RP.A.3d
Understand ratio concepts and use ratio reasoning to solve problems.

Convert to the given unit.

1. 42 ft = [ ] yd

   conversion factor: $\frac{1\ yd}{3\ ft}$

   42 ft × $\frac{1\ yd}{3\ ft}$

   42 ft = 14 yd

2. 2,350 m = [ ] km

3. 18 ft = [ ] in.

4. 289 m = [ ] dm

5. 5 mi = [ ] yd

6. 35 mm = [ ] cm

Compare. Write <, >, or =.

7. 1.9 dm ◯ 1,900 mm

8. 12 ft ◯ 4 yd

9. 56 cm ◯ 56,000 km

10. 98 in. ◯ 8 ft

11. 64 cm ◯ 630 mm

12. 2 mi ◯ 10,560 ft

Problem Solving Real World

13. The giant swallowtail is the largest butterfly in the United States. Its wingspan can be as large as 16 centimeters. What is the maximum wingspan in millimeters?

14. The 102nd floor of the Sears Tower in Chicago is the highest occupied floor. It is 1,431 feet above the ground. How many yards above the ground is the 102nd floor?

15. **WRITE** ▸Math Explain why units can be simplified first when measurements are multiplied.

Lesson Check (6.RP.A.3d)

1. Justin rides his bicycle 2.5 kilometers to school. Luke walks 1,950 meters to school. How much farther does Justin ride to school than Luke walks to school?

2. The length of a room is $10\frac{1}{2}$ feet. What is the length of the room in inches?

Spiral Review (6.NS.C.8, 6.RP.A.3a, 6.RP.A.3c)

3. Each unit on the map represents 1 mile. What is the distance between the campground and the waterfall?

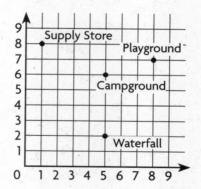

4. On a field trip, 2 vans can carry 32 students. How many students can go on a field trip when there are 6 vans?

5. According to a 2008 survey, $\frac{29}{50}$ of all teens have sent at least one text message in their lives. What percent of teens have sent a text message?

6. Of the students in Ms. Danver's class, 6 walk to school. This represents 30% of her students. How many students are in Ms. Danver's class?

© Houghton Mifflin Harcourt Publishing Company

FOR MORE PRACTICE
GO TO THE
Personal Math Trainer

Name _____

Convert Units of Capacity

Essential Question How can you use ratio reasoning to convert from one unit of capacity to another?

Common Core Ratios and Proportional Relationships—6.RP.A.3d
MATHEMATICAL PRACTICES
MP2, MP6

Capacity measures the amount a container can hold when filled. In the customary measurement system, some common units of capacity are fluid ounces, cups, pints, quarts, and gallons. You can convert between units by multiplying the given units by an appropriate conversion factor.

Customary Units of Capacity

8 fluid ounces (fl oz)	= 1 cup (c)
2 cups	= 1 pint (pt)
2 pints	= 1 quart (qt)
4 cups	= 1 quart
4 quarts	= 1 gallon (gal)

Unlock the Problem Real World

A dairy cow produces about 25 quarts of milk each day. How many gallons of milk does the cow produce each day?

- How are quarts and gallons related?

  _____

- Why can you multiply a quantity by $\frac{1 \text{ gal}}{4 \text{ qt}}$ without changing the value of the quantity?

  _____

  _____

 Convert 25 quarts to gallons.

Choose a conversion factor. **Think:** I'm converting *to* gallons *from* quarts.

1 gallon = 4 quarts, so use the rate $\frac{1 \text{ gal}}{4 \text{ qt}}$.

Multiply 25 qt by the conversion factor.

$$25 \text{ qt} \times \frac{1 \text{ gal}}{4 \text{ qt}} = \frac{25 \text{ qt}}{1} \times \frac{1 \text{ gal}}{4 \text{ qt}} = 6\,\frac{}{4} \text{ gal}$$

The fractional part of the answer can be renamed using the smaller unit.

$$6\,\frac{}{4} \text{ gal} = \underline{\quad} \text{ gallons}, \underline{\quad} \text{ quart}$$

So, the cow produces _____ gallons, _____ quart of milk each day.

 How many pints of milk does a cow produce each day?

Choose a conversion factor. **Think:** I'm converting *to* pints *from* quarts.

2 pints = 1 quart, so use the rate $\dfrac{\boxed{} \text{ pt}}{\text{qt}}$.

Multiply 25 qt by the conversion factor.

$$25 \text{ qt} \times \frac{\boxed{} \text{ pt}}{\text{qt}} = \frac{25 \text{ qt}}{1} \times \frac{\boxed{} \text{ pt}}{\text{qt}} = \underline{\quad} \text{ pt}$$

So, the cow produces _____ pints of milk each day.

Metric Units You can use a similar process to convert metric units of capacity. Just like metric units of length, metric units of capacity are related by powers of 10.

Metric Units of Capacity

1,000 milliliters (mL) = 1 liter (L)
100 centiliters (cL) = 1 liter
10 deciliters (dL) = 1 liter
1 dekaliter (daL) = 10 liters
1 hectoliter (hL) = 100 liters
1 kiloliter (kL) = 1,000 liters

🔑 **Example** A piece of Native American pottery has a capacity of 1.7 liters. What is the capacity of the pot in dekaliters? What is the capacity in milliliters?

🔑 **One Way** Use a conversion factor.

1.7 liters = ▨ dekaliters

Choose a conversion factor.

1 dekaliter = 10 liters, so use the rate

$$\frac{\text{daL}}{\text{L}}.$$

Multiply 1.7 L by the conversion factor.

$$\frac{1.7\,\cancel{L}}{1} \times \frac{\text{daL}}{\cancel{L}} = \underline{\hspace{2cm}} \text{daL}$$

So, 1.7 liters is equivalent to _____ dekaliter.

🔑 **Another Way** Use powers of 10.

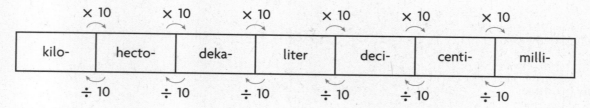

× 10	× 10	× 10	× 10	× 10	× 10	
kilo-	hecto-	deka-	liter	deci-	centi-	milli-

÷ 10   ÷ 10   ÷ 10   ÷ 10   ÷ 10   ÷ 10

1.7 liters = ▨ milliliters

Use the chart.

Milliliters are 3 places to the right of liters. So, move the decimal point 3 places to the right.

1.7   1700.

So, 1.7 liters is equal to _____ milliliters.

Math Talk

MATHEMATICAL PRACTICES ⑥

Explain Why can't you convert between units in the customary system by moving the decimal point left or right?

- **MATHEMATICAL PRACTICE ⑥ Describe a Method** Describe how you would convert kiloliters to milliliters.

Name _____

Convert to the given unit.

1. 5 quarts = ■ cups

   conversion factor: $\dfrac{c}{qt}$

   5 quarts = $\dfrac{5\ qt}{1} \times \dfrac{4\ c}{1\ qt}$ = _____ c

2. 6.7 liters = _____ hectoliters

3. 5.3 kL = _____ L

4. 36 qt = _____ gal

5. 5,000 mL = _____ cL

Math Talk MATHEMATICAL PRACTICES ⑥

Compare the customary and metric systems. In which system is it easier to convert from one unit to another?

On Your Own

6. It takes 41 gallons of water for a washing machine to wash a load of laundry. How many quarts of water does it take to wash one load?

   _____

7. Sam squeezed 237 milliliters of juice from 4 oranges. How many liters of juice did Sam squeeze?

   _____

8. **MATHEMATICAL PRACTICE ② Reason Quantitatively** A bottle contains 3.78 liters of water. Without calculating, determine whether there are more or less than 3.78 deciliters of water in the bottle. Explain your reasoning.

   _____

   _____

9. **GO DEEPER** Tonya has a 1-quart, a 2-quart, and a 3-quart bowl. A recipe asks for 16 ounces of milk. If Tonya is going to triple the recipe, what is the smallest bowl that will hold the milk?

   _____

   _____

Practice: Copy and Solve Compare. Write <, >, or =.

10. 700,000 L ◯ 70 kL

11. 6 gal ◯ 30 qt

12. 54 kL ◯ 540,000 dL

13. 10 pt ◯ 5 qt

14. 500 mL ◯ 50 L

15. 14 c ◯ 4 qt

Unlock the Problem

16. **THINK SMARTER** Jeffrey is loading cases of bottled water onto a freight elevator. There are 24 one-pint bottles in each case. The maximum weight that the elevator can carry is 1,000 pounds. If 1 gallon of water weighs 8.35 pounds, what is the maximum number of full cases Jeffrey can load onto the elevator?

a. What do you need to find?

_____

_____

_____

b. How can you find the weight of 1 case of bottled water? What is the weight?

_____

_____

_____

_____

_____

c. How can you find the number of cases that Jeffrey can load onto the elevator?

_____

_____

_____

_____

_____

_____

_____

_____

_____

_____

d. What is the maximum number of full cases Jeffrey can load onto the elevator?

_____

---

17. **GO DEEPER** Monica put 1 liter, 1 deciliter, 1 centiliter, and 1 milliliter of water into a bowl. How many milliliters of water did she put in the bowl?

_____

18. **THINK SMARTER** Select the conversions that are equivalent to 235 liters. Mark all that apply.

- **(A)** 235,000 milliliters
- **(B)** 0.235 milliliters
- **(C)** 235,000 kiloliters
- **(D)** 0.235 kiloliters

Convert Units of Capacity

COMMON CORE STANDARD—6.RP.A.3d
*Understand ratio concepts and use ratio
reasoning to solve problems.*

Convert to the given unit.

1. 7 gallons = ☐ quarts

conversion factor: $\frac{4 \text{ qt}}{1 \text{ gal}}$

$7 \text{ gal} \times \frac{4 \text{ qt}}{1 \text{ gal}}$

7 gal = 28 qt

2. 5.1 liters = ☐ kiloliters

Move the decimal point **3** places to the left.

5.1 liters = **0.0051** kiloliters

3. 20 qt = ☐ gal

4. 40 L = ☐ mL

5. 33 pt = ☐ qt ☐ pt

_____

_____

_____

6. 29 cL = ☐ daL

7. 7.7 kL = ☐ cL

8. 24 fl oz = ☐ pt ☐ c

_____

_____

_____

Problem Solving *Real World*

9. A bottle contains 3.5 liters of water. A second bottle contains 3,750 milliliters of water. How many more milliliters are in the larger bottle than in the smaller bottle?

10. Arnie's car used 100 cups of gasoline during a drive. He paid $3.12 per gallon for gas. How much did the gas cost?

_____

_____

11. **WRITE** ▸*Math* Explain how units of length and capacity are similar in the metric system.

_____

_____

Lesson Check (6.RP.A.3d)

1. Gina filled a tub with 25 quarts of water. What is this amount in gallons and quarts?

2. Four horses are pulling a wagon. Each horse drinks 45,000 milliliters of water each day. How many liters of water will the horses drink in 5 days?

Spiral Review (6.NS.C.8, 6.RP.A.2, 6.RP.A.3b, 6.RP.A.3c, 6.RP.A.3d)

3. The map shows Henry's town. Each unit represents 1 kilometer. After school, Henry walks to the library. How far does he walk?

4. An elevator travels 117 feet in 6.5 seconds. What is the elevator's speed as a unit rate?

5. Julie's MP3 player contains 860 songs. If 20% of the songs are rap songs and 15% of the songs are R&B songs, how many of the songs are other types of songs?

6. How many kilometers are equivalent to 3,570 meters?

FOR MORE PRACTICE
GO TO THE
Personal Math Trainer

Name _____

Convert Units of Weight and Mass

Essential Question How can you use ratio reasoning to convert from one unit of weight or mass to another?

Common Core **Ratios and Proportional Relationships—6.RP.A.3d**
MATHEMATICAL PRACTICES
MP1, MP2, MP3, MP4

The weight of an object is a measure of how heavy it is. Units of weight in the customary measurement system include ounces, pounds, and tons.

Customary Units of Weight

1 pound (lb) = 16 ounces (oz)
1 ton (T) = 2,000 pounds

 Unlock the Problem Real World

The largest pearl ever found weighed 226 ounces. What was the pearl's weight in pounds?

- How are ounces and pounds related?

  _____

- Will you expect the number of pounds to be greater than 226 or less than 226? Explain.

  _____

 Convert 226 ounces to pounds.

Choose a conversion factor.
Think: I'm converting *to* pounds *from* ounces.

1 lb = 16 oz, so use the rate $\dfrac{\boxed{}\text{ lb}}{\boxed{}\text{ oz}}$.

Multiply 226 ounces by the conversion factor.

$$226 \text{ oz} \times \frac{1 \text{ lb}}{16 \text{ oz}} = \frac{226 \text{ o\!\!\!/z}}{1} \times \frac{1 \text{ lb}}{16 \text{ o\!\!\!/z}} = \boxed{}\ \frac{\boxed{}}{16} \text{ lb}$$

Think: The fractional part of the answer can be renamed using the smaller unit.

$$\frac{\boxed{}}{16} \text{ lb} = \underline{\quad} \text{ lb}, \underline{\quad} \text{ oz}$$

So, the largest pearl weighed _____ pounds, _____ ounces.

 The largest emerald ever found weighed 38 pounds. What was its weight in ounces?

Choose a conversion factor.
Think: I'm converting *to* ounces *from* pounds.

16 oz = 1 lb, so use the rate $\dfrac{\boxed{}\text{ oz}}{\boxed{}\text{ lb}}$.

Multiply 38 lb by the conversion factor.

$$38 \text{ lb} \times \frac{16 \text{ oz}}{1 \text{ lb}} = \frac{38 \text{ l\!\!\!/b}}{1} \times \frac{16 \text{ oz}}{1 \text{ l\!\!\!/b}} = \underline{\qquad} \text{ oz}$$

So, the emerald weighed _____ ounces.

1. **MATHEMATICAL PRACTICE 4 Model Mathematics** Explain how you could convert the emerald's weight to tons.

_____

Metric Units The amount of matter in an object is called the mass. Metric units of mass are related by powers of 10.

Metric Units of Mass

1,000 milligrams (mg) = 1 gram (g)
100 centigrams (cg) = 1 gram
10 decigrams (dg) = 1 gram
1 dekagram (dag) = 10 grams
1 hectogram (hg) = 100 grams
1 kilogram (kg) = 1,000 grams

🔑 **Example** Corinne caught a trout with a mass of 2,570 grams. What was the mass of the trout in centigrams? What was the mass in kilograms?

🔑 **One Way** Use a conversion factor.

2,570 grams to centigrams

Choose a conversion factor.   100 cg = 1 g, so use the rate ▭ $\frac{cg}{g}$.

Multiply 2,570 g by the conversion factor. $\frac{2{,}570 \cancel{g}}{1} \times \frac{100 \text{ cg}}{1 \cancel{g}} = $ _____ cg

So, the trout's mass was _____ centigrams.

🔑 **Another Way** Use powers of 10.

Recall that metric units are related to each other by factors of 10.

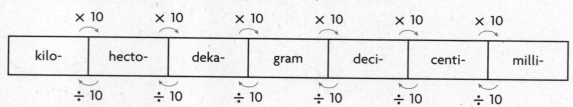

× 10	× 10	× 10	× 10	× 10	× 10
kilo-	hecto-	deka-	gram	deci-	centi-	milli-
÷ 10	÷ 10	÷ 10	÷ 10	÷ 10	÷ 10

2,570 grams to kilograms

Use the chart.

Kilograms are 3 places to the left of grams.   2570.   2.570
Move the decimal point 3 places to the left.

So, 2,570 grams = _____ kilograms.

Math Talk

MATHEMATICAL PRACTICES ②

Reason Quantitatively
Compare objects with masses of 1 dg and 1 dag. Which has a greater mass? Explain.

2. **MATHEMATICAL PRACTICE ①** **Describe Relationships** Suppose hoots and goots are units of weight, and 2 hoots = 4 goots. Which is heavier, a hoot or a goot? Explain.

_____

_____

Name _____

Share and Show MATH BOARD

Convert to the given unit.

1. 9 pounds = [ ] ounces

   conversion factor: $\dfrac{\boxed{}\ \text{oz}}{\boxed{}\ \text{lb}}$

   9 pounds = 9 lb × $\dfrac{16\ \text{oz}}{1\ \text{lb}}$ = _____ oz

2. 3.77 grams = _____ dekagram

☑ 3. Amanda's computer weighs 56 ounces. How many pounds does it weigh?

☑ 4. A honeybee can carry 40 mg of nectar. How many grams of nectar can a honeybee carry?

_____

_____

Math Talk MATHEMATICAL PRACTICES ③

Compare How are metric units of capacity and mass alike? How are they different?

On Your Own

Convert to the given unit.

5. 4 lb = _____ oz

6. 7.13 g = _____ cg

7. 3 T = _____ lb

8. The African Goliath frog can weigh up to 7 pounds. How many ounces can the Goliath frog weigh?

9. GO DEEPER The mass of a standard hockey puck must be at least 156 grams. What is the minimum mass of 8 hockey pucks in kilograms?

_____

_____

Practice: Copy and Solve Compare. Write <, >, or =.

10. 250 lb ◯ 0.25 T

11. 65.3 hg ◯ 653 dag

12. 5 T ◯ 5,000 lb

13. THINK SMARTER Masses of precious stones are measured in carats, where 1 carat = 200 milligrams. What is the mass of a 50-dg diamond in carats?

_____

Problem Solving • Applications Real World

Use the table for 14–17.

14. Express the weight range for bowling balls in pounds.

_____

15. GO DEEPER How many more pounds does the heaviest soccer ball weigh than the heaviest baseball? Round your answer to the nearest hundredth.

_____

16. THINK SMARTER A manufacturer produces 3 tons of baseballs per day and packs them in cartons of 24 baseballs each. If all of the balls are the minimum allowable weight, how many cartons of balls does the company produce each day?

_____

17. MATHEMATICAL PRACTICE ⑤ **Communicate** Explain how you could use mental math to estimate the number of soccer balls it would take to produce a total weight of 1 ton.

_____

_____

_____

_____

Sport Ball Weights (in ounces)	
baseball 5–5.25	handball 2.1–2.3
bowling ball 160–256	soccer ball 14–16

····· **WRITE** *Math* • **Show Your Work** ·····

18. THINK SMARTER The Wilson family's newborn baby weighs 84 ounces. Choose the numbers to show the baby's weight in pounds and ounces.

5	
6	pounds
7	

3	
4	ounces
5	

Convert Units of Weight and Mass

Common Core **COMMON CORE STANDARD—6.RP.A.3d**
Understand ratio concepts and use ratio reasoning to solve problems.

Convert to the given unit.

1. 5 pounds = [____] ounces

conversion factor: $\dfrac{16 \text{ oz}}{1 \text{ lb}}$

5 pounds = 5 ~~lb~~ × $\dfrac{16 \text{ oz}}{1 \text{ ~~lb~~}}$ = **80**oz

2. 2.36 grams = [____] hectograms

Move the decimal point **2** places to the left.

2.36 grams = **0.0236** hectogram

3. 30 g = [____] dg

4. 17.2 hg = [____] g

5. 400 lb = [____] T

6. 38,600 mg = [____] dag

7. 87 oz = [____] lb [____] oz

8. 0.65 T = [____] lb

Problem Solving (Real World)

9. Maggie bought 52 ounces of swordfish selling for $6.92 per pound. What was the total cost?

10. Three bunches of grapes have masses of 1,000 centigrams, 1,000 decigrams, and 1,000 grams, respectively. What is the total combined mass of the grapes in kilograms?

11. **WRITE** ▶*Math* Explain how you would find the number of ounces in 0.25T.

_____

_____

© Houghton Mifflin Harcourt Publishing Company

Lesson Check (6.RP.A.3d)

1. The mass of Denise's rock sample is 684 grams. The mass of Pauline's rock sample is 29,510 centigrams. How much greater is the mass of Denise's sample than Pauline's sample?

_____

2. A sign at the entrance to a bridge reads: Maximum allowable weight 2.25 tons. Jason's truck weighs 2,150 pounds. How much additional weight can he carry?

_____

Spiral Review (6.RP.A.1, 6.RP.A.2, 6.RP.A.3a, 6.RP.A.3b, 6.RP.A.3c)

3. There are 23 students in a math class. Twelve of them are boys. What is the ratio of girls to total number of students?

_____

4. Miguel hiked 3 miles in 54 minutes. At this rate, how long will it take him to hike 5 miles?

_____

5. Marco borrowed $150 from his brother. He has paid back 30% so far. How much money does Marco still owe his brother?

_____

6. How many milliliters are equivalent to 2.7 liters?

_____

© Houghton Mifflin Harcourt Publishing Company

FOR MORE PRACTICE
GO TO THE
Personal Math Trainer

Name _____

✓ Mid-Chapter Checkpoint

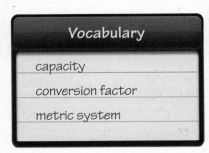

Vocabulary

Choose the best term from the box to complete the sentence.

Vocabulary
capacity
conversion factor
metric system

1. A _____ is a rate in which the two quantities are equal, but use different units. (p. 315)

2. _____ is the amount a container can hold. (p. 321)

Concepts and Skills

Convert units to solve. (6.RP.A.3d)

3. A professional football field is 160 feet wide. What is the width of the field in yards?

_____

4. Julia drinks 8 cups of water per day. How many quarts of water does she drink per day?

_____

5. The mass of Hinto's math book is 4,458 grams. What is the mass of 4 math books in kilograms?

_____

6. Turning off the water while brushing your teeth saves 379 centiliters of water. How many liters of water can you save if you turn off the water the next 3 times you brush your teeth?

_____

Convert to the given unit. (6.RP.A.3d)

7. 34.2 mm = _____ cm

8. 42 in. = _____ ft

9. 1.4 km = _____ hm

10. 4 gal = _____ qt

11. 53 dL = _____ daL

12. 28 c = _____ pt

13. Trenton's laptop is 32 centimeters wide. What is the width of the laptop in decimeters? (6.RP.A.3d)

_____

14. A truck is carrying 8 cars weighing an average of 4,500 pounds each. What is the total weight in tons of the cars on the truck? (6.RP.A.3d)

_____

15. GO DEEPER Ben's living room is a rectangle measuring 10 yards by 168 inches. By how many feet does the length of the room exceed the width? (6.RP.A.3d)

_____

16. Jessie served 13 pints of orange juice at her party. How many quarts of orange juice did she serve? (6.RP.A.3d)

_____

17. Kaylah's cell phone has a mass of 50,000 centigrams. What is the mass of her phone in grams? (6.RP.A.3d)

_____

Name _____

Transform Units

Essential Question How can you transform units to solve problems?

You can sometimes use the units of the quantities in a problem to help you decide how to solve the problem.

 Common Core

Ratios and Proportional Relationships—6.RP.A.3d

MATHEMATICAL PRACTICES
MP1, MP3, MP6

 Unlock the Problem Real World

A car's gas mileage is the average distance the car can travel on 1 gallon of gas. Maria's car has a gas mileage of 20 miles per gallon. How many miles can Maria travel on 9 gallons of gas?

- Would you expect the answer to be greater or less than 20 miles? Why?

_____

_____

 Analyze the units in the problem.

STEP 1 Identify the units.

You know two quantities: the car's gas mileage and the amount of gas.

Gas mileage: 20 miles per gallon $= \dfrac{20}{1}$ _____

Amount of gas: 9 _____

You want to know a third quantity: the distance the car can travel.

Distance: ■ _____

_____

STEP 2 Determine the relationship among the units.

Think: The answer needs to have units of miles. If I multiply $\frac{20 \text{ miles}}{1 \text{ gallon}}$ by 9 gallons, I can simplify the units. The product will have units of

_____, which is what I want.

_____

STEP 3 Use the relationship.

$$\frac{20 \text{ mi}}{1 \text{ gal}} \times 9 \text{ gal} = \frac{20 \text{ mi}}{1 \, \cancel{\text{gal}}} \times \frac{9 \, \cancel{\text{gal}}}{1} = \underline{\hspace{2cm}}$$

So, Maria can travel _____ on 9 gallons of gas.

1. Explain why the units of gallons are crossed out in the multiplication step above.

_____

_____

Sometimes you may need to convert units before solving a problem.

🔑 Example

The material for a rectangular awning has an area of 315 square feet. If the width of the material is 5 yards, what is the length of the material in feet? (Recall that the area of a rectangle is equal to its length times its width.)

STEP 1 Identify the units.

You know two quantities: the area of the material and the width of the material.

Area: 315 sq ft = 315 ft × ft

Width: 5 _____

You want to know a third quantity: the length of the material.

Length: ▮ ft

STEP 2 Determine the relationship among the units.

Think: The answer needs to have units of feet. So, I should convert the width from yards to feet.

Width: $\dfrac{5 \text{ yd}}{1} \times \dfrac{ \text{ft}}{1 \text{ yd}} = \boxed{}$ ft

Think: If I divide the area by the width, the units will simplify. The quotient will have units of _____, which is what I want.

STEP 3 Use the relationship.

Divide the area by the width to find the length.

315 sq ft ÷ _____ ft

Write the division using a fraction bar.

$\dfrac{\boxed{} \text{ sq ft}}{15 \text{ ft}}$

Write the units of area as a product and divide the common units.

$\dfrac{\boxed{} \text{ ft} \times \text{ft}}{\text{ft}} = \boxed{}$ ft

So, the length of the material is _____.

> **Math Idea**
> You can write units of area as products.
> sq ft = ft × ft

 Math Talk

MATHEMATICAL PRACTICES ①

Analyze How can examining the units in a problem help you solve the problem?

2. **MATHEMATICAL PRACTICE ③ Apply** Explain how knowing how to find the area of a rectangle could help you solve the problem above.

_____

_____

3. **MATHEMATICAL PRACTICE ⑥ Explain** why the answer is in feet.

_____

_____

_____

Name _____

Share and Show MATH BOARD

✓ **1.** A dripping faucet leaks 12 gallons of water per day. How many gallons does the faucet leak in 6 days?

Quantities you know: $\frac{12}{1}$ _____ and _____ days

Quantity you want to know: ▪ _____

$$\frac{\text{gal}}{1 \text{ day}} \times \text{days} = \underline{}$$

So, the faucet leaks _____ in 6 days.

✓ **2.** Bananas sell for $0.44 per pound. How much will 7 pounds of bananas cost?

_____

3. Grizzly Park is a rectangular park with an area of 24 square miles. The park is 3 miles wide. What is its length in miles?

_____

On Your Own

Multiply or divide the quantities.

4. $\frac{24 \text{ kg}}{1 \text{ min}} \times 15 \text{ min}$

_____

5. 216 sq cm ÷ 8 cm

_____

6. $\frac{17 \text{ L}}{1 \text{ hr}} \times 9 \text{ hr}$

_____

7. **GO DEEPER** The rectangular rug in Marcia's living room measures 12 feet by 108 inches. What is the rug's area in square feet?

_____

8. **MATHEMATICAL PRACTICE ①** **Make Sense of Problems** A box-making machine makes cardboard boxes at a rate of 72 boxes per minute. How many minutes does it take to make 360 boxes?

_____

Personal Math Trainer

9. **THINK SMARTER ＋** The area of an Olympic-size swimming pool is 1,250 square meters. The length of the pool is 5,000 centimeters. Select True or False for each statement.

9a. The length of the pool is 50 meters. ○ True ○ False

9b. The width of the pool is 25 meters. ○ True ○ False

9c. The area of the pool is 1.25 square kilometers ○ True ○ False

Connect to Reading

Make Predictions

A *prediction* is a guess about something in the future. A prediction is more likely to be accurate if it is based on facts and logical reasoning.

The Hoover Dam is one of America's largest producers of hydroelectric power. Up to 300,000 gallons of water can move through the dam's generators every second. Predict the amount of water that moves through the generators in half of an hour.

FACT		PREDICTION
300,000 gallons per second	→	? gallons in half of an hour

Use what you know about transforming units to make a prediction.

You know the rate of the water through the generators, and you are given an amount of time.

Rate of flow: $\dfrac{\boxed{}\text{ gal}}{1\text{ sec}}$; time: $\dfrac{1}{2}$ _____

You want to find the amount of water.

Amount of water: ■ gallons

Convert the amount of time to seconds to match the units in the rate.

$\dfrac{1}{2}$ hr = $\boxed{}$ min

$\dfrac{30\ \cancel{\text{min}}}{1} \times \dfrac{\boxed{}\text{ sec}}{1\ \cancel{\text{min}}} = \underline{\hspace{2cm}}$ sec

Multiply the rate by the amount of time to find the amount of water.

$\dfrac{\boxed{}\text{ gal}}{\text{sec}} \times \dfrac{\underline{\hspace{1cm}}\text{ sec}}{1} = \underline{\hspace{2cm}}$ gal

So, a good prediction of the amount of water that moves through the generators in half of an hour is _____.

Transform units to solve.

10. An average of 19,230 people tour the Hoover Dam each week. Predict the number of people touring the dam in a year.

11. **THINK SMARTER** The Hoover Dam generates an average of about 11,506,000 kilowatt-hours of electricity per day. Predict the number of kilowatt-hours generated in 7 weeks.

© Houghton Mifflin Harcourt Publishing Company • Image Credits: (t) ©Ron Chapple Stock/Alamy Images

Transform Units

 COMMON CORE STANDARD—6.RP.A.3d
Understand ratio concepts and use ratio reasoning to solve problems.

Multiply or divide the quantities.

1. $\dfrac{62\text{ g}}{1\text{ day}} \times 4\text{ days}$

$\dfrac{62\text{ g}}{1\text{ day}} \times \dfrac{4\text{ days}}{1} = 248\text{ g}$

2. $322\text{ sq yd} \div 23\text{ yd}$

$\dfrac{322\text{ sq yd}}{23\text{ yd}}$

$\dfrac{322\text{ yd} \times \text{yd}}{23\text{ yd}} = 14\text{ yd}$

3. $\dfrac{128\text{ kg}}{1\text{ hr}} \times 10\text{ hr}$

4. $136\text{ sq km} \div 8\text{ km}$

5. $\dfrac{88\text{ lb}}{1\text{ day}} \times 12\text{ days}$

6. $154\text{ sq mm} \div 11\text{ mm}$

7. $\dfrac{\$150}{1\text{ sq ft}} \times 20\text{ sq ft}$

8. $234\text{ sq ft} \div 18\text{ ft}$

Problem Solving *Real World*

9. Green grapes are on sale for $2.50 a pound. How much will 9 pounds cost?

10. A car travels 32 miles for each gallon of gas. How many gallons of gas does it need to travel 192 miles?

11. **WRITE** ▸*Math* Write and solve a problem in which you have to transform units. Use the rate 45 people per hour in your question.

_____

_____

_____

Lesson Check (6.RP.A.3d)

1. A rectangular parking lot has an area of 682 square yards. The lot is 22 yards wide. What is the length of the parking lot?

2. A machine assembles 44 key chains per hour. How many key chains does the machine assemble in 11 hours?

Spiral Review (6.RP.A.3a, 6.RP.A.3c)

3. Three of these ratios are equivalent to $\frac{8}{20}$. Which one is NOT equivalent?

$$\frac{2}{5} \qquad \frac{12}{24} \qquad \frac{16}{40} \qquad \frac{40}{100}$$

4. The graph shows the money that Marco earns for different numbers of days worked. How much money does he earn per day?

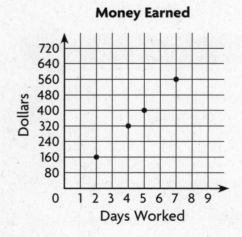

Money Earned

5. Megan answered 18 questions correctly on a test. That is 75% of the total number of questions. How many questions were on the test?

FOR MORE PRACTICE
GO TO THE
Personal Math Trainer

Name _____

Problem Solving • Distance, Rate, and Time Formulas

Essential Question How can you use the strategy *use a formula* to solve problems involving distance, rate, and time?

PROBLEM SOLVING — Lesson 6.5**

Common Core Ratios and Proportional Relationships—6.RP.A.3d
MATHEMATICAL PRACTICES MP1, MP3, MP7

You can solve problems involving distance, rate, and time by using the formulas below. In each formula, d represents distance, r represents rate, and t represents time.

Distance, Rate, and Time Formulas		
To find distance, use $d = r \times t$	To find rate, use $r = d \div t$	To find time, use $t = d \div r$

Unlock the Problem (Real World)

Helena drives 220 miles to visit Niagara Falls. She drives at an average speed of 55 miles per hour. How long does the trip take?

Use the graphic organizer to help you solve the problem.

Read the Problem

What do I need to find?

I need to find the _____ the trip takes.

What information do I need to use?

I need to use the _____ Helena travels and the _____ of speed her car is moving.

How will I use the information?

First I will choose the formula _____ because I need to find time. Next I will substitute for d and r. Then I will _____ to find the time.

Solve the Problem

• First write the formula for finding time.

$$t = d \div r$$

• Next substitute the values for d and r.

$$t = \text{_____ mi} \div \frac{\boxed{} \text{ mi}}{1 \text{ hr}}$$

• Rewrite the division as multiplication by the reciprocal of $\frac{55 \text{ mi}}{1 \text{ hr}}$.

$$t = \frac{\boxed{} \text{ mi}}{1} \times \frac{1 \text{ hr}}{\boxed{} \text{ mi}} = \text{_____ hr}$$

MATHEMATICAL PRACTICES ⑦

Look for Structure How do you know which formula to use?

So, the trip takes _____ hours.

Chapter 6 341**

🔑 Try Another Problem

Santiago's class traveled to the Museum of Natural Science for a field trip. To reach the destination, the bus traveled at a rate of 65 miles per hour for 2 hours. What distance did Santiago's class travel?

Choose a formula.

$$d = r \times t \qquad r = d \div t \qquad t = d \div r$$

Use the graphic organizer below to help you solve the problem.

Read the Problem	Solve the Problem
What do I need to find?	
What information do I need to use?	
How will I use the information?	

So, Santiago's class traveled _____ miles.

Math Talk

MATHEMATICAL PRACTICES ①

Evaluate How could you check your answer by solving the problem a different way?

1. **What if** the bus traveled at a rate of 55 miles per hour for 2.5 hours? How would the distance be affected?

   _____

2. **MATHEMATICAL PRACTICE ⑦ Identify Relationships** Describe how to find the rate if you are given the distance and time.

   _____

   _____

Name _____

Unlock the Problem

√ Choose the appropriate formula.
√ Include the unit in your answer.

1. Mariana runs at a rate of 180 meters per minute. How far does she run in 5 minutes?

   First, choose a formula.

   _____

   Next, substitute the values into the formula and solve.

   _____

   So, Mariana runs _____ in 5 minutes.

2. **THINK SMARTER** **What if** Mariana runs for 20 minutes at the same speed? How many kilometers will she run?

   _____

3. A car traveled 130 miles in 2 hours. How fast did the car travel?

   _____

4. A subway car travels at a rate of 32 feet per second. How far does it travel in 16 seconds?

   _____

5. A garden snail travels at a rate of 2.6 feet per minute. At this rate, how long will it take for the snail to travel 65 feet?

   _____

6. **GO DEEPER** A squirrel can run at a maximum speed of 12 miles per hour. At this rate, how many seconds will it take the squirrel to run 3 miles?

   _____

7. **THINK SMARTER** A cyclist rides 8 miles in 32 minutes. What is the speed of the cyclist in miles per hour?

   _____

WRITE *Math* • **Show Your Work**

© Houghton Mifflin Harcourt Publishing Company

On Your Own

8. A pilot flies 441 kilometers in 31.5 minutes. What is the speed of the airplane?

_____

9. **GO DEEPER** Chris spent half of his money on a pair of headphones. Then he spent half of his remaining money on CDs. Finally, he spent his remaining $12.75 on a book. How much money did Chris have to begin with?

_____

WRITE ▸ _Math_
Show Your Work

10. **THINK SMARTER** André and Yazmeen leave at the same time and travel 75 miles to a fair. André drives 11 miles in 12 minutes. Yazmeen drives 26 miles in 24 minutes. If they continue at the same rates, who will arrive at the fair first? Explain.

_____

_____

11. **MATHEMATICAL PRACTICE 3** **Make Arguments** Bonnie says that if she drives at an average rate of 40 miles per hour, it will take her about 2 hours to drive 20 miles across town. Does Bonnie's statement make sense? Explain.

_____

_____

Personal Math Trainer

12. **THINK SMARTER +** Claire says that if she runs at an average rate of 6 miles per hour, it will take her about 2 hours to run 18 miles. Do you agree or disagree with Claire? Use numbers and words to support your answer.

_____

_____

_____

_____

Problem Solving • Distance, Rate, and Time Formulas

Common Core

COMMON CORE STANDARD—6.RP.A.3d
Understand ratio concepts and use ratio reasoning to solve problems.

Read each problem and solve.

1. A downhill skier is traveling at a rate of 0.5 mile per minute. How far will the skier travel in 18 minutes?

$d = r \times t$

$d = \dfrac{0.5 \text{ mi}}{1 \text{ min}} \times 18 \text{ min}$

$d = 9 \text{ miles}$

2. How long will it take a seal swimming at a speed of 8 miles per hour to travel 52 miles?

_____

3. A dragonfly traveled at a rate of 35 miles per hour for 2.5 hours. What distance did the dragonfly travel?

_____

4. A race car travels 1,212 kilometers in 4 hours. What is the car's rate of speed?

_____

5. Kim and Jay leave at the same time to travel 25 miles to the beach. Kim drives 9 miles in 12 minutes. Jay drives 10 miles in 15 minutes. If they both continue at the same rate, who will arrive at the beach first?

_____

6. **WRITE** ▸*Math* Describe the location of the variable *d* in the formulas involving rate, time, and distance.

_____

_____

_____

Lesson Check (6.RP.A.3d)

1. Mark cycled 25 miles at a rate of 10 miles per hour. How long did it take Mark to cycle 25 miles?

_____

2. Joy ran 13 miles in $3\frac{1}{4}$ hours. What was her average rate?

_____

Spiral Review (6.RP.A.3a, 6.RP.A.3c, 6.RP.A.3d)

3. Write two ratios that are equivalent to $\frac{9}{12}$.

_____

_____

_____

4. In the Chang family's budget, 0.6% of the expenses are for internet service. What fraction of the family's expenses is for internet service? Write the fraction in simplest form.

_____

_____

_____

5. How many meters are equivalent to 357 centimeters?

_____

6. What is the product of the two quantities shown below?

$$\frac{60 \text{ mi}}{1 \text{ hr}} \times 12 \text{ hr}$$

_____

FOR MORE PRACTICE
GO TO THE
Personal Math Trainer

✓ Chapter 6 Review/Test

Personal Math Trainer
Online Assessment
and Intervention

1. A construction crew needs to remove 2.5 tons of river rock during the construction of new office buildings.

   The weight of the rocks is | 800 |
   | 2,000 | pounds.
   | 5,000 |

2. Select the conversions that are equivalent to 10 yards. Mark all that apply.

   (A) 20 feet   (C) 30 feet

   (B) 240 inches   (D) 360 inches

3. Meredith runs at a rate of 190 meters per minute. Use the formula $d = r \times t$ to find how far she runs in 6 minutes.

4. The table shows data for 4 cyclists during one day of training. Complete the table by finding the speed for each cyclist. Use the formula $r = d \div t$.

Cyclist	Distance (mi)	Time (hr)	Rate (mi per hr)
Alisha	36	3	
Jose	39	3	
Raul	40	4	
Ruthie	22	2	

© Houghton Mifflin Harcourt Publishing Company

GO DIGITAL Assessment Options
Chapter Test

5. For numbers 5a–5c, choose <, >, or =.

5a. 5 kilometers 〔 < > = 〕 5,000 meters

5b. 254 centiliters 〔 < > = 〕 25.4 liters

5c. 6 kilogram 〔 < > = 〕 600 gram

6. A recipe calls for 16 fluid ounces of light whipping cream. If Anthony has 1 pint of whipping cream in his refrigerator, does he have enough for the recipe? Explain your answer using numbers and words.

7. For numbers 7a–7d, choose <, >, or =.

7a. 43 feet 〔 < > = 〕 15 yards   7c. 10 pints 〔 < > = 〕 5 quarts

7b. 5 tons 〔 < > = 〕 5000 pounds   7d. 6 miles 〔 < > = 〕 600 yards

8. **GO DEEPER** The distance from Caleb's house to the school is 1.5 miles, and the distance from Ashlee's house to the school is 3,520 feet. Who lives closer to the school, Caleb or Ashlee? Use numbers and words to support your answer.

Name _____

9. Write the mass measurements in order from least to greatest.

| 7.4 kilograms | 7.4 decigrams | 7.4 centigrams |

_____ _____ _____

10. An elephant's heart beats 28 times per minute. Complete the product to find how many times its heart beats in 30 minutes.

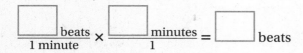

$$\frac{\boxed{}\text{ beats}}{1 \text{ minute}} \times \frac{\boxed{}\text{ minutes}}{1} = \boxed{}\text{ beats}$$

11. The length of a rectangular football field, including both end zones, is 120 yards. The area of the field is 57,600 square feet. For numbers 11a–11d, select True or False for each statement.

11a. The width of the field is   ○ True   ○ False
       480 yards.

11b. The length of the field is   ○ True   ○ False
       360 feet.

11c. The width of the field is   ○ True   ○ False
       160 feet.

11d. The area of the field is   ○ True   ○ False
       6,400 square yards.

12. Harry received a package for his birthday. The package weighed 357,000 centigrams. Select the conversions that are equivalent to 357,000 centigrams. Mark all that apply.

○ 3.57 kilograms

○ 357 dekagrams

○ 3,570 grams

○ 3,570,000 decigrams

13. Mr. Martin wrote the following problem on the board.

> Juanita's car has a gas mileage of 21 miles per gallon. How many miles can Juanita travel on 7 gallons of gas?

Alex used the expression $\frac{21 \text{ miles}}{1 \text{ gallon}} \times \frac{1}{7 \text{ gallons}}$ to find the answer. Explain Alex's mistake.

14. Mr. Chen filled his son's wading pool with 20 gallons of water.

20 gallons is equivalent to
| 80 |
| 60 |
| 40 |
quarts.

15. Nadia has a can of vegetables with a mass of 411 grams. Write equivalent conversions in the correct boxes.

4.11   41.1   0.411

kilograms	hectograms	dekagrams

16. Steve is driving 440 miles to visit the Grand Canyon. He drives at an average rate of 55 miles per hour. Explain how you can find the amount of time it will take Steve to get to the Grand Canyon.

Houghton Mifflin Harcourt Publishing Company

17. Lucy walks one time around the lake. She walks for 1.5 hours at an average rate of 3 miles per hour. What is the distance, in miles, around the lake?

_____ miles

18. The parking lot at a store has a width of 20 yards 2 feet and a length of 30 yards.

20 yards 2 feet

30 yards

Part A

Derrick says that the width could also be written as 22 feet. Explain whether you agree or disagree with Derrick.

Part B

The cost to repave the parking lot is $2 per square foot. Explain how much it would cost to repave the parking lot.

19. THINKSMARTER ➕ Jake is using a horse trailer to take his horses to his new ranch.

Part A

Complete the table by finding the weight, in pounds, of Jake's horse trailer and each horse.

	Weight (T)	Weight (lb)
Horse	0.5	
Trailer	1.25	

Part B

Jake's truck can tow a maximum weight of 5,000 pounds. What is the maximum number of horses he can take in his trailer at one time without going over the maximum weight his truck can tow? Use numbers and words to support your answer.

20. A rectangular room measures 13 feet by 132 inches. Tonya said the area of the room is 1,716 square feet. Explain her mistake, then find the area in square feet.

Glossary

Pronunciation Key

a	add, map	f	fit, half	n̄	nice, tin	p	pit, stop	û(r) burn, term
ā	ace, rate	g	go, log	ng	ring, song	r	run, poor	yo͞o fuse, few
â(r)	care, air	h	hope, hate	o	odd, hot	s	see, pass	v	vain, eve
ä	palm, father	i	it, give	ō	open, so	sh	sure, rush	w	win, away
b	bat, rub	ī	ice, write	ô	order, jaw	t	talk, sit	y	yet, yearn
ch	check, catch	j	joy, ledge	oi	oil, boy	th	thin, both	z	zest, muse
d	dog, rod	k	cool, take	ou	pout, now	t͟h	this, bathe	zh	vision, pleasure
e	end, pet	l	look, rule	o͝o	took, full	u	up, done	
ē	equal, tree	m	move, seem	o͞o	pool, food	u̇	pull book	

ə the schwa, an unstressed vowel representing the sound spelled *a* in **a**bove, *e* in sick**e**n, *i* in poss**i**ble, *o* in mel**o**n, *u* in circ**u**s

Other symbols:
- · separates words into syllables
- ′ indicates stress on a syllable

A

absolute value [ab′sə·lo͞ot val′yo͞o] **valor absoluto** The distance of an integer from zero on a number line (p. 165)

acute angle [ə·kyo͞ot′ ang′gəl] **ángulo agudo** An angle that has a measure less than a right angle (less than 90° and greater than 0°)
Example:

acute triangle [ə·kyo͞ot′ trī′ang·gəl] **triángulo acutángulo** A triangle that has three acute angles

addend [ad′end] **sumando** A number that is added to another in an addition problem

addition [ə·dish′ən] **suma** The process of finding the total number of items when two or more groups of items are joined; the inverse operation of subtraction

Addition Property of Equality [ə·dish′ən präp′ər·tē əv ē·kwôl′ə·tē] **propiedad de suma de la igualdad** The property that states that if you add the same number to both sides of an equation, the sides remain equal

additive inverse [ad′ə·tiv in′v ûrs] **inverso aditivo** The number which, when added to the given number, equals zero

algebraic expression [al·jə·brā′ik ek·spresh′ən] **expresión algebraica** An expression that includes at least one variable (p. 369)
Examples: x + 5, 3*a* − 4

angle [ang′gəl] **ángulo** A shape formed by two rays that share the same endpoint
Example:

area [âr′ē·ə] **área** The measure of the number of unit squares needed to cover a surface (p. 533)

array [ə•rā′] **matriz** An arrangement of objects in rows and columns
Example:

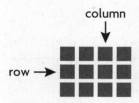

Associative Property of Addition [ə•sō′shē•ə•āt•iv präp′ər•tē əv ə•dish′ən] **propiedad asociativa de la suma** The property that states that when the grouping of addends is changed, the sum is the same
Example: $(5 + 8) + 4 = 5 + (8 + 4)$

Associative Property of Multiplication [ə•sō′shē•ə•tiv präp′ər•tē əv mul•tə•pli•kā′shən] **propiedad asociativa de la multiplicación** The property that states that when the grouping of factors is changed, the product is the same
Example: $(2 \times 3) \times 4 = 2 \times (3 \times 4)$

bar graph [bär graf] **gráfica de barras** A graph that uses horizontal or vertical bars to display countable data
Example:

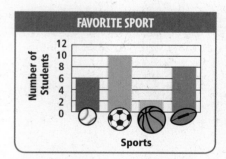

base [bās] (arithmetic) **base** A number used as a repeated factor (p. 357)
Example: $8^3 = 8 \times 8 \times 8$. The base is 8.

base [bās] (geometry) **base** In two dimensions, one side of a triangle or parallelogram which is used to help find the area. In three dimensions, a plane figure, usually a polygon or circle, which is used to partially describe a solid figure and to help find the volume of some solid figures. See also *height*.
Examples:

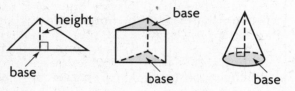

benchmark [bench′märk] **punto de referencia** A familiar number used as a point of reference

billion [bil′yən] **millardo** 1,000 millions; written as 1,000,000,000

box plot [bäks plät] **diagrama de caja** A graph that shows how data are distributed using the median, quartiles, least value, and greatest value (p. 714)
Example:

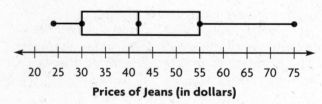

Prices of Jeans (in dollars)

capacity [kə•pas′i•tē] **capacidad** The amount a container can hold (p. 321)
Examples: $\frac{1}{2}$ gallon, 2 quarts

Celsius (°C) [sel′sē•əs] **Celsius (°C)** A metric scale for measuring temperature

closed figure [klōzd fig′yər] **figura cerrada** A figure that begins and ends at the same point

coefficient [kō•ə•fish′ənt] **coeficiente** A number that is multiplied by a variable (p. 376)
Example: 6 is the coefficient of *x* in 6*x*

common denominator [käm′ən dē•näm′ə•nāt•ər] **denominador común** A common multiple of two or more denominators
Example: Some common denominators for $\frac{1}{4}$ and $\frac{5}{6}$ are 12, 24, and 36.

common factor [käm′ən fak′tər] **factor común** A number that is a factor of two or more numbers (p. 23)

common multiple [käm′ən mul′tə•pəl] **múltiplo común** A number that is a multiple of two or more numbers

Commutative Property of Addition [kə•myoot′ ə•tiv präp′ər•tē əv ə•dish′ən] **propiedad conmutativa de la suma** The property that states that when the order of two addends is changed, the sum is the same
Example: $4 + 5 = 5 + 4$

Commutative Property of Multiplication [kə•myoot′ə•tiv präp′ər•tē əv mul•tə•pli•kāsh′ən] **propiedad conmutativa de la multiplicación** The property that states that when the order of two factors is changed, the product is the same
Example: $4 \times 5 = 5 \times 4$

compatible numbers [kəm•pat′ə•bəl num′bərz] **números compatibles** Numbers that are easy to compute with mentally

composite figure [kəm•päz′it fig′yər] **figura compuesta** A figure that is made up of two or more simpler figures, such as triangles and quadrilaterals (p. 571)
Example:

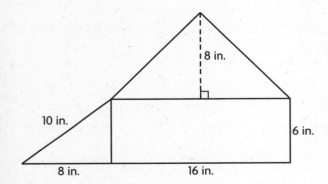

composite number [kəm•päz′it num′bər] **número compuesto** A number having more than two factors
Example: 6 is a composite number, since its factors are 1, 2, 3, and 6.

cone [kōn] **cono** A solid figure that has a flat, circular base and one vertex
Example:

congruent [kən•groo′ənt] **congruente** Having the same size and shape (p. 539)
Example:

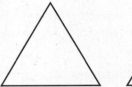

conversion factor [kən•vûr′zhən fak′tər] **factor de conversión** A rate in which two quantities are equal, but use different units (p. 315)

coordinate plane [kō•ôrd′n•it plān] **plano cartesiano** A plane formed by a horizontal line called the *x*-axis and a vertical line called the *y*-axis (p. 177)
Example:

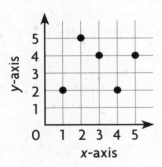

cube [kyo͞ob] **cubo** A solid figure with six congruent square faces
Example:

cubic unit [kyo͞o'bik yo͞o'nit] **unidad cúbica** A unit used to measure volume such as cubic foot (ft³), cubic meter (m³), and so on

data [dāt'ə] **datos** Information collected about people or things, often to draw conclusions about them (p. 649)

decagon [dek'ə·gän] **decágono** A polygon with 10 sides and 10 angles
Examples:

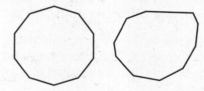

decimal [des'ə·məl] **decimal** A number with one or more digits to the right of the decimal point

decimal point [des'ə·məl point] **punto decimal** A symbol used to separate dollars from cents in money, and the ones place from the tenths place in decimal numbers

degree (°) [di·grē'] **grado (°)** A unit for measuring angles or for measuring temperature

degree Celsius (°C) [di·grē' sel'sē·əs] **grado Celsius** A metric unit for measuring temperature

degree Fahrenheit (°F) [di·grē' fâr'ən·hīt] **grado Fahrenheit** A customary unit for measuring temperature

denominator [de·näm'ə·nāt·ər] **denominador** The number below the bar in a fraction that tells how many equal parts are in the whole or in the group

Example: $\frac{3}{4}$ ← denominator

dependent variable [de·pen'dənt vâr'ē·ə·bəl] **variable dependiente** A variable whose value depends on the value of another quantity (p. 491)

difference [dif'ər·əns] **diferencia** The answer to a subtraction problem

digit [dij'it] **dígito** Any one of the ten symbols 0, 1, 2, 3, 4, 5, 6, 7, 8, 9 used to write numbers

dimension [də·men'shən] **dimensión** A measure in one direction

distribution [dis·tri·byo͞o'shən] **distribución** The overall shape of a data set

Distributive Property [di·strib'yo͞o·tiv präp'ər·tē] **propiedad distributiva** The property that states that multiplying a sum by a number is the same as multiplying each addend in the sum by the number and then adding the products (p. 24)
Example: $3 \times (4 + 2) = (3 \times 4) + (3 \times 2)$
$$3 \times 6 = 12 + 6$$
$$18 = 18$$

divide [də·vīd'] **dividir** To separate into equal groups; the inverse operation of multiplication

dividend [div'ə·dend] **dividendo** The number that is to be divided in a division problem
Example: $36 \div 6$; $6\overline{)36}$ The dividend is 36.

divisible [də•viz'ə•bəl] **divisible** A number is divisible by another number if the quotient is a counting number and the remainder is zero
Example: 18 is divisible by 3.

division [də•vizh'ən] **división** The process of sharing a number of items to find how many groups can be made or how many items will be in a group; the operation that is the inverse of multiplication

Division Property of Equality [də•vizh'ən präp'ər•tē əv ē•kwôl'ə•tē] **propiedad de división de la igualdad** The property that states that if you divide both sides of an equation by the same nonzero number, the sides remain equal

divisor [də•vī'zər] **divisor** The number that divides the dividend
Example: 15 ÷ 3; 3)‾15‾ The divisor is 3.

dot plot [dot plät] **diagrama de puntos** A graph that shows frequency of data along a number line (p. 661)
Example:

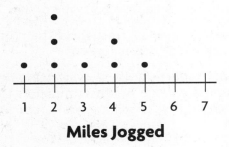

Miles Jogged

edge [ej] **arista** The line where two faces of a solid figure meet
Example:

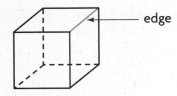

equation [i•kwā'zhən] **ecuación** An algebraic or numerical sentence that shows that two quantities are equal (p. 421)

equilateral triangle [ē•kwi•lat'ər•əl trī'ang•gəl] **triángulo equilátero** A triangle with three congruent sides
Example:

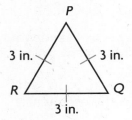

equivalent [ē•kwiv'ə•lənt] **equivalente** Having the same value

equivalent decimals [ē•kwiv'ə•lənt des'ə•məlz] **decimales equivalentes** Decimals that name the same number or amount
Example: 0.4 = 0.40 = 0.400

equivalent expressions [ē•kwiv'ə•lənt ek•spresh'ənz] **expresiones equivalentes** Expressions that are equal to each other for any values of their variables (p. 401)
Example: 2x + 4x = 6x

equivalent fractions [ē•kwiv'ə•lənt frak'shənz] **fracciones equivalentes** Fractions that name the same amount or part
Example: $\frac{3}{4} = \frac{6}{8}$

equivalent ratios [ē•kwiv'ə•lənt rā'shē•ōz] **razones equivalentes** Ratios that name the same comparison (p. 223)

estimate [es'tə•mit] *noun* **estimación (s)** A number close to an exact amount

estimate [es'tə•māt] *verb* **estimar (v)** To find a number that is close to an exact amount

evaluate [ē•val′yoō•āt] **evaluar** To find the value of a numerical or algebraic expression (p. 363)

even [ē′vən] **par** A whole number that has a 0, 2, 4, 6, or 8 in the ones place

expanded form [ek•span′did fôrm] **forma desarrollada** A way to write numbers by showing the value of each digit
Example: 832 = 800 + 30 + 2

exponent [eks′pōn•ənt] **exponente** A number that shows how many times the base is used as a factor (p. 357)
Example: $10^3 = 10 \times 10 \times 10$; 3 is the exponent.

> **Word History**
>
> *Exponent* comes from the combination of the Latin roots *ex* ("out of") + *ponere* ("to place"). In the 17th century, mathematicians began to use complicated quantities. The idea of positioning a number by raising it "out of place" is traced to René Descartes.

expression [ek•spresh′ən] **expresión** A mathematical phrase or the part of a number sentence that combines numbers, operation signs, and sometimes variables, but does not have an equal or inequality sign

face [fās] **cara** A polygon that is a flat surface of a solid figure
Example:

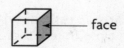
face

fact family [fakt fam′ə•lē] **familia de operaciones** A set of related multiplication and division, or addition and subtraction, equations
Example: 7 × 8 = 56; 8 × 7 = 56;
56 ÷ 7 = 8; 56 ÷ 8 = 7

factor [fak′tər] **factor** A number multiplied by another number to find a product

factor tree [fak′tər trē] **árbol de factores** A diagram that shows the prime factors of a number
Example:

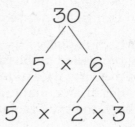

Fahrenheit (°F) [fâr′ən•hīt] **Fahrenheit (°F)** A customary scale for measuring temperature

formula [fôr′myoō•lə] **fórmula** A set of symbols that expresses a mathematical rule
Example: A = b × h

fraction [frak′shən] **fracción** A number that names a part of a whole or a part of a group

frequency [frē′kwən•sē] **frecuencia** The number of times an event occurs (p. 661)

frequency table [frē′kwən•sē tā′bəl] **tabla de frecuencia** A table that uses numbers to record data about how often an event occurs (p. 662)

greatest common factor (GCF) [grāt′est käm′ən fak′tər] **máximo común divisor (MCD)** The greatest factor that two or more numbers have in common (p. 23)
Example: 6 is the GCF of 18 and 30.

grid [grid] **cuadrícula** Evenly divided and equally spaced squares on a figure or flat surface

height [hīt] **altura** The length of a perpendicular from the base to the top of a plane figure or solid figure
Example:

height

hexagon [hek′sə•gän] **hexágono** A polygon with six sides and six angles
Examples:

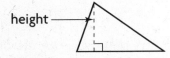

histogram [his′tə•gram] **histograma** A type of bar graph that shows the frequencies of data in intervals. (p. 667)
Example:

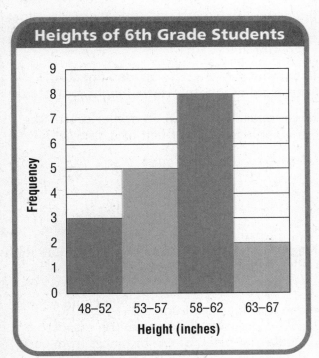

Heights of 6th Grade Students

Height (inches)

Frequency

horizontal [hôr•i•zänt′əl] **horizontal** Extending left and right

hundredth [hun′drədth] **centésimo** One of one hundred equal parts
Examples: 0.56, $\frac{56}{100}$, fifty-six hundredths

Identity Property of Addition [ī•den′tə•tē präp′ər•tē əv ə•dish′ən] **propiedad de identidad de la suma** The property that states that when you add zero to a number, the result is that number

Identity Property of Multiplication [ī•den′tə•tē präp′ər•tē əv mul•tə•pli•kāsh′ən] **propiedad de identidad de la multiplicación** The property that states that the product of any number and 1 is that number

independent variable [in•dē•pen′dənt′ vâr′ē•ə•bəl] **variable independiente** A variable whose value determines the value of another quantity (p. 491)

inequality [in•ē•kwôl′ə•tē] **desigualdad** A mathematical sentence that contains the symbol <, >, ≤, ≥, or ≠ (p. 465)

integers [in′tə•jərz] **enteros** The set of whole numbers and their opposites (p. 139)

interquartile range [in′tûr•kwôr′tīl rānj] **rango intercuartil** The difference between the upper and lower quartiles of a data set (p. 726)

intersecting lines [in•tər•sekt′ing līnz] **líneas secantes** Lines that cross each other at exactly one point
Example:

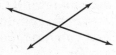

inverse operations [in′vûrs äp•pə•rā′shənz] **operaciones inversas** Opposite operations, or operations that undo each other, such as addition and subtraction or multiplication and division (p. 439)

key [kē] **clave** The part of a map or graph that explains the symbols

kite [kīt] **cometa** A quadrilateral with exactly two pairs of congruent sides that are next to each other; no two sides are parallel
Example:

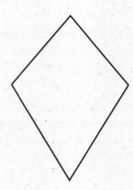

ladder diagram [lad'ər dī'ə•gram] **diagrama de escalera** A diagram that shows the steps of repeatedly dividing by a prime number until the quotient is 1

lateral area [lat'ər•əl âr'ē•ə] **área lateral** The sum of the areas of the lateral faces of a solid (p. 616)

lateral face [lat'ər•əl fās] **cara lateral** Any surface of a polyhedron other than a base

least common denominator (LCD) [lēst käm'ən dē•näm'ə•nāt•ər] **mínimo común denominador (m.c.d.)** The least common multiple of two or more denominators
Example: The LCD for $\frac{1}{4}$ and $\frac{5}{6}$ is 12.

least common multiple (LCM) [lēst käm'ən mul'tə•pəl] **mínimo común múltiplo (m.c.m.)** The least number that is a common multiple of two or more numbers (p. 17)

like terms [līk tûrmz] **términos semejantes** Expressions that have the same variable with the same exponent (p. 395)

line [līn] **línea** A straight path in a plane, extending in both directions with no endpoints
Example:

line graph [līn graf] **gráfica lineal** A graph that uses line segments to show how data change over time

line of symmetry [līn əv sim'ə•trē] **eje de simetría** A line that divides a figure into two halves that are reflections of each other (p. 184)

line segment [līn seg'mənt] **segmento** A part of a line that includes two points called endpoints and all the points between them
Example:

line symmetry [līn sim'ə•trē] **simetría axial** A figure has line symmetry if it can be folded about a line so that its two parts match exactly. (p. 184)

linear equation [lin'ē•ər ē•kwā'zhən] **ecuación lineal** An equation that, when graphed, forms a straight line (p. 517)

linear unit [lin'ē•ər yōō'nit] **unidad lineal** A measure of length, width, height, or distance

lower quartile [lō'ər kwôr'tīl] **primer cuartil** The median of the lower half of a data set (p. 713)

mean [mēn] **media** The sum of a set of data items divided by the number of data items (p. 681)

mean absolute deviation [mēn ab'sə•lōōt dē•vē•ā'shən] **desviación absoluta respecto a la media** The mean of the distances from each data value in a set to the mean of the set (p. 720)

measure of center [mezh′ər əv sent′ər] **medida de tendencia central** A single value used to describe the middle of a data set (p. 681)
Examples: mean, median, mode

measure of variability [mezh′ər əv vâr′ē•ə•bil′ə•tē] **medida de dispersión** A single value used to describe how the values in a data set are spread out (p. 725)
Examples: range, interquartile range, mean absolute deviation

median [mē′dēən] **mediana** The middle value when a data set is written in order from least to greatest, or the mean of the two middle values when there is an even number of items (p. 681)

midpoint [mid′point] **punto medio** A point on a line segment that is equally distant from either endpoint

million [mil′yən] **millón** 1,000 thousands; written as 1,000,000

mixed number [mikst num′bər] **número mixto** A number that is made up of a whole number and a fraction
Example: $1\frac{5}{8}$

mode [mōd] **moda** The value(s) in a data set that occurs the most often (p. 681)

multiple [mul′tə•pəl] **múltiplo** The product of two counting numbers is a multiple of each of those numbers

multiplication [mul•tə•pli•kā′shən] **multiplicación** A process to find the total number of items made up of equal-sized groups, or to find the total number of items in a given number of groups; It is the inverse operation of division.

Multiplication Property of Equality [mul•tə•pli•kā′shən präp′ər•tē əv ē•kwôl′ə•tē] **propiedad de multiplicación de la igualdad** The property that states that if you multiply both sides of an equation by the same number, the sides remain equal

multiplicative inverse [mul′tə•pli•kāt•iv in′vûrs] **inverso multiplicativo** A reciprocal of a number that is multiplied by that number resulting in a product of 1 (p. 108)

multiply [mul′tə•plī] **multiplicar** When you combine equal groups, you can multiply to find how many in all; the inverse operation of division

negative integer [neg′ə•tiv in′tə•jər] **entero negativo** Any integer less than zero
Examples: ⁻4, ⁻5, and ⁻6 are negative integers.

net [net] **plantilla** A two-dimensional pattern that can be folded into a three-dimensional polyhedron (p. 597)
Example:

not equal to (≠) [not ē′kwəl tōō] **no igual a** A symbol that indicates one quantity is not equal to another

number line [num′bər līn] **recta numérica** A line on which numbers can be located
Example:

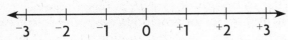

numerator [nōō′mər•āt•ər] **numerador** The number above the bar in a fraction that tells how many equal parts of the whole are being considered
Example: $\frac{3}{4}$ ← numerator

numerical expression [nōō•mer′i•kəl ek•spresh′ən] **expresión numérica** A mathematical phrase that uses only numbers and operation signs (p. 363)

obtuse angle [äb•tōōs′ ang′gəl] **ángulo obtuso**
An angle whose measure is greater than 90°
and less than 180°
Example:

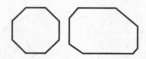

obtuse triangle [äb•tōōs′ trī′ang•gəl] **triángulo
obtusángulo** A triangle that has one obtuse
angle

octagon [äk′tə•gän] **octágono** A polygon with
eight sides and eight angles
Examples:

odd [od] **impar** A whole number that has a 1, 3,
5, 7, or 9 in the ones place

open figure [ō′pən fig′yər] **figura abierta** A figure
that does not begin and end at the same point

opposites [äp′ə•zits] **opuestos** Two numbers
that are the same distance, but in opposite
directions, from zero on a number line (p. 139)

order of operations [ôr′dər əv äp•ə•rā′shənz]
orden de las operaciones A special set of rules
which gives the order in which calculations are
done in an expression (p. 363)

ordered pair [ôr′dərd pâr] **par ordenado** A pair of
numbers used to locate a point on a grid. The
first number tells the left-right position and
the second number tells the up-down position.
(p. 177)

origin [ôr′ə•jin] **origen** The point where the two
axes of a coordinate plane intersect; (0,0)
(p. 177)

outlier [out′lī•ər] **valor atípico** A value much
higher or much lower than the other values in
a data set (p. 687)

overestimate [ō′vər•es•tə•mit] **sobrestimar**
An estimate that is greater than the exact
answer

parallel lines [pâr′ə•lel līnz] **líneas paralelas** Lines
in the same plane that never intersect and are
always the same distance apart
Example:

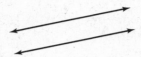

parallelogram [pâr•ə•lel′ə•gram] **paralelogramo**
A quadrilateral whose opposite sides are parallel
and congruent
Example:

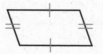

parentheses [pə•ren′thə•sēz] **paréntesis** The
symbols used to show which operation or
operations in an expression should be done
first

partial product [pär′shəl präd′əkt] **producto parcial**
A method of multiplying in which the ones,
tens, hundreds, and so on are multiplied
separately and then the products are added
together

pattern [pat′ərn] **patrón** An ordered set of
numbers or objects; the order helps you
predict what will come next
Examples: 2, 4, 6, 8, 10

pentagon [pen′tə•gän] **pentágono** A polygon
with five sides and five angles
Examples:

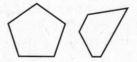

percent [pər•sent′] **porcentaje** The comparison of a number to 100; percent means "per hundred" (p. 269)

perimeter [pə•rim′ə•tər] **perímetro** The distance around a closed plane figure

period [pir′ē•əd] **período** Each group of three digits separated by commas in a multidigit number
Example: 85,643,900 has three periods.

perpendicular lines [pər•pən•dik′yōō•lər līnz] **líneas perpendiculares** Two lines that intersect to form four right angles
Example:

pictograph [pik′tə•graf] **pictografía** A graph that displays countable data with symbols or pictures
Example:

HOW WE GET TO SCHOOL	
Walk	✹ ✹ ✹
Ride a Bike	✹ ✹ ✹ ✹
Ride a Bus	✹ ✹ ✹ ✹ ✹ ◗
Ride in a Car	✹ ✹

Key: Each ✹ = 10 students

place value [plās val′yōō] **valor posicional** The value of each digit in a number based on the location of the digit

plane [plān] **plano** A flat surface that extends without end in all directions
Example:

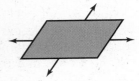

plane figure [plān fig′yər] **figura plana** A figure that lies in a plane; a figure having length and width

point [point] **punto** An exact location in space

polygon [päl′i•gän] **polígono** A closed plane figure formed by three or more line segments
Examples:

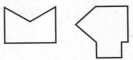

Polygons   Not Polygons

polyhedron [päl•i•hē′drən] **poliedro** A solid figure with faces that are polygons
Examples:

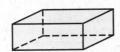

positive integer [päz′ə•tiv in′tə•jər] **entero positivo** Any integer greater than zero

prime factor [prīm fak′tər] **factor primo** A factor that is a prime number

prime factorization [prīm fak•tə•rə•zā′shən] **descomposición en factores primos** A number written as the product of all its prime factors (p. 11)

prime number [prīm num′bər] **número primo** A number that has exactly two factors: 1 and itself
Examples: 2, 3, 5, 7, 11, 13, 17, and 19 are prime numbers. 1 is not a prime number.

prism [priz′əm] **prisma** A solid figure that has two congruent, polygon-shaped bases, and other faces that are all rectangles
Examples:

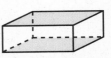

rectangular prism   triangular prism

product [präd′əkt] **producto** The answer to a multiplication problem

pyramid [pir′ə•mid] **pirámide** A solid figure with a polygon base and all other faces as triangles that meet at a common vertex
Example:

quadrants [kwä′drənts] **cuadrantes** The four regions of the coordinate plane separated by the *x*- and *y*-axes (p. 183)

quadrilateral [kwä•dri•lat′ər•əl] **cuadrilátero** A polygon with four sides and four angles
Example:

quotient [kwō′shənt] **cociente** The number that results from dividing
Example: 8 ÷ 4 = 2. The quotient is 2.

range [rānj] **rango** The difference between the greatest and least numbers in a data set (p. 726)

rate [rāt] **tasa** A ratio that compares two quantities having different units of measure (p. 218)

ratio [rā′shē•ō] **razón** A comparison of two numbers, *a* and *b*, that can be written as a fraction $\frac{a}{b}$ (p. 211)

rational number [rash′•ən•əl num′bər] **número racional** Any number that can be written as a ratio $\frac{a}{b}$ where *a* and *b* are integers and $b \neq 0$. (p. 151)

ray [rā] **semirrecta** A part of a line; it has one endpoint and continues without end in one direction
Example:

reciprocal [ri•sip′rə•kəl] **recíproco** Two numbers are reciprocals of each other if their product equals 1. (p. 108)

rectangle [rek′tang•gəl] **rectángulo** A parallelogram with four right angles
Example:

rectangular prism [rek•tang′gyə•lər priz′əm] **prisma rectangular** A solid figure in which all six faces are rectangles
Example:

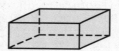

reflection [ri•flek′shən] **reflexión** A movement of a figure to a new position by flipping it over a line; a flip
Example:

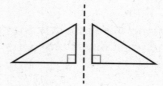

regroup [rē•grōōp′] **reagrupar** To exchange amounts of equal value to rename a number
Example: 5 + 8 = 13 ones or 1 ten 3 ones

regular polygon [reg'yə•lər päl'i•gän] **polígono regular** A polygon in which all sides are congruent and all angles are congruent (p. 565)

relative frequency table [rel'ə•tiv frē'kwən•sē tā'bəl] **tabla de frecuencia relativa** A table that shows the percent of time each piece of data occurs (p. 662)

remainder [ri•mān'dər] **residuo** The amount left over when a number cannot be divided equally

rhombus [räm'bəs] **rombo** A parallelogram with four congruent sides
Example:

Word History

Rhombus is almost identical to its Greek origin, *rhombos*. The original meaning was "spinning top" or "magic wheel," which is easy to imagine when you look at a rhombus, an equilateral parallelogram.

right triangle [rīt trī'ang•gəl] **triángulo rectángulo** A triangle that has a right angle
Example:

round [round] **redondear** To replace a number with one that is simpler and is approximately the same size as the original number
Example: 114.6 rounded to the nearest ten is 110 and to the nearest unit is 115.

sequence [sē'kwəns] **secuencia** An ordered set of numbers

simplest form [sim'pləst fôrm] **mínima expresión** A fraction is in simplest form when the numerator and denominator have only 1 as a common factor

simplify [sim'plə•fī] **simplificar** The process of dividing the numerator and denominator of a fraction or ratio by a common factor

solid figure [sä'lid fig'yər] **cuerpo geométrico** A three-dimensional figure having length, width, and height (p. 597)

solution of an equation [sə•loo'shən əv ən ē•kwā'zhən] **solución de una ecuación** A value that, when substituted for the variable, makes an equation true (p. 421)

solution of an inequality [sə•loo'shən əv ən in•ē•kwôl'ə•tē] **solución de una desigualdad** A value that, when substituted for the variable, makes an inequality true (p. 465)

square [skwâr] **cuadrado** A polygon with four equal, or congruent, sides and four right angles

square pyramid [skwâr pir'ə•mid] **pirámide cuadrada** A solid figure with a square base and with four triangular faces that have a common vertex
Example:

square unit [skwâr yoo'nit] **unidad cuadrada** A unit used to measure area such as square foot (ft^2), square meter (m^2), and so on

standard form [stan'dərd fôrm] **forma normal** A way to write numbers by using the digits 0–9, with each digit having a place value
Example: 456 ← standard form

statistical question [stə•tis'ti•kəl kwes'chən] **pregunta estadística** A question that asks about a set of data that can vary (p. 649)
Example: How many desks are in each classroom in my school?

Substitution Property of Equality [sub•stə•tōō'shən präp'ər•tē əv ē•kwôl'ə•tē] **propiedad de sustitución de la igualdad** The property that states that if you have one quantity equal to another, you can substitute that quantity for the other in an equation

subtraction [səb•trak'shən] **resta** The process of finding how many are left when a number of items are taken away from a group of items; the process of finding the difference when two groups are compared; the inverse operation of addition

Subtraction Property of Equality [səb•trak'shən präp'ər•tē əv ē•kwôl'ə•tē] **propiedad de resta de la igualdad** The property that states that if you subtract the same number from both sides of an equation, the sides remain equal

sum [sum] **suma o total** The answer to an addition problem

surface area [sûr'fis âr'ē•ə] **área total** The sum of the areas of all the faces, or surfaces, of a solid figure (p. 603)

T

tally table [tal'ē tā'bəl] **tabla de conteo** A table that uses tally marks to record data

tenth [tenth] **décimo** One of ten equal parts
Example: 0.7 = seven tenths

terms [tûrmz] **términos** The parts of an expression that are separated by an addition or subtraction sign (p. 376)

thousandth [thou'zəndth] **milésimo** One of one thousand equal parts
Example: 0.006 = six thousandths

three-dimensional [thrē də•men'shə•nəl] **tridimensional** Measured in three directions, such as length, width, and height

three-dimensional solid [thrē də•men'shə•nəl säl'id] **figura tridimensional** See *solid figure*

trapezoid [trap'i•zoid] **trapecio** A quadrilateral with at least one pair of parallel sides (p. 551)
Examples:

tree diagram [trē dī'ə•gram] **diagrama de árbol** A branching diagram that shows all possible outcomes of an event

trend [trend] **tendencia** A pattern over time, in all or part of a graph, where the data increase, decrease, or stay the same

triangle [trī'ang•gəl] **triángulo** A polygon with three sides and three angles
Examples:

triangular prism [trī•ang'gyə•lər priz'əm] **prisma triangular** A solid figure that has two triangular bases and three rectangular faces

two-dimensional [tōō də•men'shə•nəl] **bidimensional** Measured in two directions, such as length and width

two-dimensional figure [tōō də•men'shə•nəl fig'yər] **figura bidimensional** See *plane figure*

underestimate [un•dər•es′tə•mit] **subestimar** An estimate that is less than the exact answer

unit cube [yōō′nit kyōōb] **cubo unitaria** A cube that has a length, width, and height of 1 unit

unit fraction [yōō′nit frak′shən] **fraccion unitaria** A fraction that has 1 as a numerator

unit rate [yōō′nit rāt] **tasa por unidad** A rate expressed so that the second term in the ratio is one unit (p. 218)
Example: 55 mi per hr

unit square [yōō′nit skwâr] **cuadrado de una unidad** A square with a side length of 1 unit, used to measure area

unlike fractions [un′līk frak′shənz] **fracciones no semejantes** Fractions with different denominators

upper quartile [up′ər kwôr′tīl] **tercer cuartil** The median of the upper half of a data set (p. 713)

variable [vâr′ē•ə•bəl] **variable** A letter or symbol that stands for an unknown number or numbers (p. 369)

Venn diagram [ven dī′ə•gram] **diagrama de Venn** A diagram that shows relationships among sets of things
Example:

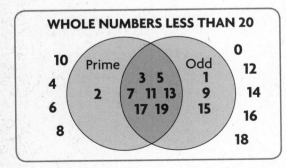

vertex [vûr′teks] **vértice** The point where two or more rays meet; the point of intersection of two sides of a polygon; the point of intersection of three (or more) edges of a solid figure; the top point of a cone; the plural of *vertex* is *vertices*
Examples:

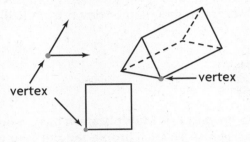

vertical [vûr′ti•kəl] **vertical** Extending up and down

volume [väl′yōōm] **volumen** The measure of the space a solid figure occupies (p. 623)

weight [wāt] **peso** How heavy an object is

whole number [hōl num′bər] **número entero** One of the numbers 0, 1, 2, 3, 4, . . . ; the set of whole numbers goes on without end

x-axis [eks ak′sis] **eje de la x** The horizontal number line on a coordinate plane (p. 177)

x-coordinate [eks kō•ôrd′n•it] **coordenada x** The first number in an ordered pair; tells the distance to move right or left from (0,0) (p. 177)

y-axis [wī ak′sis] **eje de la y** The vertical number line on a coordinate plane (p. 177)

y-coordinate [wī kō•ôrd′•n•it] **coordenada y** The second number in an ordered pair; tells the distance to move up or down from (0,0) (p. 177)

Zero Property of Multiplication [zē′rō präp′ər•tē əv mul•tə•pli•kā′shən] **propiedad del cero de la multiplicación** The property that states that when you multiply by zero, the product is zero

Correlations

 COMMON CORE STATE STANDARDS

Standards You Will Learn

Mathematical Practices		Some examples are:
MP1	Make sense of problems and persevere in solving them.	Lessons 1.1, 2.6, 2.9, 6.3, 6.5, 7.6, 8.7, 12.8, 13.2, 13.7
MP2	Reason abstractly and quantitatively.	Lessons 1.1, 2.3, 3.1, 7.3, 7.4, 7.9, 11.2, 12.7, 13.5
MP3	Construct viable arguments and critique the reasoning of others.	Lessonss 1.2, 2.3, 3.5, 6.4, 7.7, 8.1, 11.4, 12.5, 13.7
MP4	Model with mathematics.	Lessons 1.4, 2.5, 2.8, 6.3, 7.2, 8.2, 10.4, 12.4, 13.3
MP5	Use appropriate tools strategically.	Lessons 2.8, 3.4, 5.1, 6.3, 8.3, 9.2, 12.3, 12.8, 13.7
MP6	Attend to precision.	Lessons 1.6, 2.9, 3.5, 7.4, 7.9, 8.1, 13.6, 13.7, 13.8
MP7	Look for and make use of structure.	Lessons 1.2, 2.9, 3.1, 5.2, 6.5, 8.6, 13.1, 13.4, 13.8
MP8	Look for and express regularity in repeated reasoning.	Lessons 1.9, 2.7, 3.2, 4.5, 6.1, 7.1, 10.2, 12.5, 13.1
Domain: Ratios and Proportional Relationships		**Student Edition Lessons**
Understand ratio concepts and use ratio reasoning to solve problems.		
6.RP.A.1	Understand the concept of a ratio and use ratio language to describe a ratio relationship between two quantities.	Lessons 4.1, 4.2
6.RP.A.2	Understand the concept of a unit rate a/b associated with a ratio $a:b$ with $b \neq 0$, and use rate language in the context of a ratio relationship.	Lessons 4.2, 4.6

Domain: Ratios and Proportional Relationships (Continued)

6.RP.A.3	Use ratio and rate reasoning to solve real-world and mathematical problems, e.g., by reasoning about tables of equivalent ratios, tape diagrams, double number line diagrams, or equations.	
	a. Make tables of equivalent ratios relating quantities with whole-number measurements, find missing values in the tables, and plot the pairs of values on the coordinate plane. Use tables to compare ratios.	Lessons 4.3, 4.4, 4.5, 4.8
	b. Solve unit rate problems including those involving unit pricing and constant speed.	Lessons 4.6, 4.7
	c. Find a percent of a quantity as a rate per 100 (e.g., 30% of a quantity means 30/100 times the quantity); solve problems involving finding the whole, given a part and the percent.	Lessons 5.1, 5.2, 5.3, 5.4, 5.5, 5.6
	d. Use ratio reasoning to convert measurement units; manipulate and transform units appropriately when multiplying or dividing quantities.	Lessons 6.1, 6.2, 6.3, 6.4, 6.5

Standards You Will Learn

Domain: The Number System		
Apply and extend previous understandings of multiplications and division to divide fractions by fractions.		
6.NS.A.1	Interpret and compute quotients of fractions, and solve word problems involving division of fractions by fractions, e.g., by using visual fraction models and equations to represent the problem.	Lessons 2.5, 2.6, 2.7, 2.8, 2.9, 2.10
Compute fluently with multi-digit numbers and find common factors and multiples.		
6.NS.B.2	Fluently divide multi-digit numbers using the standard algorithm.	Lesson 1.1
6.NS.B.3	Fluently add, subtract, multiply, and divide multi-digit decimals using the standard algorithm for each operation.	Lessons 1.6, 1.7, 1.8, 1.9
6.NS.B.4	Find the greatest common factor of two whole numbers less than or equal to 100 and the least common multiple of two whole numbers less than or equal to 12. Use the distributive property to express a sum of two whole numbers 1–100 with a common factor as a multiple of a sum of two whole numbers with no common factor.	Lessons 1.2, 1.3, 1.4, 1.5, 2.3, 2.4

Apply and extend previous understandings of numbers to the system of rational numbers.

6.NS.C.5	Understand that positive and negative numbers are used together to describe quantities having opposite directions or values (e.g., temperature above/below zero, elevation above/below sea level, credits/ debits, positive/negative electric charge); use positive and negative numbers to represent quantities in real-world contexts, explaining the meaning of 0 in each situation.	Lesson 3.1, 3.3
6.NS.C.6	Understand a rational number as a point on the number line. Extend number line diagrams and coordinate axes familiar from previous grades to represent points on the line and in the plane with negative number coordinates.	
	a. Recognize opposite signs of numbers as indicating locations on opposite sides of 0 on the number line; recognize that the opposite of the opposite of a number is the number itself, e.g., $-(-3) = 3$, and that 0 is its own opposite.	Lessons 3.1, 3.3
	b. Understand signs of numbers in ordered pairs as indicating locations in quadrants of the coordinate plane; recognize that when two ordered pairs differ only by signs, the locations of the points are related by reflections across one or both axes.	Lesson 3.8
	c. Find and position integers and other rational numbers on a horizontal or vertical number line diagram; find and position pairs of integers and other rational numbers on a coordinate plane.	Lessons 2.1, 3.1, 3.3, 3.7

Apply and extend previous understandings of numbers to the system of rational numbers. *(Continued)*

6.NS.C.7	Understand ordering and absolute value of rational numbers.	
	a. Interpret statements of inequality as statements about the relative position of two numbers on a number line diagram.	Lessons 2.2, 3.2, 3.4
	b. Write, interpret, and explain statements of order for rational numbers in real-world contexts.	Lessons 3.2, 3.4
	c. Understand the absolute value of a rational number as its distance from 0 on the number line; interpret absolute value as magnitude for a positive or negative quantity in a real-world situation.	Lesson 3.5
	d. Distinguish comparisons of absolute value from statements about order.	Lesson 3.6
6.NS.C.8	Solve real-world and mathematical problems by graphing points in all four quadrants of the coordinate plane. Include use of coordinates and absolute value to find distances between points with the same first coordinate or the same second coordinate.	Lessons 3.9, 3.10

Domain: Expressions and Equations

Apply and extend previous understandings of arithmetic to algebraic expressions.

6.EE.A.1	Write and evaluate numerical expressions involving whole-number exponents.	Lessons 7.1, 7.2
6.EE.A.2	Write, read, and evaluate expressions in which letters stand for numbers.	
	a. Write expressions that record operations with numbers and with letters standing for numbers.	Lesson 7.3
	b. Identify parts of an expression using mathematical terms (sum, term, product, factor, quotient, coefficient); view one or more parts of an expression as a single entity.	Lesson 7.4
	c. Evaluate expressions at specific values of their variables. Include expressions that arise from formulas used in real-world problems. Perform arithmetic operations, including those involving whole-number exponents, in the conventional order when there are no parentheses to specify a particular order (Order of Operations).	Lessons 7.5, 10.1, 10.3, 10.5, 10.6, 10.7, 11.3, 11.4, 11.6
6.EE.A.3	Apply the properties of operations to generate equivalent expressions.	Lessons 7.7, 7.8

Apply and extend previous understandings of arithmetic to algebraic expressions. *(Continued)*

6.EE.A.4	Identify when two expressions are equivalent (i.e., when the two expressions name the same number regardless of which value is substituted into them). *For example, the expressions $y + y + y$ and $3y$ are equivalent because they name the same number regardless of which number y stands for.*	Lesson 7.9

Reason about and solve one-variable equations and inequalities.

6.EE.B.5	Understand solving an equation or inequality as a process of answering a question: which values from a specified set, if any, make the equation or inequality true? Use substitution to determine whether a given number in a specified set makes an equation or inequality true.	Lessons 8.1, 8.8
6.EE.B.6	Use variables to represent numbers and write expressions when solving a real-world or mathematical problem; understand that a variable can represent an unknown number, or, depending on the purpose at hand, any number in a specified set.	Lesson 7.6
6.EE.B.7	Solve real-world and mathematical problems by writing and solving equations of the form $x + p = q$ and $px = q$ for cases in which p, q and x are all nonnegative rational numbers.	Lessons 8.2, 8.3, 8.4, 8.5, 8.6, 8.7, 10.1
6.EE.B.8	Write an inequality of the form $x > c$ or $x < c$ to represent a constraint or condition in a real-world or mathematical problem. Recognize that inequalities of the form $x > c$ or $x < c$ have infinitely many solutions; represent solutions of such inequalities on number line diagrams.	Lessons 8.9, 8.10

Represent and analyze quantitative relationships between dependent and independent variables.

| 6.EE.C.9 | Use variables to represent two quantities in a real-world problem that change in relationship to one another; write an equation to express one quantity, thought of as the dependent variable, in terms of the other quantity, thought of as the independent variable. Analyze the relationship between the dependent and independent variables using graphs and tables, and relate these to the equation. *For example, in a problem involving motion at constant speed, list and graph ordered pairs of distances and times, and write the equation d = 65t to represent the relationship between distance and time.* | Lessons 9.1, 9.2, 9.3, 9.4, 9.5 |

Domain: Geometry

Solve real-world and mathematical problems involving area, surface area, and volume.

| 6.G.A.1 | Find the area of right triangles, other triangles, special quadrilaterals, and polygons by composing into rectangles or decomposing into triangles and other shapes; apply these techniques in the context of solving real-world and mathematical problems. | Lessons 10.1, 10.2, 10.3, 10.4, 10.5, 10.6, 10.7, 10.8, 11.7 |
| 6.G.A.2 | Find the volume of a right rectangular prism with fractional edge lengths by packing it with unit cubes of the appropriate unit fraction edge lengths, and show that the volume is the same as would be found by multiplying the edge lengths of the prism. Apply the formulas $V = lwh$ and $V = bh$ to find volumes of right rectangular prisms with fractional edge lengths in the context of solving real-world and mathematical problems. | Lessons 11.5, 11.6, 11.7 |

Solve real-world and mathematical problems involving area, surface area, and volume. (Continued)

6.G.A.3	Draw polygons in the coordinate plane given coordinates for the vertices; use coordinates to find the length of a side joining points with the same first coordinate or the same second coordinate. Apply these techniques in the context of solving real-world and mathematical problems.	Lesson 10.9
6.G.A.4	Represent three-dimensional figures using nets made up of rectangles and triangles, and use the nets to find the surface area of these figures. Apply these techniques in the context of solving real-world and mathematical problems.	Lessons 11.1, 11.2, 11.3, 11.4, 11.7

Domain: Statistics and Probability

Develop understanding of statistical variability.

6.SP.A.1	Recognize a statistical question as one that anticipates variability in the data related to the question and accounts for it in the answers. *For example, "How old am I?" is not a statistical question, but "How old are the students in my school?" is a statistical question because one anticipates variability in students' ages.*	Lesson 12.1
6.SP.A.2	Understand that a set of data collected to answer a statistical question has a distribution which can be described by its center, spread, and overall shape.	Lessons 12.6, 13.1, 13.4, 13.6, 13.7, 13.8
6.SP.A.3	Recognize that a measure of center for a numerical data set summarizes all of its values with a single number, while a measure of variation describes how its values vary with a single number.	Lessons 12.6, 13.4, 13.6

Summarize and describe distributions.

6.SP.B.4	Display numerical data in plots on a number line, including dot plots, histograms, and box plots.	Lessons 12.3, 12.4, 12.8, 13.2
6.SP.B.5	Summarize numerical data sets in relation to their context, such as by:	
	a. Reporting the number of observations.	Lesson 12.2
	b. Describing the nature of the attribute under investigation, including how it was measured and its units of measurement.	Lesson 12.2
	c. Giving quantitative measures of center (median and/or mean) and variability (interquartile range and/or mean absolute deviation), as well as describing any overall pattern and any striking deviations from the overall pattern with reference to the context in which the data were gathered.	Lessons 12.5, 12.6, 12.7, 13.1, 13.3, 13.4, 13.8
	d. Relating the choice of measures of center and variability to the shape of the data distribution and the context in which the data were gathered.	Lessons 12.7, 13.5, 13.7

Index

MathBoard. In every student edition. Some examples are: 6, 7, 12, 71, 77, 83, 141, 147, 153, 212, 218, 225, 271, 276, 283, 317, 323, 329, 359, 365, 371, 429, 435, 441, 493, 499, 505, 535, 541, 547, 599, 605, 611, 651, 657, 663, 709, 715, 721

Mathematical Practices

1. Make sense of problems and persevere in solving them. In many lessons. Some examples are: 6, 104, 121, 558, 600
2. Reason abstractly and quantitatively. In many lessons. Some examples are: 19, 632
3. Construct viable arguments and critique the reasoning of others. In many lessons. Some examples are: 88, 166, 498, 747
4. Model with mathematics. In many lessons. Some examples are: 24, 96, 396
5. Use appropriate tools strategically. In many lessons. Some examples are: 251, 330
6. Attend to precision. In many lessons. Some examples are: 45, 243, 611
7. Look for and make use of structure. In many lessons. Some examples are: 13, 256
8. Look for and express regularity in repeated reasoning. In many lessons. Some examples are: 109, 192, 359, 540, 552, 707

Math Idea, 5, 18, 76, 139, 145, 165, 315, 336, 357, 369, 402, 421, 465, 533, 584, 661, 733

Math in the Real World Activities, 3, 67, 137, 209, 267, 313, 355, 419, 489, 531, 595, 647, 705

Math on the Spot videos. In every student edition lesson. Some examples are: 8, 14, 20, 72, 78, 84, 142, 148, 154, 214, 220, 226, 272, 278, 284, 318, 324, 338, 360, 366, 372, 424, 430, 442, 494, 497, 506, 536, 542, 554, 600, 606, 612, 652, 658, 664, 710, 716, 722

Math Talk. In all Student Edition lessons, 7, 11, 12, 13, 17, 19, 23, 25, 29, 38, 39, 44, 49, 51, 56, 57, 69, 70, 71, 75, 76, 77, 81, 83, 87, 89, 96, 103, 107, 108, 109, 113, 114, 120, 121, 125, 139, 140, 141, 145, 146, 147, 151, 152, 153, 157, 158, 159, 165, 167, 172, 173, 178, 179, 184, 185, 189, 190, 191, 195, 196, 211, 212, 218, 219, 223, 225, 229, 236, 237, 243, 245, 249, 255, 257, 270, 276, 282, 289, 290, 295, 296, 301, 302, 303, 315, 316, 317, 322, 323, 328, 329, 336, 341, 342, 357, 358, 359, 363, 365, 369, 371, 376, 377, 381, 382, 383, 389, 390, 391, 395, 402, 403, 407, 408, 409, 421, 422, 423, 427, 429, 433, 434, 439, 441, 445, 446, 451, 452, 453, 457, 458, 460, 465, 466, 467, 471, 472, 478, 479, 491, 493, 497, 503, 504, 511, 512, 513, 517, 519, 533, 535, 540, 545, 557, 558, 559, 565, 567, 571, 573, 577, 578, 599, 604, 609, 611, 615, 617, 623, 624, 629, 631, 635, 636, 650, 651, 656, 657, 662, 669, 675, 681, 683, 707, 714, 715, 720, 725, 726, 727, 734, 735, 739, 745, 746, 747, 751

Mean
defined, 648, 681
as fair share and balance point, 675–678
finding, 681–684
set of data, 705

Mean absolute deviation, 719–722
defined, 720
dot plot, 721–722

Measurement
conversion factor, 314
converting units of capacity, 321–323
converting units of length, 313, 315–318
converting units of mass, 327–330
converting units of volume, 313
converting units of weight, 313, 327–333

Measure of center, 681–684
applying, 739–742
defined, 681
effect of outliers, 687–690

Measure of variability, 706, 725–728
applying, 739–742
choose an appropriate, 733–736
defined, 725

Median
defined, 648, 681
finding, 681–684
outlier, 687–690

Meter, 314, 322

Metric units of measure
capacity, 322
converting, 316, 322
length, 316–317
mass, 328

Mid-Chapter Checkpoint, 35–36, 93–94, 163–164, 241–242, 287–288, 333–334, 387–388, 463–464, 509–510, 563–564, 621–622, 673–674, 731–732

Miles, 315

Mililiters, 322

Milligrams, 328

Millimeters, 316

Mixed numbers, 68
converting to decimals, 69–72
division, 119–122
model division, 113–116
writing, 69

Mode
defined, 648, 681
finding, 681–684

Model fraction division, 95–98

Model mixed number division, 113–116

Model percents, 269–272

Model ratios, 211–214

© Houghton Mifflin Harcourt Publishing Company

Volume
cube, 630
defined, 596, 623
fractions and, 623–626
prism, 630
rectangular prisms, 623–626, 629–631

Weight
converting units, 327–330
customary units, 327
defined, 314
units, 327–330

What If, 31, 43, 78, 96, 127, 342, 397, 459, 492, 505

What's the Error, 72, 104, 148, 154, 318, 366, 384, 424, 430, 454, 554, 606

Whole numbers, 138
compare, 67
dividing decimals by, 49–52
greatest common factor, 23–26
least common multiple, 17–20
multiplication
by decimals, 267

Word sentence
writing equation, 428–429
writing inequality, 471–474

Write Math, In every Student Edition lesson. Some examples are: 8, 14, 26, 78, 97, 98, 160, 220, 232, 297, 330, 343, 366, 378, 384, 430, 579, 580, 600, 625, 721

Writing
algebraic expressions, 369–372
equations, 427–430
equivalent algebraic equations, 401–404
inequalities, 471–473
ratios, and rates, 217–220

x-**axis,** 177
x-**coordinate,** 177

Yard, 315
y-**axis,** 177
y-**coordinate,** 177

Table of Measures

METRIC	CUSTOMARY

Length

1 meter (m) = 1,000 millimeters (mm)	1 foot (ft) = 12 inches (in.)
1 meter = 100 centimeters (cm)	1 yard (yd) = 3 feet
1 meter = 10 decimeters (dm)	1 yard = 36 inches
1 dekameter (dam) = 10 meters	1 mile (mi) = 1,760 yards
1 hectometer (hm) = 100 meters	1 mile = 5,280 feet
1 kilometer (km) = 1,000 meters	

Capacity

1 liter (L) = 1,000 milliliters (mL)	1 cup (c) = 8 fluid ounces (fl oz)
1 liter = 100 centiliters (cL)	1 pint (pt) = 2 cups
1 liter = 10 deciliters (dL)	1 quart (qt) = 2 pints
1 dekaliter (daL) = 10 liters	1 quart = 4 cups
1 hectoliter (hL) = 100 liters	1 gallon (gal) = 4 quarts
1 kiloliter (kL) = 1,000 liters	

Mass/Weight

1 gram (g) = 1,000 milligrams (mg)	1 pound (lb) = 16 ounces (oz)
1 gram = 100 centigrams (cg)	1 ton (T) = 2,000 pounds
1 gram = 10 decigrams (dg)	
1 dekagram (dag) = 10 grams	
1 hectogram (hg) = 100 grams	
1 kilogram (kg) = 1,000 grams	

TIME

1 minute (min) = 60 seconds (sec)	1 year (yr) = about 52 weeks
1 hour (hr) = 60 minutes	1 year = 12 months (mo)
1 day = 24 hours	1 year = 365 days
1 week (wk) = 7 days	1 decade = 10 years
	1 century = 100 years
	1 millennium = 1,000 years

SYMBOLS

$=$	is equal to	10^2	ten squared
$\neq$	is not equal to	10^3	ten cubed
$\approx$	is approximately equal to	2^4	the fourth power of 2
$>$	is greater than	$\lvert {}^-4 \rvert$	the absolute value of $^-4$
$<$	is less than	$\%$	percent
$\geq$	is greater than or equal to	$(2, 3)$	ordered pair (x, y)
$\leq$	is less than or equal to	$^\circ$	degree

FORMULAS

Perimeter and Circumference

Polygon	$P = $ sum of the lengths of sides
Rectangle	$P = 2l + 2w$
Square	$P = 4s$

Area

Rectangle	$A = lw$
Parallelogram	$A = bh$
Triangle	$A = \frac{1}{2}bh$
Trapezoid	$A = \frac{1}{2}(b_1 + b_2)h$
Square	$A = s^2$

Volume

Rectangular Prism	$V = lwh$ or Bh
Cube	$V = s^3$

Surface Area

Cube	$S = 6s^2$